C21025

CW00670614

Britain's First Labour Government

Also by John Shepherd

BRITAIN'S SECOND LABOUR GOVERNMENT, 1929–31: A REAPPRAISAL (*edited with Jonathan Davis and Chris Wrigley*)

ON THE MOVE: ESSAYS IN LABOUR AND TRANSPORT HISTORY

PRESENTED TO PHILIP BAGWELL (*edited with Chris Wrigley*)

GEORGE LANSBURY: AT THE HEART OF OLD LABOUR

Also by Keith Laybourn

LABOUR HEARTLAND (*with Jack Reynolds*)

THE RISE OF LABOUR

BRITAIN ON THE BREADLINE

THE CENTENNIAL HISTORY OF THE ILP (*edited*)

THE GENERAL STRIKE OF 1926

PHILIP SNOWDEN: A BIOGRAPHY

THE EVOLUTION OF BRITISH SOCIAL POLICY AND THE WELFARE STATE

UNDER THE RED FLAG (*with Dylan Murphy*)

UNEMPLOYMENT AND EMPLOYMENT POLICIES CONCERNING WOMEN IN BRITAIN, 1900–1951

MARXISM IN BRITAIN: DISSENT, DECLINE AND RE-EMERGENCE, 1945–*c*.2000

Britain's First Labour Government

John Shepherd
Professor of History, University of Huddersfield

Keith Laybourn
Diamond Jubilee Professor, University of Huddersfield

First published 2006 by
First published in paperback 2013 by
PALGRAVE MACMILLAN

Palgrave Macmillan in the UK is an imprint of Macmillan Publishers Limited, registered in England, company number 785998, of Houndmills, Basingstoke, Hampshire RG21 6XS.

Palgrave Macmillan in the US is a division of St Martin's Press LLC, 175 Fifth Avenue, New York, NY 10010.

Palgrave Macmillan is the global academic imprint of the above companies and has companies and representatives throughout the world.

Palgrave® and Macmillan® are registered trademarks in the United States, the United Kingdom, Europe and other countries.

ISBN: 978–1–403–91572–6 hardback
ISBN: 978–1–137–31186–3 paperback

This book is printed on paper suitable for recycling and made from fully managed and sustained forest sources. Logging, pulping and manufacturing processes are expected to conform to the environmental regulations of the country of origin.

A catalogue record for this book is available from the British Library.

A catalog record for this book is available from the Library of Congress.

10   9   8   7   6   5   4   3   2   1
22   21   20   19   18   17   16   15   14   13

Printed and bound in Great Britain by
CPI Antony Rowe, Chippenham and Eastbourne

For Jan and Julia

Contents

Illustrations

Tables

Preface to the Paperback Edition

The rise and fall of political parties and governments continues to fascinate both historians and political scientists alike. Minority administrations, political pacts and coalition governments have intrigued them even more so as political parties have faced the need to compromise and sacrifice their cherished beliefs in the pursuit of political gains. In 2013, coalitions of different parties must work together to govern Australia, Greece, Italy and other European countries and to find solutions to the current global economic and financial crisis. Following the May 2010 general election and a fevered five days of inter-party negotiations that followed, Britain is now governed by a coalition of Tory and Liberal Democrat parties for the first time since the Second World War. Single-party government is no longer the British norm. The study of coalitions and minority governments, hung parliaments and political pacts is now developing into something of a genre in its own right.

Britain's First Labour Government was published in 2006, the first full-scale study of Ramsay MacDonald's Labour Government (1924) since Richard Lyman's pioneering book appeared in 1957. It remains the only full-length modern account to date of Labour's first minority administration that lasted only 287 days. The research for this book was based on a wide range of archival material, not available to Richard Lyman in the 1950s, including access to government sources and the Ramsay MacDonald Collections in The National Archives and John Rylands Library, as well as the private papers of many of those involved in the history of Labour during the twentieth-century.

Disraeli famously declared that England does not love coalitions. Yet, even taking into account the post-war years of Labour and Conservative administrations from 1945-2013, the British parliamentary system has not always resulted in single-party government. Since 1900 there have been coalition or minority government for 24 years, as well as a long history of pacts or general understandings between political parties. In 1903, for example, Herbert Gladstone, Liberal Chief Party Whip, and Ramsay MacDonald, Secretary of the Labour Representation Committee (Labour Party in 1906), agreed a secret pact that was an important landmark in the 1906 Liberal electoral landslide and the evolution of the British Labour Party. In 1977 James Callaghan, Labour Prime Minister, and David Steel, signed the famous 'Lib-Lab Pact' that sustained the minority Labour administration in office during a highly critical time. Britain witnessed coalition government during the First and Second World Wars. In peacetime, the National Governments from 1931-1940 were coalitions (though with an increasing Conservative majority after September 1932). In 1924 and 1929-1931 Ramsay MacDonald's Labour Governments first took office as minority administrations. Though maintained in office by Liberal votes, there was never an electoral arrangement or overt agreement that underpinned these inter-war administrations. In fact, in 1924 Ramsay MacDonald, who wished to destroy the Liberal Party, pursued a moderate programme of mainly non-socialist reforms and challenged the Liberals to bring down his government, if they dared. How his minority government survived for nearly ten months without a formal alliance remains a fascinating topic that is analysed in *Britain's First Labour Government*.

This study also explores how the 1924 minority government with 191 MPs was able to govern backed by only about 30 per cent of the MPs in the House of Commons. In addition, Labour's position in the House of Lords was limited, with Conservative and Liberal peers being significantly more highly represented. At the same time, the politics of MacDonald's Cabinet formation were intriguing. Besides socialists and trade unionist, the Labour Leader chose ex-Liberals and Conservatives (including a former Viceroy of India), part of significant shifts in political allegiance towards Labour in the post-First world War years.

Not surprisingly little was expected of the first Labour government. However, in 1924 John Wheatley's Housing Act was a singular success in encouraging the building of council housing, at a time when there was a severe shortage of housing for rent. Philip Snowden, the Chancellor of the Exchequer, initiated the National Grid. Even more important, Ramsay MacDonald, who was also Foreign Secretary as well as Prime Minister, achieved international acclaim for his attempts to pave the way for a permanent peace in Europe, although his work was later undone by the subsequent Baldwin's Conservative government.

In addition, in surviving between January and November 1924, this minority Labour government exceeded the hope of most contemporaries and helped to establish the Labour Party as one of the two major parties of government in British politics. But why was the Government formed and why did the administration fall over the Soviet treaties and the famous Campbell case – or, as Beaverbrook asked in a famous article, 'Who Killed Cock Robin? These are among other important questions explored in *Britain's First Labour Government*. In addition, Labour's defeat in the 1924 general election and the significance of the infamous 'Red scare', the *Zinoviev Letter,* complete the story.

Any quick summary of MacDonald's first Labour government might reflect that it was a minority administration, lucky to be in office, of short duration and achieved little except in housing and fleeting successes in foreign policy. It has at times been portrayed as a mere *cul de sac* in the overall history of the Labour Party. *Britain's First Labour Government* challenges such notions and maintains that its true role was more central than this assessment suggests. The 1924 minority Labour administration was a sensitive indicator of how much Labour had progressed since the Labour Representation Committee was founded in London in 1900. In particular, MacDonald's first Labour government was a useful mile-post by which the party could assess its progress, scrutinise its policies and develop its organisational strategies and skills. Above all, the 1924 Labour government was vital in legitimising Labour as the representative of the progressive forces in British politics, and helped to dispatch the Liberal Party to political oblivion for more than eighty years.

John Shepherd   Keith Laybourn
Dry Drayton, Cambridgeshire   Pudsey, West Yorkshire

Acknowledgements

We are grateful for the permission of HM Queen Elizabeth II to quote from material in The Royal Archives, Windsor. We are also indebted to the following for permission to use copyright material: British School of Political and Economic Science; the Bodleian Library; Churchill Archives, Cambridge; Labour History and Archive Centre at the John Rylands Library, Manchester; Manchester Reference Library; The National Archives; The Robinson Library, University of Newcastle; Shulbrede Archive. We would like to acknowledge that the James Ramsay MacDonald diaries were 'meant as notes to guide and revive the memory as regards happenings and must on no account be published as they are'. We have only used small extracts from his diaries. Every effort has been taken to trace copyright holders and to avoid infringement of copyright. We apologise unreservedly to any copyright holders who have inadvertently been overlooked.

We particularly would like to acknowledge the formative influence in our historical research of Jack Reynolds (1915–1988), David Wright (1937–1995), Professor Eric Hobsbawm, Professor Kenneth O. Morgan and Professor Chris Wrigley. We would also wish to thank Steven Bird, former Archivist at the Labour History and Archive Study Centre at the John Rylands Library, Manchester, and his colleagues for access to the records of the British Labour Party and for expert advice during our visits. Philip Dunn at the Labour Party photographic archive was very helpful in supplying the photographs which illustrate this volume. We would like to acknowledge the expert help we have received from the staff at many British libraries and for granting access to manuscript collections in their possession: The Bodleian Library, The British Library, The British Library of Political and Economic Science, Cambridge University Library, Keele University Library, The Modern Records Centre, The Robinson Library, University of Newcastle, The National Archives.

We are most grateful to Professor Kenneth O. Morgan, Dr Janet Shepherd and Professor Chris Wrigley who read the typescript in preparation and provided extremely valuable comments and wise counsel. Any errors or omissions that remain are our responsibility alone. We also thank Dr David Musgrove and Greg Neale for publishing our article on 'Labour's Red Letter Day' in *The BBC History Magazine* and for the opportunity to present papers on our research at the Cambridge branch of The

Historical Association and Anglia Ruskin University, Cambridge, and for the constructive views of the participants. We also wish to thank Dr Huw Richards, Casper Sylvest, Dr Jon Davis, Dr Paul Corthorn, Carol Probert, Professor Paul Ward, John Fisher and Beverley Harding for their assistance and advice. We are most grateful to Laura Ponsonby and Catherine and Ian Russell for their hospitality and access to the Lord Ponsonby Papers at Shulbrede Priory.

At Palgrave we have been most fortunate in our two commissioning editors, Luciana O'Flaherty and Michael Strang and their colleagues, Ruth Ireland and Daniel Bunyard. We thank them for their constant encouragement and unfailing patience. We are most grateful for support and help of Clare Mence, Assistant Editor, in making this paperback edition possible. We would also like to thank Penny Simmons for seeing this book through to publication.

We dedicate this book to our wives, Jan and Julia. Without their unstinting support and help completion would be a distant prospect.

John Shepherd   Keith Laybourn
Dry Drayton, Cambridgeshire   Pudsey, West Yorkshire

Abbreviations

ASLEF	Associated Society of Locomotive Engineers and Firemen
BBC	British Broadcasting Company (later Corporation)
BSP	British Socialist Party
CID	Committee of Imperial Defence
CCWTE	Central Committee on Women's Training and Employment
CPGB	Communist Party of Great Britain
DPP	Director of Public Prosecutions
ECCI	Executive committee of the Communist International
FO	Foreign Office
ILP	Independent Labour Party
LRC	Labour Representation Committee
MFGB	Miners' Federation of Great Britain
MP	Member of Parliament
NAC	National Administrative Council
NEC	National Executive Committee
NLC	National Liberal Club
NUR	National Union of Railwaymen
PCF	*Bolshevik Parti Communiste Français*
PLP	Parliamentary Labour Party
PPS	Parliamentary Private Secretary
SDF	Social Democratic Federation
SFIO	*Section Francaise de l'Internationale Ouvriere*
STC	Supply and Transport Committee
SJCIWO	Standing Joint Committee of Industrial Women's Organisations
TGWU	Transport and General Workers' Union
TUC	Trades Union Congress
UDC	Union of Democratic Control
WBCG	Workers' Birth Control Group
WLL	Women's Labour League

1

From Foundation Conference to Government

On leaving his Whitehall office on a cold January evening in 1924, Thomas Jones, Assistant Cabinet Secretary, saw the newspaper placards announcing: 'Lenin Dead [*official*]. Ramsay MacDonald Premier.'[1] After six weeks of political uncertainty and rumours, Britain's first-ever Labour government had taken office with its Scottish leader as prime minister and foreign secretary. The general election in December 1923 had produced an inconclusive result – Conservatives 258, Labour 191 and Liberals 158. Stanley Baldwin, the Conservative Prime Minister, had waited to resign until defeated in the new Parliament on 21 January 1924. At this time, democratically elected left-wing governments had already taken office in Western Europe – in Sweden (as a Social Democratic – Liberal coalition in 1917 and in 1920 as a minority administration) and in Germany (where the SPD joined the 1918 coalition in the Weimar Republic).[2] In Australia, seen as a laboratory for social democratic politics, the ministry formed by Anderson Dawson in Queensland in 1899 before federation – albeit for a few days – was the first Labour ministry in the world. Also in Australia in 1904 Chris Watson's Labour administration became was the world's first national Labour government. New Zealand was also a pioneer of Labour administrations, where the first Labour MP was elected in 1905, the New Zealand Labour Party founded in 1916 and a majority Labour government led by Michael Savage was returned in 1935.[3] And here in Britain a number of Labour Party members had served in the Coalition Governments during the First World War.[4]

In a devastating taunt in 1920, that still resounded in British politics years later, Winston Churchill told his cheering audience in Sunderland that Labour was 'quite unfitted for the responsibility of Government'. The opposition party had no constructive programme and was identified with class rather than national interests.[5] After King George V invited MacDonald to form an administration, he famously wrote in his diary: 'Today 23 years ago dear Grandmama died. I wonder what she would have thought of a Labour government!'[6] The imminence of a socialist administration full of revolutionaries – that might easily levy a wealth tax or bring in state nationalisation – caused a mood of alarm and despondency in governing circles. For a while, hare-brained schemes abounded to obstruct Labour's path to power and control over Britain's destiny. Even then, if the unthinkable took place, Sir Frederick Banbury, MP for the City of London, pledged he would personally lead the Coldstream Guards into Parliament to protect the Constitution.[7] Before long, more sensible counsel prevailed about the political changes taking place. 'A socialist govt. actually in power. But don't get uneasy about your investments and your antiques. Nothing will be removed or abstracted . . . They are all engaged in looking as respectable as lather and blather will make them,' David Lloyd George, former Liberal Prime Minister, reassured his daughter, Megan.[8]

For those on the political Left, the advent of the first Labour government in Britain offered a different vision after the trauma and carnage on the Western Front and empty promises of a 'Land Fit for Heroes'. In prospect was a new dawn in a world shattered by economic collapse, enflamed by political revolution and teetering on the brink of international conflict. R. H. Tawney was, like his fellow intellectuals G. D. H. Cole, Harold Laski, H. N. Brailsford, J. A. Hobson and Leonard Woolf, a major influence on socialist thought and policy in the 1920s. He naturally welcomed the new Labour administration, and not only for the fresh initiatives it could bring to contemporary problems of foreign policy, unemployment, housing and education. 'A new force, with a different standard of political values, will hence forth play its part in directly moulding British policy,' the Christian socialist predicted.[9] Yet, within less than a year, MacDonald's government had come to an end amid accusations of a Communist conspiracy that hastened its downfall.

Since then, 11 Labour administrations have taken office in Britain. Yet, in twentieth-century British politics 1945, 1966, 1997 and 2001 remain landmark years for Labour election victories and taking power – rather than 1923 or 1924. The names of Clement Attlee, Harold Wilson, James Callaghan, and obviously Tony Blair, are more likely to be recalled on the top of the Clapham omnibus as Labour Prime Ministers than Ramsay MacDonald. Today the first-ever Labour government, from January–November 1924, is a distant memory. It is possibly remembered for the manner of its defeat over the fake Zinoviev Letter, published by the *Daily Mail* shortly before polling day as a so-called Communist plot 'to stir up the masses of the British proletariat'. This revelation allegedly ruined Labour chances in the October 1924 election – the first of various shadowy anti-Labour stunts that have entered the party's folklore, including the 1931 Post Office Savings Bank rumours and the stillborn 'Government of National Emergency' to replace the Wilson ministry in 1968. Even as late as 1998, Robin Cook, New Labour's Foreign Secretary, established an official inquiry into the Zinoviev Letter and the role of British Intelligence, the Foreign Office and the Tory press. Despite opening hitherto secret British, American and Russian archives, more questions were probably raised than answered about the infamous 'Red Scare' of 1924.[10]

Eighty-odd years on, the composition of Ramsay MacDonald's 1924 administration, what it set out to implement and actually accomplished during its short spell in office, remain significant issues. It emerged during a period of major party realignment after the collapse of the Lloyd George Coalition government. The years from 1922 to 1924 saw three general elections and four different Prime Ministers and administrations in Britain. Labour had established itself in terms of Crown and Parliament and paved the way for a future majority government. In retrospect, the first Labour Cabinet was a remarkable and broad-based collection of figures – Labourites, trade unionists, socialists and even former Liberals and Conservatives – that reflected the uneasy coalition that made up the post-war Labour Party. Outside the Cabinet, other appointments in 1924 were also important indicators of the times: in the decade when women finally gained the parliamentary vote, Margaret Bondfield became the first woman British government minister, and in 1929 the first woman member of a British Cabinet, a token acknowledgement at least of the presence of women and women's issues in the traditional male-dominated world of British politics.[11] In 1924 Major Clement Attlee was chosen as the Under-Secretary of State for War, as well as MacDonald's Parliamentary Private Secretary – he went on to be party leader in 1935 and, ten years later, Prime Minister of the first majority Labour government.[12]

Unquestionably, MacDonald was Labour's dominant figure in the 1920s, theorist as well as party leader, and widely acknowledged within the party as such; with a mission, on gaining the newly created position of party leader in 1922, to pull together the warring factions among his party's members. Beatrice Webb observed MacDonald's charismatic hold over the party: '[He] rules absolutely and the other Labour members stick to him as their only salvation from confusion . . . [S]o long as he chooses to remain leader of the Labour Party he will do so.'[13] Undoubtedly, MacDonald believed in the inevitability of socialism; but in 1924 the capital levy – feared by the middle and upper classes – was silently abandoned and only modest social reforms, rather than any scheme of common ownership, formed part of Labour's programme. Traditionally, only the Wheatley Housing Act and some easing of European tensions by MacDonald – in his burdensome dual role as Foreign Secretary as well as Prime Minister – are usually seen as achievements of any note by the 1924 ministry.

Seven years later, the controversial collapse of the second Labour government – that opened the way to the locust years of Conservative-dominated National Governments – has long since overshadowed MacDonald's first administration.[14] It is not difficult to see why the 1924 government was quickly forgotten rather than celebrated as the advent of Labour in power. No twentieth-century party leader has received as much loathing among Labour supporters as Ramsay MacDonald for his part in the historic events during the political crisis of August 1931. The bitter recriminations of former Cabinet ministers – many of whom served in the 1924 ministry – subsequently coloured assessments of MacDonald's earlier performance as the charismatic party leader and Prime Minister. In the future, 1931 entered party mythology as the litmus test of those Labour politicians wishing to demonstrate party loyalty.[15] In 1938 Lachlan MacNeill Weir, who had succeeded Attlee as MacDonald's Parliamentary Private Secretary from 1924, published his most damning work – *The Tragedy of Ramsay MacDonald* – with accusations of careerism and treachery by the Labour leader. It left a harsh and devastating reputation that only time has just begun to erode.[16]

In addition, the 1924 administration has attracted little attention from historians and political scientists. Published almost fifty years ago, American historian, Richard Lyman's account of the first Labour government in Britain – now out of print – has to date been the only full-scale study.[17] In the 1950s Lyman made judicious use of contemporary literature, public documents and newspapers, as well as interviews with Labour politicians, including Sir Charles Trevelyan, the only surviving member of Ramsay MacDonald's Cabinet. However, new archives – including the private papers of Ramsay MacDonald, the Labour Party archives, and the Cabinet records – have since been opened to researchers in subsequent years. Lyman demonstrated that in office Labour was a party of moderation, especially under Ramsay MacDonald, a magnetic premier determined to display his government's respectability and ability to play the parliamentary game. Lyman's account established the orthodox picture of the first MacDonald government, a minority administration largely dependent on Liberal votes within a three-party system, until brought down by the furore over the Anglo-Soviet Treaties and the Campbell Case. Also, as a short-lived ministry mainly concerned with daily administration, Labour appeared to achieve little in domestic affairs apart from John Wheatley's major Housing Act, which set in motion local authority building programmes of council houses for rent. On unemployment – the massive domestic issue confronting British society – Labour ministers disappointedly had nothing original to offer on the seemingly intractable problem of an increasing number of jobless. After some initial hesitation, MacDonald also became his own Foreign Secretary, handling his portfolio with considerable skill. His personal style of diplomacy and his adept chairmanship of the international London conference were acclaimed for promoting the Dawes Plan, thereby easing European tensions over the Ruhr crisis. He did nothing, however, to revise the discredited Treaty of Versailles, despite the presence of former associates from the Union of Democratic Control in his administration and his own internationalist leanings.

As Labour left office in October 1924, the *Labour Magazine* claimed that the ministry's short stint in office had the 'quality of an epic'. This assessment, that MacDonald's government managed to secure more positive legislative accomplishments than administrations of longer duration, set in train the official party view of Labour on the parliamentary road to socialism at Westminster.[18] Any criticism of Labour's record could be explained away in terms of the Westminster voting arithmetic that prevented the introduction of a socialist programme. The notion of 'The Forward March of Labour' now underpinned official Labour histories, an invented tradition proudly first fostered in the 1920s in various editions of Bracher's *Herald Book of Labour Members* and Herbert Tracey's three-volume work, *The Book of the Labour Party*.[19]

However, left-wing critics took a different view, regarding Labour's performance in office as lamentable. The failure to implement socialism was laid at the door of the Labour leadership in rejecting any form of direct action outside the parliamentary system. Ralph Miliband adopted this line of argument in his *Parliamentary Socialism*, one of the most influential critiques of the history of the Labour Party published after the Second World War. The 1924 administration – notable for its outward respectability and avowed concern for the national welfare – belied any notion that it was recruited from a party of revolt. MacDonald's ministry was the first of a number of Labour governments – even during the halcyon days of the post-war Attlee ministry – censured for not adopting more radical and independent policies at home and abroad.[20] For the political Left, the history of the 1924 Labour government marks the beginning of the betrayal by party leaders, empowered by parliamentary democracy, to transform British capitalism and to secure a socialist society as envisaged by its party's founders.[21]

In 1977 David Marquand's monumental biography of James Ramsay MacDonald devoted three of its 30 chapters to the period of the first Labour government.[22] Marquand concluded that MacDonald's leadership was largely responsible for harnessing the different elements within his party; for demonstrating that government was not solely the province of the aristocracy and bourgeoisie; and for his stunning conduct of international policy in 1924. At the same time, the Labour leader was blamed for his administration losing office, even though the 1924 election saw the devastating rout of the Liberal Party.[23]

Recent years have seen a plethora of publications on the history of the Labour Party, particularly in 2000 when several important books marked Labour's centennial year – each including a brief survey of the 1924 administration in Labour's forward march. By any account, a defining characteristic of this short-lived administration was the appointment of the Clydesider and Independent Labour Party MP, John Wheatley, to the Ministry of Health with a portfolio of housing, the poor law and local government. His Housing Act was the ministry's most noteworthy domestic achievement in launching a durable construction programme of rented council housing based on union – employer cooperation. As Pat Thane has written, the percentage of government expenditure on social services was generally on an upward curve during the inter-war years – despite chronic economic difficulties. This trend included an improvement in unemployment benefit in 1924, as well as measures for the future. The first Labour government set up the Royal Commission on national health insurance as well as the Hadow Committee on secondary education. However, like a number of other measures, these reports did not see light of day before the fall of the ministry.[24] Andrew Thorpe has noted that the precarious balance of the political parties at Westminster limited Labour's performance in policy terms. Liberal abstentions alone could allow the Conservatives to oust the minority Labour government.[25]

David Howell's scholarly study of the Labour Party in the decade before the 1931 collapse has provided important fresh insights into the 1924 and 1929–31 MacDonald governments.[26] His analysis examines the various components of the progressive party that MacDonald largely built with its different identities – including the trade unions, the Labour Party, the Parliamentary Labour Party (PLP), the ILP, the Fabian Society, the women's movement and the intake of Liberal politicians – in order to explain how they interacted to shape politics between 1922 and 1931. Though not focused specifically on the first Labour government, *MacDonald's Party* provides a valuable historical context as to how the 1924 administration and its problems might be assessed and more broadly understood.

No assessment of the 1924 administration can ignore its antecedents or avoid the question of how far its beginnings configured its political trajectory along the parliamentary route to government. In 2000 the Labour Party celebrated its centennial year by honouring Keir Hardie and his fellow pioneers who, a hundred years before at the height of the Boer War, had gathered in a joint conference of trade union delegates together with socialist representatives of the Independent Labour Party, Social Democratic Federation and Fabian Society convened by the Trades Union Congress.[27] In reality, the origins of this historic Labour alliance of socialists and trade unionists predated the foundation conference of the Labour Representation Committee (LRC) and can be traced back to the abortive 'socialist unity' debates of the Social Democratic Federation (SDF) and the ILP in the 1890s that prompted the ILP leadership to seek an alliance with the unions to tap their greater finance and organisational strength.[28]

Yet, only nine spectators were present on 27–28 February 1900 in the public gallery at the Memorial Hall in Farringdon Street, London, to witness the foundation of the LRC, as it was known until 1906 when the Labour Party title was adopted. This uneasy alliance of British trade union and socialist delegates, seeking to increase Labour representation at Westminster, made no specific commitment to any socialist ideology, but resolved to set up 'a distinct Labour group in Parliament, who shall have their own whips and agree upon their policy'. In the 1900 general election two LRC candidates – Keir Hardie and Richard Bell (the latter essentially a Lib-Lab) – were returned to Parliament and were joined by three others – David Shackleton, Will Crooks and Arthur Henderson – in by-elections in 1902–3. Ramsay MacDonald, who had abandoned the Liberals to join the new ILP in 1894, was elected unpaid LRC secretary and, doubling up his family home in Lincoln's Inn Fields as the LRC's first office, undertook invaluable pioneering work with his wife, Margaret, in building the party organisation. In attempting to return MacDonald to Downing Street in October 1924, J. S. Middleton, the party secretary, admiringly recalled those pioneering days: 'From the moment he took hold of the Labour Representation Committee he consecrated every ounce of his energy and every passion of his soul to building up the Labour Party.'[29]

In effect, the LRC was primarily a political party largely founded and financed by certain unions in an attempt to secure their corporate existence in law during a climate of adverse court judgments. Affiliations to the new party increased dramatically from 1901 following the adverse Taff Vale judgement that threatened union funds. Keir Hardie's historic alliance of Labour and the trade unions became the bedrock of the party's history, albeit with cracks and fault lines, during the next hundred years. As Ernest Bevin, the redoubtable General Secretary of the Transport and General Workers' Union, once famously reminded the annual party conference with some inaccuracy, the Labour Party had been 'born out of the bowels of the TUC'. Between 1918 and 1929 the percentage of union-sponsored MPs declined: in 1918, 51 out of 61 Labour MPs (80 per cent), with the figures dropping to 102 out of 191 in 1924 (53 per cent) and to 115 out of 287 in 1929 (40 per cent).[30] Income from the trade union affiliation fees and other monies remained essential to Labour prosperity. In 1924 the attitude of the Labour administration to union priorities and expectations proved a significant test of the special relationship between the industrial and political wings of the Labour Party. Yet, even in 1900, the 129 delegates represented a broad church filled not only by a phalanx of no-nonsense trade unionists, but also socialists of various hues, plus Lib-Lab politicians, intellectuals and journalists. In 1924 the composition of MacDonald's administration reflected this coalition of different interests and conflicting rivalries within the party as a whole.

Labour is the only substantial political party founded in the twentieth century that has survived in British politics for more than a few decades. By the turn of the century, in 2005, as New Labour with Tony Blair as Prime Minister, it had won a remarkable third successive term in office. Yet in 1900 the fledgeling party had an uncertain future with no guarantee that it would increase its affiliated membership or last, let alone form two governments within the next 30 years. Unlike the Conservatives and Liberals, Labour was the party with its origins firmly outside Parliament that needed sponsorship and finance to promote parliamentary representation. The previous half-century had been strewn with failed attempts by organisations to elect working men to Parliament – mainly in alliance with the Liberal Party, such as the Labour Representation League in the 1870s and the Labour Electoral Association established after the Southport TUC in 1885 which sunk without trace ten years later. In the 1880s and 1890s the revival of socialism had brought into being the SDF, the Fabian Society and the ILP – all destined to play varying roles in the future in the history of the Labour Party.

Socialist fortunes were at their lowest ebb in the 1895 election when the 32 defeated SDF and ILP candidates – who included Keir Hardie who lost his seat at West Ham South – could total only 40,000 votes.[31]

In 1900, besides the LRC, three other bodies were established to promote working- class MPs – the Scottish Workers' Parliamentary Elections Committee, an expanded electoral fund run by the Miners' Federation of Great Britain, and the National Democratic League, an alliance of radicals and socialists. All three were short-lived independent ventures that soon vanished from the political scene, the first two being absorbed by the growing Labour Party.[32] Hardie's Labour alliance of trade unionists and socialists not only defined the shape of the new party for the next 30 years as the political expression of working-class interests and hopes, but also marginalised any attempt to establish a Socialist party – such as the British Socialist Party in 1911 – on the Left of British politics.[33] The Communist Party of Great Britain, founded in 1920, suffered a similar fate. Ramsay MacDonald was adamant in excluding Communists from the Labour Party in the 1920s.[34]

In 1906 the Liberal Party secured its most decisive win at a general election in modern times. Twenty-nine LRC MPs, soon to be 30, were returned to the Commons to form the new Parliamentary Labour Party (PLP), providing Labour not only with a new name but also its distinct identity within the progressive framework in Edwardian politics. As Robert Taylor has observed, the PLP has played a significant role during the last century as Labour has moved from being a pressure group to a party of government. During the 1906 Parliament the PLP – white males from working-class origins and mainly trade union backgrounds, mostly religious, nearly half teetotallers, with an average age of 46 – at first occupied the opposition benches, often voting with the Liberal government. But this new collective group – roughly half of whom saw themselves as socialists – also provided a distinctive voice to working-class demands for old-age pensions, feeding poor children, a national minimum wage, tackling unemployment and trade union legislation.[35] The beginnings of the parliamentary careers of the main figures in the 1924 Labour government can be also traced back to these years when they first entered the Commons. As party secretary, MacDonald's major contribution had been the secret electoral pact he had struck in 1903 with the Liberal Chief Whip, Herbert Gladstone. It cleared the way for this solid bloc of newcomers – including MacDonald himself and Philip Snowden – to be returned in the Liberal landslide victory. The new contingent of independent Labour members in 1906 displaced almost all the remaining old guard of the Lib-Lab MPs, who were also effectively reduced at a stroke by the affiliation of the Miners' Federation of Great Britain to the Labour Party in 1909. By December 1910 the PLP had increased to 42 MPs, who lobbied for important trade union legislation. This 'Progressive Alliance' with Labour as the junior partner to the Liberal government also yielded the introduction of MPs' salaries in return for Labour support for the National Insurance Act (1911).[36]

The number of constituency parties affiliated to the national party between 1906 and 1914 increased from 73 to 179, an expansion which, in part, reflected Labour's progress at municipal level with 500 representatives by the eve of the First World War. Nonetheless, as Kenneth Morgan has noted, the party in the constituencies was a conglomeration of local representation committees, trades councils, unions, ILP groups and similar bodies that affiliated to the national party in the days before individual membership.[37] Outside the traditionally masculine world of Westminster, Labour's early years also coincided with the upsurge in women's political campaigning, particularly for the parliamentary vote. The Women's Labour League, which eventually gained affiliation to the Labour Party during the First World War, played a significant role in promoting women's issues and lobbying for representation at national and municipal levels.[38] In 1912 Arthur Henderson, the Labour Party secretary, concluded an electoral alliance with the National Union of Women's Suffrage Societies.

Yet, despite its advances in the coalfields and industrial towns, the Labour Party was in still relatively weak in national organisation and representation, particularly in the south of England, outside parts of London, and in the rural areas. Even with an increasing number of MPs in the three elections of 1906 and 1910, the Labour Party remained a parliamentary pressure group in 1914 – rather than a future government. During these years, the resurgence of grassroots 'Labour unrest' – in part inspired by syndicalism – provided an extra-parliamentary alternative to the Labour leadership's strategy at Westminster.[39] Between December 1910 and the outbreak of war in 1914, the party lost 16 by-elections – in most cases finishing bottom of the poll. Yet, there were some hopeful signs. In many cases, Labour's share of the votes in these by-elections had increased substantially. From 1909–13 municipal results were more encouraging and in the ballots under the Trade Union Act of 1913 all the trade unions voted, sometimes by narrow majorities, to establish political funds for the Labour Party.[40] However, despite Arthur Henderson's efforts with Labour organisation and discipline as party secretary, in 1914 Labour appeared to have little prospect of superseding either of the two main parties.[41]

Yet in 1918 Labour emerged after the First World War as the unmistakable party of the future on the democratic Left. In Britain the impact of war had transformed politics – particularly the relationship of the Liberal and Labour Parties. Trevor Wilson's famous metaphor likened the downfall of the Liberal Party to the fate of a healthy pedestrian run down by a runaway omnibus. In 1916 the unexpected division within the Liberal Party leadership between Asquith and Lloyd George split the party irreversibly, and with devastating effect.[42] It also triggered an exodus of the more radical Liberals, who easily found their new home in the Labour Party. Arthur Henderson, who took over the chairmanship of the Labour Party after MacDonald's resignation over British entry into the war, become a member of the Liberal coalition governments, first under Asquith and then, in 1916–17, as one of the five ministers in the Lloyd George War Cabinet.

In 1917 revolutions in Russia ended the tyranny of the Tsarist regime and brought the Bolsheviks to power. These events had worldwide significance, inspired revolutionary movements throughout much of Europe, and had a major impact on the development of the British Labour Party. A member of the Labour Research Department, the Fabian Margaret Cole recalled that 'on the way to the office we bought our newspapers and read with incredulous eyes that the Russian *people*, the workers, soldiers, peasants, had really risen and cast out the Tsar and his government, who were to our minds, the arch symbols of black oppression in the world.'[43] Henderson returned from an official mission to the Petrograd provisional government with a new international perspective on the war and the belief that the Labour Party should be reshaped as a future democratic alternative government to the revolutionary upheaval he witnessed in Russia.[44] His expulsion from the War Cabinet over the 'doormat incident' concerning the Stockholm Conference in 1917 left him free to concentrate on overhauling Labour's Head Office and party organisation. In particular, the expansion of the unions – whose cooperation was essential for the war effort – benefited Labour. In certain industries, the regulation of wages and prices by the state not only created full employment and improved living standards, but also altered union perceptions of the state as a future agent of social and political change. Despite MacDonald's resignation of the PLP chairmanship in August 1914 as Labour voted for war credits at Westminster, and ILP opposition to the war, the PLP had suffered no permanent division within its ranks. By 1917 trade unionists and socialists found common ground in planning post-war reconstruction.[45]

The effects of wartime social and political changes were not lost on the Labour leadership ready to modernise the party organisation in preparation for normal peacetime politics. The Representation of the People Act (1918) virtually tripled the number of voters – from 7.7 million to 21.4 million – by enfranchising all men and women aged 30 and over. Other significant changes – particularly for Labour – included the redistribution of constituencies and the abolition of electoral returning officers' charges. In 1918 Labour's new constitution – mainly the work of Arthur Henderson and the Fabian Sidney Webb – introduced individual membership to expand the party and also committed it to public ownership in its famous Clause IV – 'the common ownership of the means of production and best obtainable system of popular administration and control of each industry or service'. The party's election programme for the 1918 election, *Labour and the New Social Order*, advocated land nationalisation, public ownership of mines, railways, electric production and life assurance – a collection of party resolutions that has provoked debates over the years as to how far the Labour Party was a socialist party. In these post-war years, Labour therefore faced the prospect of moving on from being a parliamentary pressure group to eventually becoming the governing party. The Labour leadership worked actively towards creating a national party by broadening the party's appeal beyond the traditional working-class to middle-class members and voters. Nine advisory committees were established to draw on middle-class expertise, as former Liberals joined the Labour Party in some numbers.[46] Henderson declared in 1918: 'the scheme of reorganisation which has been adopted contemplates the creation of a genuine national party on a broader basis of membership.' He added that widening the party's support beyond working-class voters would be achieved by the promotion of 'the political, social and economic emancipation of the people, and more particularly of those who depend upon their own exertions *by hand or by brain* for the means of life.'[47] In the 1920s, Labour appeared as the party whose time had come – closely identified with a strengthened trade union movement and with scores of newly enfranchised voters ready to support the new class-based party on the political Left.

Besides changes to the party's national organisation, Labour was also making remarkable progress in municipal politics in the inter-war years, in part based on the introduction of individual membership and the establishment and growth of local Labour Parties. In 1923 around 600 constituencies possessed a directly affiliated Divisional or Borough Labour Party and Trades and Labour Council. By 1924 only three constituencies in Britain lacked some kind of local party to undertake political work.[48] In the post-war years, a notable feature of a number of local parties was the creation of women's sections. Before the war, besides the local trade union movement and the suffrage campaign, women had been active in the Women's Labour League and the Women's Cooperative Guild. Now, after groundbreaking work during wartime in the labour and trade union movements, women started to play a key role in certain local Labour communities, joining in greater numbers as individual members, while more men remained affiliated to the party through their trade union.[49]

In November 1919, Labour had swept to power in different parts of Britain. It gained control of 12 out of the 28 metropolitan borough councils in London, as well as the counties of Durham, Monmouthshire and Glamorgan, and the city of Bradford. The East London heartland produced some remarkable results for Labour. In Poplar, where George Lansbury became Labour's first mayor – breaking with tradition by taking office 'without robes, mace or cocked hat' – 39 out of 42 Labour candidates were returned in the borough election. In Clement Attlee's Stepney 40 Labour councillors were elected out of the 60 who stood at the polls. Similarly, in nearby Bethnal Green, 24 of the 28 Labour candidates were successful. In the post-war years, Labour's rapid – albeit uneven – advance in municipal affairs in different regions had important implications in terms of central – local government relations and for the national Labour leadership determined to demonstrate its constitutional and moderate case as a governing party. Where the party gained the opportunity to exercise power over important municipal services and administration, Labour had the opportunity to bring about real political change. Lansbury made this point most emphatically: 'Labour councillors must be different from those we have displaced or why displace them? Our policy is that quite revolutionary one of using *all* the powers Parliament has given us in order to serve the commonweal.'[50] At the same time, overwhelming problems of unemployment and the provision of adequate social services faced Labour's new representatives, as well as accusations by political opponents of municipal extravagance. 'Labour men and women must enter on the municipal fight with a clear conception of their aim and a realisation that municipal work is part of the means of changing the basis of society from profit-making to Life,' Attlee declared.[51]

In Poplar, the Labour councillors left few municipal stones unturned in attempting fundamental change: generous outdoor relief for paupers and the unemployed, improved municipal services and welfare programmes, and the introduction of a minimum wage for municipal workers, including equal pay for women, were all implemented.

Moreover, the adamantine belief of the Labour councillors that they could influence government policy on national issues of unemployment and poverty resulted in a famous challenge to central authority that thrust 'Poplarism' into the political vocabulary. The 'Poplar Rates Revolt' of 1921 – when 30 Labour councillors willingly suffered imprisonment in defence of their local community – took its place in Labour history alongside the Tolpuddle Martyrs, the Newport Chartist march, the London Dock Strike, the 'Revolt on the Clyde', and the 'Hands Off Russia!' campaign.[52] By extending Labour's role in local government, the Poplar councillors had challenged a minimalist central government and the gradualist philosophy of Ramsay MacDonald and the national Labour leadership. The populist Lansbury envisaged a different type of Labour Party pledged to replace capitalism and imperialism with socialism. '[I]n a nutshell this means diverting wealth from wealthy ratepayers to the poor. Those who pretend that a sound Labour policy can be pursued nationally or locally without making the rich poorer should find another party,' he proclaimed.

MacDonald would have no truck with the unconstitutional methods of a Labour local authority. When he took office in 1924, the second edition of his *Socialism: Critical and Constructive* contained this significant riposte: 'It cannot be over-emphasized that public doles, Poplarism, strikes for increased wages, limitation of output, not only are not Socialism, but may mislead the spirit and policy of the Socialist movement.' The clash between the national Labour leadership and local crusading councillors in Poplar reflected similar tensions visible throughout the party's history.[53] Poplarism also drew the fire of the young Herbert Morrison, secretary of the London Labour Party, formed only in 1914. London was an excellent example of Labour growth at municipal level during the inter-war years. The German SPD provided a clear cut example of the development of a powerful party machine and this strongly influenced Morrison in building the London Labour Party as a mirror image of the Berlin SPD. He noted: 'I have never forgotten what Stephen Sanders, MP, told us before the war with regard to Berlin: "that the Social Democratic Party Executive could sit on the top floor of the *Vorwarts* building, pass a manifesto paragraph by paragraph, have it put in type and circulated to every tenement in the city of Berlin by the next morning." We cannot do this yet in London, but we ought to be able to do it. And some day we will do it.'[54] In 1921 Morrison's intervention secured the release of the imprisoned Poplar councillors to stop the spread of this independent action to other boroughs and reassure anxious middle-class voters. Morrison's emphasis on capturing the critical middle ground in politics in the inter-war years can be seen in his well-known rhetorical question of 'Can Labour win London without the middle classes?'

Marketing Labour to the voters was usually associated with the post-1945 era; and after 1994 with 'New Labour's' red roses, blue serge suits and 'spin'. However, the 1920s heralded a new era of mass communications in politics and electioneering, albeit far removed from modern opinion polls and television. The Labour Press and Publicity Department was founded in 1917. Somewhat remarkably, Philip Snowden and Sidney Webb had more than a rudimentary awareness of the psychology and market research in modern electioneering, as well traditional canvassing, manifestos and leaflets. Snowden argued for appealing to 'matter of fact people' rather than the intellectual elite. *The Labour Organiser* – the journal of the Labour Party agents – also played an important role in promoting the party to the electorate in the 1920s. New election advertisements appeared, including Labour's appealing 1923 campaign poster *Greet the Dawn: Give Labour its Chance*. In 1924 the party's literature had a new logo – a torch, shovel and quill symbol incorporating the word 'Liberty'. The Conservatives significantly failed to employ an advertising agency until 1929 when two firms, Holford Bottomley and S. H. Benson – later associated with the National governments in the 1930s – were taken on.[55]

In the 1920s, Ramsay MacDonald remained Labour's most captivating platform orator – though, compared to the emollient Baldwin, he performed awkwardly when radio broadcasts were introduced. Other Labour figures, particularly the popular George Lansbury, had reputations for commanding large public audiences, but where Labour could not compete was in press coverage. The *Daily Herald* was the party's only newspaper in opposition to the major capitalist organs of Fleet Street, but it was dogged by recurrent financial crises. From 1912–22 Lansbury had been associated with the paper as one of its founders, then editor-proprietor and from 1922–25 as its general manager. Though in 1922 the newspaper's ownership passed into the hands of the Labour Party and the trade unions, the *Daily Herald* remained a stern critic at times of the first Labour government. In 1925 MacDonald employed the newspaper to run a competition to replace Jim Connell's socialist *Red Flag* – composed on a train between Charing Cross and New Cross – with a new party anthem. Despite 300 entries in the contest, this was one marketing ploy by the Labour leadership that fell on stony ground. The *Red Flag* survived and its vibrant verses have continued to ring out at party conferences and socialist gatherings to the present day.[56]

However, it is can be too easy simply to identify the extension of the franchise, and the development of working-class solidarity, or some impressive advances in local politics and new marketing techniques, as the only reasons for the expansion of the Labour Party in the post-war years. During this time, the realignment of the three major parties did not polarise British politics merely as Labour as the workers' party and the Conservatives as the party of the wealthy. In the inter-war years, a significant proportion of working-class voters did not vote Labour, the party was weak in major cities other than Sheffield, and before 1945 the party only managed to form two minority Labour governments. In the 1923 election Labour obtained less than a third (30.7 per cent) of the votes cast. More election agents and an improved party organisation, as well as the failure of the Liberals to hang on to their working-class voters, were also highly significant factors underpinning the party's advance.

Despite the potential for success in a new post-war era, Labour's progress remained incremental and patchy. Between 1918 and 1924 in parts of Britain, such as Scotland, West Yorkshire and South Wales, there is some evidence Labour benefited from class voting that produced a political allegiance to it as a workerist party.[57] In particular, a considerable electoral base had been built up in coalfield areas, where miners dominated constituencies. In the 1920s, Labour polled less well, however, in mixed working-class constituencies – even in areas adjacent to coalfield communities.[58] As Prime Minister of the 1918–22 Coalition government, Lloyd George had earlier warned of the threat that the Labour Party presented, once peacetime politics prevailed. In 1920 he told his Minister of Agriculture, Lee of Fareham, of his determination to 'get to grips with the real enemy – Labour'.[59] With only 57 MPs after the 1918 Coupon election, Labour still formed an important part of the opposition to the Coalition government and its massive majority. By 1922 Lloyd George had fallen from power, the British political party system was in flux, and there followed three elections in as many years during which Labour's fortunes soared. In 1922 MacDonald secured the newly created post of Labour leader, capping a remarkable political comeback for someone dubbed the most hated man in Britain following his courageous and principled stand against his country's participation in the Great War. The Parliamentary Labour Party became the official opposition to the Bonar Law and Baldwin Governments. The Liberals were pushed into third place in both the 1922 and 1923 elections.[60]

As the main opposition party, Labour might now be regarded as a serious challenger for power and an alternative government in the future – certainly from 1922 – rather than a party of protest. At this election,

MacDonald, Snowden and Thomas were reunited with Clynes in Parliament. Once Henderson joined them after a by-election, Labour's 'Big Five' formed the leadership that dominated Labour politics until 1931. Significantly, all had been in Parliament before the First World War and Henderson and Clynes had experience of wartime government. Other Labour figures, also returned to the 1922 Parliament, were destined to play significant roles in the future – men like Attlee, Lansbury, Greenwood and Alexander were returned along with ex-Liberals, Trevelyan, Ponsonby and Noel Buxton. In the period 1922–23 MacDonald dominated the opposition benches, making a particular mark on foreign policy on issues such as the French occupation of the Ruhr.

After the 1923 general election, the prospects for Labour were different and especially promising for those who had worked so tirelessly – often for 40 or more years – to seize power away from the Gilbertian world of Conservative and Liberal politics. 'The electoral battle is over, and we have won an amazing victory. Probably within six weeks a Labour ministry will be in power for the first time in English history . . . I wish I could reproduce for you the excitement the new situation has created,' a buoyant Harold Laski wrote to his longstanding American friend, Justice Oliver Wendell Holmes.[61]

In British political life, Laski established a reputation as Labour's outstanding political theorist and Marxist intellectual in the inter-war and post-war years. His career, as Laski moved among the great and the good, throws considerable light on the role of the intellectual in a changing world of Labour politics. In the 1920s a member of the Fabian Society, a friend of trade unionists – especially the miners during 'Black Friday' in April 1921 – and a prolific academic, Laski made the intellectual and practical case for a future Labour administration after the fall of the Lloyd George coalition. Though Rebecca West suggested that one believed only half what the pretentious Laski recounted – he once claimed he turned down MacDonald's offer of a Cabinet post – he was undoubtedly an influential figure who, through his teaching, writings and personal contacts, helped to shape Labour as a party that favoured parliamentary solutions rather than direct action. In the early 1920s, Laski's broad network of contacts included politicians and members of the intelligentsia, such as Sidney Webb, R. H. Tawney, Bertrand Russell, H. N Brailsford, and H. W. Massingham. Lord Haldane, who advised MacDonald, was one close associate Laski shared ideas with – especially on education – and was in regular contact with. Above all, Laski remained until the debacle of 1931 a fervent admirer of MacDonald who consulted him on various aspects of government.[62] In 1924 Laski penned the important Fabian tract No. 210, *The Position of the Two Parties and the Right of Dissolution*, about coping with minority government that probably convinced MacDonald he was on safe constitutional ground to ask George V to dissolve Parliament in October 1924.

In assuming office in January 1924, the Labour Party had demonstrated a remarkable and swift rise to power for a new political party. How far this was inevitable and whether it was expected that Labour would replace the Liberals within a British two-party system has led to considerable and continued debate among historians and political scientists.[63] Similarly, the party's history in office and opposition has been open to varying interpretations. Some writers have suggested that Labour's growth was almost inevitable as it captured trade union – and therefore working-class – support, while others have maintained that Labour's growth had more to do with the collapse of the Liberal Party during and just after the First World War.[64]

In post-war Western Europe, significant changes took place in socialist parties at varying degrees comparable to Labour's emergence as a major social democratic party in Britain. All political parties in the 1920s had to adjust to mass electorates – that now included women voters – and to confront the political, social and economic problems of a new post-war era. Socialist parties faced the challenge of new Communist parties, as well as established bourgeois parties – all competing for working-class support during times of industrial dislocation and change. In seeking ways forward, many European socialists revised attitudes towards capitalism, abandoned Marxism and the class struggle, and rethought socialist ideas and programmes. In the inter-war years, Swedish Social Democrats successfully pioneered a socialist state and welfare system, much admired by rising young British socialists like Hugh Gaitskell. Major electoral success was achieved by rejecting Marxist economics and embracing neo-Keynesian methods, redistributive taxation and a managed market economy. Elsewhere, in the 1920s, the German SPD adopted a revisionist programme and worked with bourgeois parties in the Weimar Republic especially in 1928–30, while in Belgium and the Netherlands the publication of the widely read *The Psychology of Socialism*, by the socialist, Hendrick de Man, provided a powerful rationale for alternative radical programmes to Marxism.[65] In some cases, socialists had to meet head on the dilemma of having power – in a coalition or minority – in circumstances where capitalism had not collapsed and socialism remained a distant dream. In France, where working-class support for socialism was comparatively weak and largely split between the *Section Francaise de l'Internationale Ouvriere* (SFIO) and the *Bolshevik Parti Communiste Francais* (PCF). The leading socialist, Leon Blum, drew an important theoretical distinction between the 'conquest of power', where socialism could be constructed eventually – by a mass party, with a strong economy and international peace – and 'the exercise of power', which justified taking office earlier in a non-revolutionary situation to secure limited reforms. In 1924 his SFIO concluded the temporary 'Cartel des Gauches' – an electoral alliance with Edouard Herriot's Radical Party (a strategy that eventually led to his Popular Front administration in 1936).[66]

In 1923 Britain's Labour leaders had not anticipated victory, but polling day produced the possibility of a Labour government. Sidney Webb, who had predicted in his presidential address to the party conference that Labour might take office in 1926, wrote to his close Fabian associate, William Robson, 'the one thing that neither I, nor anyone else could write now is 'What would a Labour Government do'!'[67] Webb's admission raises the question of how far Labour had prepared for power or considered a strategy for being in office. In the post-war years the party's electoral plan, despite a disappointing performance in the 1918 Coupon election, envisaged achieving the status of a national party, first as a credible opposition and then in office. Unquestionably, as we have seen, in the 1920s Ramsay MacDonald was the Labour Party's outstanding political strategist. By 1930 the London correspondent of the German newspaper *Vorwarts*, Egon Wertheimer, considered him to be 'the outstanding figure of International Socialism' following the deaths of leading European social democrats: Bebel, Jaures, Adler and Branting. 'He has become a legendary being – the personification of all that thousands of down-trodden men and women hope and dream and desire. Like Lenin, too, he is the focus of the mute hopes of a whole class.'[68] Like his European contemporaries, MacDonald had responded to the challenges of a changing world and the growth of a mass political democracy. While he was aware of, and influenced by, intellectuals such as the German revisionist, Eduard Bernstein, MacDonald sought to fashion a British form of socialism as a moderate alternative to Marxist ideas.

Between 1905 and 1921 MacDonald had set out his eclectic thinking on the reorganisation of society in 13 books of social and political theory, in the main published by the National Labour Press. Titles such as *Socialism and Society* and *Socialism* advocated cooperation rather than the class struggle. MacDonald informed his British readership: 'The mechanical and formal conception of social evolution which Marx held, together with the inadequate reason he assigned for the conduct of individuals and of classes are seed unfit for our historical soil.'[69] As Richard Lyman has written, MacDonald's prescriptions placed a greater emphasis on human qualities of mind and character, rather than specific programmes for implementation in office. In 1920 his booklet *A Policy for Labour* indicated the contents of the King's Address for an imaginary Labour government on taking office, but revealed little in terms of detailed plans for action. Only half the 13 pages covered domestic policies, with three pages vaguely on socialist measures. Nationalisation was accorded a mere paragraph of less than half a page.[70]

In 1923 when the prospect of taking office was no longer a distant dream, MacDonald mused: 'At times it is as necessary to preserve the forms of government as to produce legislative changes, even when the latter are very pressing. Can the Labour Party devise a policy which would enable it to do some useful and urgent work, like helping to settle Europe and increase the provision for dealing with unemployment, without compromise in any shape or form?'[71] MacDonald's political writings reveal his intellectual and moral belief in an evolving model of socialism – superior to capitalism – that would naturally supersede it. In this reasoning, moderation replaced the class struggle and strikes. Blum's conceptual distinction provided the justification for French socialists taking office instead of waiting for the capitalist world to collapse. Yet, under a different voting system, French socialists were never in power in the 1920s, whereas in 1923 MacDonald had no theoretical difficulties with promising the King in advance that his government would introduce 'no extreme legislation . . . or violent administrative changes carried out: *no playing up to the Clyde Division!* But an endeavour to carry on the Government on sound lines.'[72]

As we have seen, socialists critical of Labour's performance in twentieth-century British politics, particularly during the Wilson and Callaghan governments of 1964–70 and 1974–79, have blamed lack of adventure by moderate party leaders, their unbending attachment to parliamentarianism and the domination of the party by trade unions wedded to a labourist philosophy. Social reform, rather than socialism and the transformation of British capitalism, has been the prime objective. As a minority government in 1924 seemingly dependent upon Liberal votes, MacDonald and his ministers could offer a defence to such accusations of 'in office, but not in power'. Only modest and uncontroversial measures – it was believed – could hope to be achieved during their brief tenure of office. 'I used to ask, "Who is keeping us in this evening?" for at any moment a combination of Liberals and Tories could have thrown us out,' Clement Attlee, recalled with quiet humour.[73]

Richard Lyman's *First Labour Government* was published more than fifty years ago. After this passage of time, a new study provides the opportunity to offer fresh perspectives on a number of important historical issues in British politics that surround MacDonald's first ministry. As Britain went unexpectedly to the polls in December 1923, few people anticipated a Labour victory. At best, the Labour leadership predicted 1926 as the election year when Labour might succeed to power. The unexpected circumstances in which Labour assumed office in 1924 raises important questions about the composition of the new administration, its lack of ministerial experience, and what could be achieved by a ministry that could not command an absolute majority at Westminster.

In a changing world, as a democratic party led after 1922 by a more appealing leader and backed by a new Labour research and information bureau, Labour might be expected to bring in socialist measures to transform society, raise public expenditure, tackle unemployment and provide urgently needed reforms. Being in office also meant the opportunity to change the way Britain had been run for decades by drastically overhauling the machinery of government, introducing a capital levy on wealth, and to begin the process of reshaping a class-based society. J. H. Thomas, Labour Colonial Secretary, had observed that socialists before 1914 were seen 'merely as people who wore red neckties and waved red flags and sometimes made rude remarks about the monarchy'.[74] By any measure, a new left-wing administration, however moderate in scope and policy, might expect a hostile reception in governing circles from the monarchy, civil service – particularly the mandarins at the Treasury and the Foreign Office – and British intelligence in a world still shaken by the Russian Revolution. In anticipation of office Thomas had published *When Labour Rules* to assuage middle- and upper-class anxieties as to what a Labour government would do in taxation, property, constitution or foreign and imperial policy.

Labour remained a broad church as revealed by the response to the Russian Revolution in the remarkable Leeds Convention of 3 June 1917 attended by 1150 delegates – including Ramsay MacDonald – from trade unions, trades councils, local Labour parties, women's groups and peace groups. Similarly, in 1920 three different groups from the British Labour Party of varying ideological composition – George Lansbury, the official Labour Party and TUC delegation and Ramsay MacDonald – journeyed to Bolshevik Russia and Menshevik Georgia in 1920 to study the Soviet system towards the end of the period of civil war and Allied intervention. Their different conclusions reflected the varying attitudes toward socialism of the various delegates.[75]

Much was expected by the different interest groups – particularly the trade unions – of the incoming Labour government seemingly pledged to new international perspectives, to socialist objectives and to represent 'the worker by hand and brain', but faced by governing a nation deeply divided by class. Instead, the 1924 administration would test relationships within the Labour Party, not least between the Labour government and the Parliamentary Labour Party and most certainly between the Labour Party and the members throughout the country. In demonstrating Labour's respectability in office, MacDonald would have to contend not only with differing personalities within his Cabinet, but a broad-based coalition of interests that made up the Labour Party in 1924 – from the Clydeside ILP MPs suspended in June 1923 for unparliamentary behaviour to self-determining union bosses who regarded the party as its parliamentary wing.

Before 1914 Labour members at Westminster – except for MacDonald, Hardie and Henderson – had taken little interest in international policy. But in the intervening years total war had altered the international order. By 1924 Labour perspectives had shifted with the influx of former Liberals into the party and the influence of the Union of Democratic Control seeking the revision of the Versailles Treaty and the parliamentary control of foreign policy. Most interestingly, MacDonald's decision to combine the roles of Prime Minister and Foreign Secretary revealed priorities in policy making that require further comment on Labour's international outlook.

There is a sound case for arguing that 1924 marks the final demise of Liberalism. Under MacDonald's leadership, Labour successfully outstripped the Liberal Party as a serious contender for the progressive vote in British parliamentary politics, completing the process begun a quarter of a century before. One of the major debates since the 1960s has centred on the rise of the Labour Party and the decline of the Liberal Party in British politics, though historians remain keenly divided over the nature and timing of this major change in the British party system. The 1924 administration should be seen not only for the nine-month period when it demonstrated it could govern in a moderate and traditionally recognisable manner, but also for the part it played in establishing the Labour Party in the early 1920s as the major progressive party of British politics.

On resigning in October 1924, Ramsay MacDonald told George V that the first Labour government 'have shown the country that they have the capacity to govern in equal degree with the other parties in the House . . . and considering their lack of experience they have acquitted themselves with credit'.[76] MacDonald was, indeed, right to point to the achievements of his fledgeling ministry. Although like Macbeth, 'cabined, cribbed, confined', Labour, with no overall majority in 1924, had performed relatively well in office. Supposedly propped up by an ailing Liberal Party at Westminster, MacDonald's administration survived just 287 days. Nonetheless, his minority ministry fractured the political mould of almost a century by challenging the old Conservative–Liberal hegemony and finally dispatching the Liberals into the political wilderness. Although short-lived, the 1924 Labour government remains a notable subject of historical interest and long-term relevance in twentieth-century British politics. It had ensured that Britain superseded Germany in having the most influential and powerful democratic socialist party on earth.

2
'Over the Threshold'

'The Labour Party, after more than twenty years strenuous work, (is) now the Official Opposition, holding itself out to the electors as the Alternative Government,' Sidney Webb proclaimed proudly at the annual party conference in June 1923.[1] His Presidential Address painted a compelling picture of Labour's advance during the previous decade and beyond that was to take the party 'over the threshold' of power and into office.[2] Inexorably, it seemed, the Labour Party had gathered strength on all fronts. Growth in parliamentary and municipal representation was testament to the party's steady increase in membership to around four million affiliated members, sound organisation with local parties established in nearly 600 constituencies, and comprehensive political programmes in domestic and foreign policy. As seen earlier, Webb forecast precisely the future arrival of the first Labour government. He announced that 'a continuation of the rising curve of Labour votes from the 62,698 of 1900 ... (to) the 4.5 millions of 1922, would produce a clear majority of the total votes cast in Great Britain somewhere about 1926.'[3]

In June 1923 Webb also refuted Churchill's charge that Labour was not fit to govern like its Conservative and Liberal predecessors. The former civil servant had no hesitation in proclaiming that 'the Parliamentary Labour Party will be able ... to take over the responsibilities of office at least as competently as the majority of ministers of different parties whose public administration during the last forty years it happens to have been my particular business to scrutinise and study both from inside their offices and form without.' Churchill's provocative jibe, which he repeated in 1923, was very much in the minds of Labour leaders throughout the early 1920s and beyond, as they endeavoured to demonstrate their party's patriotism, moderation and respectability as suitable credentials for governing Britain and the British Empire.

As we have seen, the experience of the First World War left the Labour leadership determined in 1917–24 to build a national party with an appeal based on moderation and patriotism that went beyond working-class voters to middle Britain. A sign of this changing orientation during this period was reflected in the different titles of the party's manifestos. In 1900 Labour's first manifesto contained only an abbreviated 250 words, but by 1918 and 1922 Labour put before the electorate more detailed proposals entitled *Labour's call to the people* as it did in its 1923 manifesto entitled *Labour's appeal to the nation*. Similarly, Labour leaders in public speeches and writings stressed moderation and respectability, thereby rejecting any notion that Labour did not deserve the nation's trust as a party of government. In 1920, as seen earlier, J. H. Thomas published *When Labour Rules*, designed to dispel fears about a future socialist administration. While Labour's new policy statement *Labour and the New Social Order* (1918) included a similar reassurance against any fears of nationalisation and price controls, the party's leaders worked hard to portray the proposal of a capital levy as a benefit for the vast majority of the nation.[4]

In 1918 Labour had adopted a new constitution – the work of Arthur Henderson and the Fabian Sidney Webb – with individual party membership for the first time. The number of party members rose to 3.5 million in 1919 from 2.1 million four years before. Owing to the introduction of individual membership, considerable – albeit uneven – growth took place in the social and political composition of local Labour Parties in different parts of Britain. Labour's imbalance was demonstrated in the abnormal 1918 election where its candidates fought against the combined opposition of Liberals and Tories and the effects of the 'coupon' to support 'patriotic' candidates. Despite a modest increase from 42 MPs in the general election of December 1910 to 57 in the 1918 general election, little progress was achieved and prominent Labour figures such as MacDonald, Snowden, Lansbury and others associated with pacifism during the War were not returned at the polls. The composition of the PLP in 1918 reflected Labour's dependence on the trade unions and its concentration in certain industrial and urban heartlands. There were only six Scottish MPs, nine Welsh MPs and of the four members of the PLP returned for constituencies below the Severn–Wash line, three were from the London area.[5]

From 1918–21 the PLP was led by William Adamson, who had been elected unopposed as Chairman. A mediocre parliamentarian – he was frequently ill in 1919 and 1920 – he received a poor press from his Labour contemporaries. According to Manny Shinwell, Adamson was a 'dour and phlegmatic Scottish miners' leader very much out of his depth in the Commons'. After lunching with the Webbs, and hearing their complaint – that Labour's parliamentary leaders 'won't come and consult us' – Hugh Dalton noted in his diary: 'Much mockery of Adamson coming and announcing that, to become His Majesty's Opposition, all the Labour Party needed was two additional clerks, a typist and a messenger.' However, in 1924 MacDonald chose Adamson as Secretary of State for Scotland and again in 1929–31. In 1924 the Scottish minister's main contribution was his advocacy of Scottish Home Rule, including backing Clydesider Labour MP George Buchanan's unsuccessful Private Member's Bill in May 1924 for a single-chamber Scottish Assembly handling Scottish legislation within a Federal United Kingdom.[6]

Nevertheless, despite this unevenness in its parliamentary representation and its weak leadership in the House of Commons, Labour was regarded in political circles as the party of the future – a sufficient daunting prospect for Lloyd George to identify the socialist opposition – largely inspired by the Bolshevik revolution in Russia – as the future main enemy of his Coalition government.[7] The early 1920s were a watershed in parliamentary politics – three general elections in 1922, 1923 and 1924 – that marked a realignment of the three-party system. By the general election of 1923, the character of the Labour Party had changed considerably. From the pre-war party of protest, when the Liberals and Conservatives largely overshadowed it at Westminster, Labour had become the main opposition party poised on the brink of government.

In 1918–20 Labour made some significant – albeit limited – attempts to respond to the advent of women gaining the parliamentary vote. Dr Marion Phillips was appointed as the party's chief woman officer. Within two years women organizers were active in nine regions in building local women's sections, often based on earlier political and suffrage campaigns, in response to the advent of a female electorate. For example, the six constituency Labour parties in Leeds had between 1500 and 2000 women members. In post-war Woolwich in South London, the membership of the two Labour branches included over 1000 women.[8] Traditionally, gender divisions within the Labour Party often appeared to relegate women to routine groundwork, such as canvassing or arranging social activities, while industrial questions, foreign affairs and political strategy was deemed male territory compared to 'women's questions' such as health, children and education. However, as Matthew Worley has written, in a male-dominated political party, women were often unsung heroines who worked unstintingly in the service of Labour but also for the general advancement of women in British politics. The women's organiser for Wales, Elizabeth Andrews of the Rhondda Labour Party, devoted a lifetime until 1948 to forming women's sections, electoral work and raising the profile of women's issues in Labour politics. In the North East, including Yorkshire and Northumberland, the women's regional organiser Lillian Fenn had been instrumental in forming 118 women's sections in Durham alone by 1925, as well as contributing to the Labour Women's Advisory Council, women's events and important electoral activity.[9]

A centrepiece of the 1918 constitution was the famous Clause IV with the socialist commitment to 'the common ownership of the means of production'. The National Executive Committee (NEC) of 23 members included 13 trade union representatives, which reflected the expansion in trades union membership from 4.1 million in 1914 to 6.5 million in 1918 and over 8 million by 1920. In the same year, the annual party conference had adopted *Labour and the New Social Order* with a miscellany of socialist or collectivist resolutions. With its new constitution and policy statement, Labour built up a network of 527 Divisional or Local Labour Parties and Trades and Labour councils. However, Labour remained a broad church, an inchoate grouping of trade unionists, socialists, Fabians, cooperators, former Liberals and other progressive politicians.

In the 1922 general election – after the fall of the Lloyd George coalition government – the composition of the new Parliament was 347 Conservatives; 142 Labour; 117 Liberals (64 Liberals led by Asquith; 53 National Liberals led by Lloyd George). As David Howell has written, the 1922 election was also important for the return of an expanded and politically diversified PLP. At Westminster leading Labour figures, such as MacDonald, Snowden, Lansbury and Jowett – but not Henderson who needed a by-election victory – now sat alongside middle-class and upper-class recruits from Liberalism, including Trevelyan, Morel and Ponsonby. The composition of the new PLP executive showed a waning of trade unionists in favour of career politicians and socialist intellectuals. MacDonald's narrow victory over Clynes for the newly designated position of Labour party leader shaped Labour fortunes for the 1920s and beyond.

Surprisingly, in 1923, the second of three elections between 1922–24 provided the occasion for Labour to take office. Stanley Baldwin, who had replaced the terminally ill Andrew Bonar Law, decided on an early election, even though his party had an overall majority that could have given them five years in office. Baldwin announced to his Cabinet on 23 October plans to introduce a tariff policy as the only solution to the mounting unemployment that faced Britain. Two days later, at the Tory Party conference at Plymouth, he claimed that: 'if we go on pottering along as we are we shall have grave unemployment with us to the end of time. And I have come to the conclusion myself that the only way of fighting this subject is by protecting the home market.' The third Tory leader in seven months, Baldwin had always been a staunch protectionist. He had decided that there could be no fiscal change without an election, ostensibly due to a pledge given by his predecessor, Bonar Law. On 13 November, Baldwin indicated there was going to be a general election. George V agreed to the dissolution of Parliament on 16 November with polling day fixed for 6 December.

Baldwin's decision to abandon free trade temporarily reunited the divided Liberal opposition. The 1923 election rang with echoes of the historic contest of 1906, largely fought almost as a referendum on 'free trade versus protection'. The leading Labour figures – MacDonald, Snowden, Clynes, Henderson and, to some extent, Thomas – were all free traders and shared common ground with the Liberals in opposition to Tory plans for tariff reform. However, in the 1923 election, Labour also mounted a hard-hitting campaign against the Liberals, by broadening the issues beyond tariff reform to foreign affairs – including French occupation of the Ruhr – and Labour's ability to tackle the mounting problem of domestic unemployment.

The Labour election manifesto focused on the Conservative failure to tackle unemployment and rejected 'Tariffs as a remedy for Unemployment', condemning them as the way to the further 'impoverishment of the people' by perpetuating 'inequalities in wealth and distribution of the world's wealth'. Instead, Labour proposals contained a programme of 'national work [that] includes the establishment of a national system of electrical power supply, the development of transport by road, rail and canal, and the improvement of national resources by land drainage, reclamation, afforestation, town-planning and housing schemes. These not only provide a remedy for the present distress, but also investments for the future.'

Among other proposals was the abolition of the three-week 'gap' for the workless (the period of non-payment between covenanted benefit and uncovenanted benefit) and the proposal for a comprehensive programme of public works. One measure marked Labour out from the Liberals. The capital levy, in reality a wealth tax advocated by Snowden, Pethick Lawrence and Dalton, was heralded officially as 'a non-recurring, graduated War Debt Redemption Levy'.[10] It proved a controversial election issue that allegedly cost the party 50 seats and was quietly dropped once Labour was in office.[11] Labour also reiterated its commitment to public ownership through the control of mines, railway services and electrical power stations and the development of municipal services. On foreign policy, the Labour manifesto advocated an international conference to settle the problems of reparations and disarmament – 'the only security for nations' – and trusted that an enlarged League of Nations would secure international peace. In the final analysis the Labour manifesto appealed to the electorate to support its party candidates in order to secure a 'humane and more civilised society'. It was a powerful statement of the Labour position that was likely to enhance its parliamentary position, if not thrust it forward to power. In the event, however, political circumstances determined that Labour would be presented with power prematurely.

With a reunited Liberal Party there was always the danger to Labour prospects of a revival of Liberalism, particularly as MacDonald had only one year's experience since the war at the party helm. With the dissolution of Parliament pending the next day, the Labour leader opened the election campaign by moving a vote of censure on the Tory failure on unemployment and, in particular, on foreign affairs. 'I know perfectly well that whoever touches foreign affairs today with a new policy must be a man of infinite patience, and behind him must be a body that is willing to wait for results. Yes, but they have got to begin,' he told the House of Commons.[12] MacDonald left London by car *en route* to his own constituency of Aberavon in South Wales via enthusiastic and fervent meetings at Gloucester, Bristol, the Forest of Dean, Newport and Cardiff.[13]

The three general elections between 1922 and 1924 put a great strain upon Labour's impoverished finances. In 1923, when the election campaign expenditure totalled £194,627, the party secretary Arthur Henderson had set up an election fighting fund to assist local parties in difficulty. This initiative raised £23,565, with about half contributed by the National Union of Railwaymen and the remainder from party appeals and conference contributions. Other donations of around £4045 came from Henderson's anonymous 'friends'. In all, 158 urban constituencies and 57 rural constituencies received some kind of financial assistance from central party funds controlled by Henderson, with a greater proportion going to the urban areas.[14]

According to the *Liberal Magazine*, the Liberal losses were anticipated and the Labour Party was expected to secure around 200 seats:
'Everything was in their favour. They were opposed to protectionist
taxes; they had never been in office; they bore a plausible appearance
of being a working-class party; the general condition of the people was
about as bad as it could be.'[15]

Polling day on 6 December 1923 produced an indecisive result.
Broadly, the number of MPs returned reflected the votes cast for each
party. Though the turn out was still relatively high – 71 per cent
compared to 73 per cent in 1922 – the distribution of votes between
the three major parties produced little change from 1922: Conservatives
5.5 million votes (38.0 per cent of the total votes cast), Labour 4.4 million
(30.7 per cent) and Liberals 4.3 million (9.7 per cent). In terms of
the number of votes, the Conservatives had lost around 115,845, after
fighting 64 more seats, whereas the Liberals had gained 186,109 and
Labour recorded an increase of 121,310. However, no party now had
an overall majority in terms of the numbers of new MPs. The balance
of the three main parties in the House of Commons was Conservatives
258, Labour 191 and Liberals 159.[16]

In 1923 Labour increased its parliamentary representation. The party's
advance was strongest in and around London, where nearly 50 per cent
of the party's gains were secured; 22 MPs were returned (compared to
9 MPs in 1922) in the County of London and in the London suburbs
15 MPs were elected (7 MPs in 1922).[17] Elsewhere, though Labour
continued to move forward – gaining, for example, 18 seats from the
Lloyd George Liberals in different parts of country – the party's performance was patchy. In industrial constituencies, such as those in West
Yorkshire, East Lancashire, Tyneside and Teesside, Labour was unable
to make substantial inroads into Liberal control of seats in these areas.
Labour had made some progress in rural constituencies in 1922, but
was unable to build on this performance in 1923, whereas the Liberals
scored significant victories in farming seats. The 1923 contest was the
only general election between 1918 and 1966 where the Conservative
Party failed to secure a majority of the rural seats.[18]

In 18 constituencies where Labour withdrew its candidate to give the
Liberals a clear run against the Conservatives there was a 20 per cent
increase in the Liberal share of the vote. In 63 constituencies where
there was a Conservative–Liberal contest, Labour intervention would
have secured the seat on a minority vote and an overall majority in
the new Parliament. Labour's depleted resources in rural areas indirectly
contributed to the advent of the First Labour Government.[19]

As the prospect of Labour achieving office had became more likely there was a considerable discussion, within and without the Labour Party, about the policies it should pursue. Whilst it was obvious that MacDonald wanted moderation, many other sections of the party did not want to see a Labour government serving the needs of a capitalist society. This became a source of contention within the party. H. W. Massingham, former editor of the *Nation*, set the scene for conflict with his report on the Labour 'Victory Rally' at the Albert Hall on 8 January as MacDonald prepared his party for office.

It is worth recalling this historic event in detail through the perspective of this informed outsider who captured the moment when a new party was rising with high expectations, but had its aspiration dampened by the reality of only achieving minority government:

> To the thousands of young men and women – the average age struck one as between 20 and 30 – who poured into the Albert Hall..., the event came as an almost solemn act of dedication rather than a flaming signal of party triumph. The British Labour Party resembles the Catholic Church at least in two particulars. It has faith and an organisation, and it is the union of these two characteristics that produces the effect of disciplined enthusiasm of which these central assemblies are evidence. The order of the Albert Hall meeting was perfect, evolved as it was out of the simple and impressive ritual of the Labour demonstration and the close harmony of its poetry and aspirations with the temper of the audience... The singing, mostly of hymn tunes and led by a trained choir from the orchestra, was set to the three or four fine English poems by Morris and Carpenter, whose familiar rhythm makes the marching music of the party and spiritualises their vision of a new social order.... Here and everywhere was the evidence of the spirit not of a party so much as a religion, which it means to apply, in full confidence, to the art of government.

This tone of mingled buoyancy and seriousness, with its suggestions of a young evangelistic church in bloom of its days of faith, was not the only remarkable feature of the Albert Hall meeting. There was something more notable still and that was the harmony between leaders and followers. Mr. MacDonald had come to say a difficult word to an idealistic audience. The word was moderation.... The effort of the Labour Ministry to establish itself as a governing force would, he made clear, proceed by a dual and connected movement. It would endeavour to establish a new concordat of peace, based upon the immediate recognition of Russia and an attempt to bring

Germany back into the European system. And it would make an offer with capital to engage with it in a great scheme of productive employment. . . . Impatient idealism might have revolted, and had it done so, the life of the Labour government, if it had ever begun, would have dwindled in a short and inglorious episode. But the response was perfect. The enthusiasm of the meeting was restrained and enhanced; and it was evident that the new Government, basing itself not on class war, but on the cooperative and even the religious instincts of the whole nation, would have behind it the wonderful movement, which brought it into being.[20]

Massingham's spellbinding evocation of the Albert Hall Rally is redolent with the hopes and realities of Labour's position in 1924. The main strand identifiable in the Labour Party is the ethical and spiritual one most associated with the early independent Labour organisations, drawing upon the pioneering socialism of William Morris and Edward Carpenter, as well as the ethical objection to inequality, to project the need for a 'new social order' in Britain. This, essentially ILP, strand was generally ambivalent about the First World War and wanted to bring Germany back into the European system, by removing the reparations imposed by the Treaty of Versailles, and was also intent upon bringing the Soviet Union into the same system.

The irony of the vast Albert Hall gathering was that the essentially radical, spiritual and principled Labour Party – the very section of the party most opposed to compromise – was being confronted with MacDonald's call for moderation. Whether or not this was a deliberate strategy by the Labour Leader, operating through a journalist who was being mooted as a possible candidate for political office, is impossible to know. However, what the meeting did not convey was the sense of a collectivist movement dominated by the trade unions, who were mostly driven more by the economic considerations of their members than by idealism. In this respect, we can also turn to particular groups such as the Independent Labour Party and the Communist Party of Great Britain to identify their political objectives and their expectations of an incoming Labour government.

Formed in 1893 at Bradford after the Manningham Mills Strike by Keir Hardie, John Bruce Glasier, George Bernard Shaw, Bob Smillie, Philip Snowden, Edward Carpenter and others, the Independent Labour Party (ILP) was the largest of the socialist societies involved in founding the Labour Representation Committee (LRC). After a disastrous performance in the 1895 election, the ILP had adopted the strategy of working with the trade unions, which furnished the basis for the establishment of the LRC on 27–28 February 1900. As the LRC became the Labour Party in 1906, the ILP remained an affiliated organisation until 1932, though it was a separate party with its own MPs and annual conference. In many respects, the ILP was Labour's intellectual godparent and provided socialist ideology and propaganda based on 'the brotherhood of man'. From within its ranks in the years before the first Labour government, had emerged most of the early Labour leaders, particularly Keir Hardie, Ramsay MacDonald, Philip Snowden, and Bruce Glasier. In 1924 the ILP could claim that the new Labour Cabinet included six members of the ILP (MacDonald, Snowden, John Wheatley, Fred Jowett, Charles Trevelyan and Josiah Wedgwood – three of whom, MacDonald, Jowett and Wheatley, were on the ILP National Administrative Council [NAC]) and nine junior ministers (Clement Attlee, Arthur Ponsonby, William Graham, Morgan Jones, Emanuel Shinwell, J. Stewart, J. W. Muir, Willie Leach and Ben Spoor).[21]

Several leaders had played a prominent role in opposing the First World War, although the ILP effectively allowed individual conscience on the War. As already noted, MacDonald had resigned his chairmanship of the PLP to oppose the War while the bulk of the Labour Party – including Arthur Henderson who entered the War Cabinet – supported the war effort. MacDonald himself was attacked viciously by Horatio Bottomley's journal, *John Bull*, which publicised MacDonald's illegitimacy. 'No paid agent of Germany had served her better,' declared *The Times*, in a leading article 'Helping the Enemy' on the Labour politician on 1 October 1914 entitled 'Helping the Enemy'. MacDonald became the most hated and vilified person in British politics with his meetings frequently broken by pro-war groups.[22] In 1918 he lost his Leicester seat in the 'Coupon election' at the end of the war and his life was endangered when he became the unsuccessful Labour candidate in the Woolwich by-election in 1921. His fortunes began to change remarkably when he was returned as MP for Aberavon in 1922 and shortly afterwards was elected Labour leader. MacDonald's wartime record was fresh in the memories of those who had fought in the Great War and there was clear concern about his fitness to be Prime Minister when British national interests were at stake.

Even more disturbing for some opponents must have been the prospect of Philip Snowden becoming Chancellor of the Exchequer. A prominent ethical socialist of the pre-Great War years, Snowden had campaigned strongly against the conflict with pamphlets and parliamentary speeches connected with the tribunals of conscientious objectors, opposition to compulsory conscription and the demand for allies to declare their war aims.[23] However, he was also associated with the Leeds Convention of the Workmen's and Soldiers' Council of June 1917 organised by the United Council of the ILP and the British Socialist Party (BSP) that had been formed on the eve of the Great War. The BSP, a quasi-Marxist organisation, was pressing for peace from 1916 onwards and, working with the ILP, felt the need to respond to the February 1917 Revolution in Russia. The Leeds Conference, which MacDonald also attended, was convened with Snowden as chairman. It attracted well over 1000 delegates and passed four resolutions including hailing the Russian Revolution, advocating a general peace based upon the rights of nations to decide their own affairs, and demanding the formation of a Council of Workmen's and Soldiers' delegates in every town, urban and rural district. The movement never took off – but, unfairly, it marked Snowden down as a revolutionary.[24]

Both MacDonald and Snowden had drifted away from the ILP in the early 1920s but they were still nominally associated with it. At the same time, the ILP was also moving politically to the left and some members had a brief flirtation with Marxism. The Great War had seen the balance of power within the ILP move from London, Lancashire, West Yorkshire and South Wales to the increasing domination of industrial West Scotland. In the 1922 general election, Labour secured 142 seats against 345 Conservatives, 62 Liberals (Asquith supporters) and 53 National Liberals (Lloyd George supporters). In Scotland Labour became the dominant parliamentary party with a third share of the total votes cast and 29 of 43 constituencies. This election marked the spectacular return to Westminster of the remarkable Clydeside group of ILP MPs who had secured ten of the 15 Glasgow seats, as well as other West Scotland constituencies; 18 of the Scottish Labour MPs had travelled down to London together. Famously, David Kirkwood exclaimed to the thousands who cheered him and his fellow Clydeside MPs off at St Enoch's Station: 'when we come back, this station, this railway, will belong to the people!'[25]

Although Clifford Allen, with his middle-class and intellectual supporters, financed the rapid growth of the ILP in the 1920s, the Clydeside section – led by John Wheatley and Jimmy Maxton – controlled the party from the mid-1920s onwards. In addition, though their subsequent recollections varied, the Clydesiders had probably voted for MacDonald in the Labour leadership contest, which MacDonald had won narrowly by 61 votes to 56 in 1922. Pat Dollan later claimed the group 'united to elect Ramsay MacDonald as Leader', whereas

Emanuel Shinwell recalled James Maxton imploring him, 'Please don't vote for MacDonald.' However, their continued support for MacDonald, who had previously been developing his contacts with the Scottish group including contributing a regular column to the Glasgow *Forward*, was soon to be tested.[26]

In Parliament the Scottish ILP members soon displayed their disapproval for Parliamentary traditions and the Labour leadership's acceptance of the conventions of the House of Commons. In a famous parliamentary scene that led to the suspension of four ILP MPs, James Maxton called the Tory MP, Sir Frederick Banbury, a 'murderer' for endorsing a financial cut in the health grants to the Scottish Board of Education – a charge repeated by fellow ILPers, John Wheatley, Rev Campbell Stephen and George Buchanan. Emanuel Shinwell reiterated the charge but adopted more appropriate Parliamentary words. While the ILP rank and file and other Labour MPs cheered the group's action, the Labour front bench remained neutral by not voting against the suspension of the Clydeside MPs from the Commons.[27]

At the ILP's annual conference in 1923 there was evidence of rising tensions between the intellectual section of the ILP and the Clydesiders over the crisis provoked by the French invasion of the Ruhr coalfield area. Charles Roden Buxton, an internationalist and anti-militarist, suggested that the Ruhr should be returned to Germany. The Clydeside group agreed, but insisted that the coal miners on the Ruhr were less deprived than those in the West of Scotland. John Wheatley noted that under-consumption at home meant that 'The enemy was not beyond the sea, it was here at home.'[28] Clifford Allen disagreed and emphasised the international causes of unemployment in Britain and Europe. The basis of future division between the international and national sections of the ILP was evolving, but the general election of December 1923 changed the situation entirely.

The attitude of the ILP to the possibility of a first-ever Labour Government emerged at a well-attended lunch on 10 December of the committee of the *New Leader*, the ILP's newspaper, edited by H. N. Brailsford, with a readership from across the Labour movement. While MacDonald had officially opposed Brailsford's appointment as editor, the *New Leader* supported his leadership until the advent of the first Labour Government: 'He is the one possible leader. His personal distinction, his intellectual power, his stature as a man and a thinker rank him among the greatest of our assets,' Brailsford declared in response to the Clydesiders' protests at MacDonald's lethargic leadership.[29] Those present included Clifford Allen, H. N. Brailsford,

Ramsay MacDonald, Arthur Ponsonby, Margaret Bondfield, Fenner Brockway, Molly Hamilton and Henry Nevinson.[30] There Ponsonby noted he 'heard the latest. The majority opinion seemed to be in favour of accepting [office] if MacDonald is sent for... I was converted to this idea provided it was not accompanied by any agreement with other parties, of which there seems to be no question.' To his surprise and dismay, Ponsonby also heard of the possibility of Thomas becoming Foreign Secretary. Clifford Allen had certainly opposed any such arrangement throughout the general election and other ILP leaders asserted as much.[31] Patrick Dollan, a prominent member of the Scottish ILP, believed that a minority government should put forward reforms in education and housing and offer a foreign policy that included recognition of the Soviet Union. In the *New Leader*, he declared that there needed to be a straight conflict between capitalism and socialism and that 'Hanging on to office' by timid compromise would be a fatal mistake.[32]

Despite the fact that many members of the ILP gained office in the 1924 Labour Government, most, such as MacDonald and Snowden, were nominally members, but not financially underwritten by the ILP at the general election. As we shall see, only John Wheatley and Fred Jowett of the ILP MPs were appointed to the Cabinet while Willie Leach and Clement Attlee gained junior ministerial posts. Notwithstanding this, and the growing criticism of Jimmy Maxton and some of the Clydesiders, Clifford Allen was willing to announce to the ILP Conference held at York in April 1924 that the Labour Government was preparing the way for future developments in socialism.[33] However, as we shall see, relations worsened as Labour failed to deliver on policy, which led eventually towards the ILP's controversial and divisive programme 'Socialism in Our Time' in 1925 and 1926, with its 'reformist' core idea of providing a 'Living Wage'. This contradicted its more 'revolutionary' objective of bringing about a speedy end to capitalism. In its ambitions for the first Labour government, it is clear that the ILP was hoisting the 'Red Flag' rather than the 'Union Jack', although it was always willing to make some concessions, despite frowning upon Labour's dependence upon the Liberals. Ultimately, therefore, the ILP's leaders became increasingly frustrated as the political activities of the first Labour government took shape.

The National Executive of the Labour Party, the PLP, and even the ILP, under specific conditions of avoiding compromise, were favourable towards the formation of the first Labour government. The TUC also supported its formation together with other sections of the Labour movement's confirmation of the wisdom of taking office was apparent at the Labour Party conference in October 1924. The Executive Committee's Report answered political opponents who had previously declared 'Labour was not fit to govern' in these terms:

> The decision to form a Government was the most important the Party has ever been called upon to make, but there are few today who will dispute that the decision was a wise one. Abroad, Labour's advent to office created expectations that, in part at any rate, have been fulfilled. Internationalism is indeed a more popular faith to-day, and the League of Nations a more favoured instrument of achievement and preservation of peace among young people than seemed possible a year ago.

The Report also commented: 'A Labour Ministry has shown that it can undertake the task of Government, as sincerely, and as successfully as any of it predecessors.'[34] These observations were illustrated by numerous examples of resolutions of congratulations passed by the National Executive of the Labour Party to Labour MPs. Most obviously, the Executive Committee of the Labour Party expressed its 'appreciation of the splendid spirit of unity loyalty and devotion displayed by the entire Labour Movement', thanked Arthur Henderson for organising the 'magnificent electoral triumph' and in view of the minority parliamentary position, enjoined that they 'proceed at once to make all the necessary arrangements – financial and otherwise for the next contest which will be the most momentous in the history of the Party'.[35]

While in 1924, as we shall see, one of the first acts of the new Labour administration was to give official recognition to the Bolshevik regime in Russia, at home the Labour leadership displayed an uncompromising attitude towards British communism. Although the CPGB enjoyed some support within the ranks of the Labour Party, the Labour leaders regularly turned down its attempts to affiliate. Even though most Communist Party members had joined from the British Socialist Party – previously affiliated to the Labour Party – Labour leaders such as MacDonald, Snowden and Thomas made no secret of their overwhelming opposition to Communist presence within the party structure. During the 1920s the CPGB challenge – represented by the attempts to affiliate – was regarded as a direct threat, ready to step into the shoes of the Labour Party as the main representative body of working class voters.

In the early 1920s Lenin had encouraged the newly founded Communist Party of Great Britain to apply for affiliation, although there had been some reluctance of follow this advice. Labour Party conferences repeatedly rejected all the CPGB affiliation attempts between 1920 and 1924, opposing the last of these overwhelmingly by 4,115,000 votes to 224,000. In 1920 the Labour NEC's refusal was on the grounds that the two parties did not share a common constitution, principles and programme. In 1921, despite negotiations between representatives of both sides, no progress was made. In June 1922, at the Labour Party conference at Edinburgh, the NEC again advised against granting affiliation. It was agreed that every person nominated as a delegate, 'shall individually accept the constitution and principles of the Labour Party' – a decision reinforced by a resolution banning delegates associated with a party sponsoring parliamentary candidates not approved by the Labour Party.[36] These conference decisions directly challenged the right of unions to choose their conference delegates and also required constituency parties to exclude properly accredited Communist representatives from their ranks. As a result, local Labour Parties began to jib at excluding 'tried and trusted' members as well as delegates from trade union branches, simply because of Communist Party membership, whereas Liberal and Conservative trade unionists in theory might attend Labour conferences unopposed.

Such was the hostility to the Edinburgh amendments that the London Conference of the Labour Party, during the summer of 1923, agreed a simple compromise that all delegates should individually accept the constitution of the Labour Party. But even this did not appease many trade unionists. In December 1923, at the time of the discussion about the formation of a Labour government, a Labour Party NEC sub-committee was charged with re-examining the situation, but without any change in the position by the time Labour was in office.[37] By the 1924 Labour Party conference, Standing Orders had been altered, requiring a three-year gap before any issue could be voted on again.[38] During the 1924 debate, the Labour MP Frank Hodges attacked the CPGB's proposals for affiliation, while Harry Pollitt, the Boiler Makers' delegate who later became the CPGB general secretary, argued that Communists were doing the 'donkey work' in organising workshops and trade union branches. It made no difference to the outcome of debate as positions were already fixed.[39] During the months of Britain's first Labour government, the increasingly hostile attitude of the CPGB did not help matters.

As Andrew Thorpe has argued, the Labour leadership in the 1920s was dominated by 'the Big Five' figures of MacDonald, Snowden, Henderson,

Thomas and Clynes. With some exceptions, they came from fairly similar backgrounds and shared an ideology of labourism. Though they often squabbled amongst themselves, and were suspicious of the aloof MacDonald, they also possessed in common a rejection of political extremism. Instead, this group of Labourites believed socialism would evolve out of the success of capitalism, unlike Communists who awaited a breakdown in capitalism that would lead to revolution. These Labour leaders had also chosen the parliamentary road to socialism – hence MacDonald's retort against Poplarism and Direct Action – and believed the state was fundamentally class-neutral and open to capitalist or socialist control. In their attitude to British communism in the 1920s, they noted the CPGB's loyalty to the Third International and the Soviet system. There was also Labour's fear of the control that Moscow exerted over the CPGB and the evidence of events in Russia, such as the Soviet invasion of Georgia in 1921, the execution of Social Revolutionary leaders in 1921 – as happened later in the show trials in 1936–38. All contributed to unease and hence Labour's rejection of the CPGB's attempts to affiliate owing to incompatibility of the two parties and its expulsion of individual Communists from the party and its associated organisations by 1928.[40]

In 1924 the CPGB initially had welcomed the advent of the minority Labour government that had taken power, but expected it would come forward with a socialist programme to improve the position of the working classes. However, as we shall see, when Labour seemed to be militating against working-class interests – the outcome of the rail strike in January 1924, the strike of the dockers, the London traffic strike, and the builders' strike, all revealing that the Labour government wanted the trade unions to settle on poor terms – attitudes changed.

There could have been no greater proof that Labour had furled the Red Flag and unfurled the Union Jack than its hostile attitude towards the Communist Party of Great Britain before, during and after the formation of the 1924 Labour government. MacDonald had argued for moderation and a modest programme of social and political reform. Alternatively, members of the ILP and others in the Labour Party agreed that MacDonald should not refuse the opportunity, if invited, to form an administration – but in many cases only on the basis of a bold socialist programme put forward regardless of the administration's minority position at Westminster. Though there was ground for disagreement within Labour ranks about the strategy to be pursued once in office, there seems to have been less disagreement with the Labour leadership's resolution to distance the party from British communism.

Despite some conflicting approaches adopted by different sections of the Labour Party as it went 'over the threshold', it is clear Labour's orientation was in favour of the Union Jack and not the Red Flag. MacDonald wanted to display the essential moderation, respectability and patriotism of his party with a limited programme of relatively uncontroversial reforms upon which most party members, the party in the constituencies, the TUC and the PLP could unite. However, few Labourites favoured the massive and revolutionary changes advocated by the CPGB. Fearful that the Communists wished to use the Labour Party for its own aims, the Labour Party during the 1920s firmly distanced itself from British communism. Labour rebuffed the CPGB's attempts to affiliate to the Labour Party, to make it increasingly difficult for individual communists to be involved in the party, and Labour leaders made it abundantly clear that they believed the CPGB was controlled from Moscow. Yet it was a heavy irony that, despite Labour's political moderation and displays of unflagging patriotism, its opponents could still profitably play up Labour's association with Bolshevism. As we shall see, it was a bungled official prosecution of a British Communist and the accusation of a Soviet plot hatched in Moscow – as seemingly revealed by the infamous Zinoviev Letter – that hastened the downfall of Britain's first Labour government.

3
Labour Takes Office

In December 1923 Lord Haldane – the former Liberal Imperialist soon to be Labour Lord Chancellor – wrote to his 99-year-old mother at his home in Scotland. 'The City is in a panic at the thought of a Labour Government and is cursing Baldwin for bringing in this election. All the old ladies are writing to their brokers beseeching them to save their capital from confiscation,' Haldane told her in his daily letter. 'I have had a message from Baldwin begging me to join the Labour Government and help them out,' he added.[1] His former Liberal Party leader agreed. 'You would be amused if you saw the contents of my daily post-bag: appeals, threats, prayers from all parts, and from all sorts and conditions of men, women and lunatics, to step in and save the country from the horrors of Socialism and Confiscation,' Asquith noted – after an election that left the Liberals as the third parliamentary party at Westminster. In defeat, he reassured himself it was still possible to journey from Land's End to Oxfordshire without crossing any Tory or Labour constituencies.[2]

The outcome of the December 1923 general election – Conservatives 258 MPs, Labour 191, and Liberals 158 – left an uncertain political situation at Westminster with no party holding an absolute majority. In these circumstances, George V played a significant role in deciding who should govern the country. Though he had lost his overall majority of 75, Baldwin did not resign immediately, but remained in office on the King's advice that he should await the verdict of the new Parliament in January 1924. The King told Baldwin that neither opposition party appeared eager to take office. Moreover, there remained the daunting prospect that a Labour administration led by Ramsay MacDonald 'might introduce a Levy on Capital, increased income tax and super-tax and death duties'. In the likelihood that Parliament rejected such a socialist measure, a fervent appeal to the electorate on 'this splendid and tempting proposal' could easily result in a landslide Labour victory. Though Baldwin stood firm against any kind of coalition – 'he had killed one and would never join another' – the King hoped that some working arrangement with the Liberals might be possible to keep the Conservatives in power 'for the present'.[3]

During the next few weeks Baldwin's decision not to resign immediately resulted in some hare-brained schemes and frenzied plots to prevent Labour gaining power, such as forming a Tory–Liberal coalition, including substituting Austen Chamberlain or Lord Deby for Baldwin as Conservative leader. All came to naught. The Conservative Chancellor of the Duchy of Lancaster, J. C. C. Davidson, formerly Parliamentary Private Secretary (PPS) to Bonar Law and to Stanley Baldwin, summed up the prevailing view: 'Any dishonest combination of that sort – which means the sacrificing of principles by both Liberals and Tories to deprive Labour of their constitutional rights – is the first step down the road to revolution.'[4]

In the end official attitudes did not stand in the way of a Labour government once the Conservatives were defeated in the new Parliament. According to his biographer, George V had not only advised that Baldwin should continue as Prime Minister, but made it clear it was his constitutional duty on the fall of the Conservative administration to invite MacDonald – as the leader of the second largest party in the Commons – to form a government.[5] On 14 December, Stamfordham had told the editor of the *Spectator*, St Loe Strachey, who had proposed outlandishly that Reginald McKenna, former Liberal Home Secretary and a Director of the London City and Midland Bank, should be invited to head up a 'Government of Trustees' for two years: 'at the present moment I feel His Majesty should do his utmost not to hamper in any way Mr Ramsay MacDonald . . . I expect that the King will be interpreting the general feeling of the people of the country, that . . . the Government, whoever they should be, should have a fair chance.'[6]

Within Labour circles, as already seen, there was also considerable debate about whether or not the party should assume office, given it could not command a majority in the House of Commons. On 8 December MacDonald had returned to London from his constituency of Aberavon, to find the evening papers announcing that Baldwin would resign shortly and that the King would send for him. The Labour leader noted that opinions differed within his party about taking office in the prevailing circumstances, despite the overwhelming support of the Labour Party and the trade unions. Sydney Arnold and Hastings Lees-Smith believed only disappointment and eventual overwhelming electoral defeat would result from a minority government. Influenced by the views of the economist J. A. Hobson, MacDonald was inclined to risk office to secure a peaceful European settlement with a limited programme in domestic politics, based on unemployment schemes and improved housing, pensions, agriculture and the national debt – thereby attracting national support for a future election victory. 'Not sure yet that the party wd. give confidence to do this moderate work, but think it would,' was MacDonald's estimation at this point.[7]

On the political Left, John Wheatley, the socialist MP for Glasgow, Shettleston, who was to join the Cabinet, rejected any notion of a Labour–Liberal alliance. 'Such a coalition or compromise is impossible. Were it possible, and adopted, it would break the hearts of those gallant men and women whose sacrifices and enthusiasm have carried our movement to the gates of the promised land,' he declared.[8] On the Left, a divergence of views formed over the appropriate strategy in the confused parliamentary situation – with individuals such as Robert Smillie, David Kirkwood and Frederick Pethick Lawrence holding firm that Labour should only take office with a clear majority. On the other hand, James Maxton believed that Labour should take up the cudgels, take office and bring in a full socialist programme and, when defeated, seek an improved mandate from the country.[9]

After the general election, as already indicated, a series of consultative meetings between the Labour leadership and different Labour and trade union groups agreed on the desirability of Labour taking office, even if for less than a year. On the eve of the NEC meeting on 12 December, Beatrice and Sidney Webb held a dinner for 'Labour's Big Five' – MacDonald, Snowden, Henderson, Clynes and Thomas – at their London home, 41 Grosvenor Road. All were apprehensive about taking office, except for Henderson, but believed that MacDonald could not refuse the King's invitation to form an administration. MacDonald went through a memorandum he had prepared for the meeting on the work of a future government and the risks involved. MacDonald made a symbolic note of the occasion: 'Unanimous that moderation & honesty were our safety. Agreed to stand together.' An indelible imprint was made on the first Labour government – even before its formation.

Beatrice Webb observed that some experience of minority government would benefit Labour in the future. 'And these few weeks or months of office, if it comes off, is like a scouting expedition in the world of administration, a testing of men and measure before they are actually called to assume majority power . . . ' she noted.[10] Sidney Webb, whose memorandum on the formation of the first Labour administration was not published until nearly 40 years later, took the view MacDonald should be left to the job of assembling his first government. Subsequent meetings with the Labour Party Executive, the General Council of the Trades Union Congress (TUC) followed by a joint session of the two bodies ended the public discourse surrounding the possibility of Labour taking office.[11]

Labour had rapidly established its position since 1922–23 as the second party in British politics and His Majesty's Opposition. MacDonald had emphasised, as already noted, the dire consequences on public opinion of a refusal to take on the responsibility of government. He also frightened doubters within the Labour ranks that the party might also surrender its position at Westminster to the Tories as His Majesty's Opposition, if Asquith formed a Liberal government after Baldwin had resigned. 'The responsibility of so sudden and unexpected an assumption of office [by Labour] gave the party a shock which sobered even the wildest of the shouters,' Webb concluded.[12]

The strong likelihood that Labour would take office became evident when on 18 December Asquith met almost all the Liberal MPs at the National Liberal Club and declared he would not 'stir a finger to save' the Tory government in the new Parliament – a position endorsed by Lloyd George and Sir John Simon. Asquith's speech set the seal on a future Labour government. He told Liberal MPs that they 'really control[led] the situation' and 'if a Labour government [were] ever to be tried . . . it would hardly be . . . under safer conditions'.[13]

Asquith's public pronouncement on 18 December may well have been motivated by the possibility that he would become Prime Minister in the event MacDonald could not form an administration. As Philip Williamson has suggested, to all intents and purposes, difficulties over important ministerial appointments in the Lords, where Labour was grossly under-represented, could have prevented MacDonald assembling an administration. If so, the Liberal leader's belief that MacDonald would find it impossible to overcome this hurdle would explain his decision not to assist the Conservatives.[14] Should a short-lived Labour administration fail, Asquith had also declared that the King might resort to other ministers to form a government, rather than grant MacDonald an immediate dissolution. The Labour leader agreed with the former editor of the *Nation*, H. W. Massingham – since April 1923 a freelance journalist espousing the Labour cause – that Asquith had 'utterly mis-stated the constitutional position in regard to Dissolution'.[15] A recent recruit from

Liberalism, Massingham had been on the platform at the Albert Hall victory rally and likened the animated Labour gathering to a religious revival. MacDonald used Massingham, who had become his confidant, as a valuable intermediary – first in confirming that the City bankers would not take fright at the prospect of Labour in office and in negotiating the official recognition of the Bolshevik regime in February 1924.[16] While Massingham advised MacDonald of Asquith's intention to throw out a minority Labour government, the Labour leader emphasized the distrust he was dealing with within his own party towards their Liberal opponents.[17]

Between the end of polling and the King's invitation to form the first Labour government, MacDonald had approximately six weeks to consider his selections for office. By the time he left for the Christmas holidays at his home in Lossiemouth, on the Moray Firth in the North East of Scotland, he had received his mandate from the Labour movement to form an administration if, as seemed likely, the King offered him the opportunity to take office.

How MacDonald decided on the composition of his administration has not been totally clear, though he largely enjoyed a free hand in deciding the appointments. As already noted, Webb had proposed that MacDonald should follow constitutional practice and select his own Cabinet. In this respect, in taking office, the Labour leader did not attempt any fundamental reorganisation of government machinery – such as Cabinet reform – recommended by the influential Haldane Committee in 1918, even though its chairman, who had served in the celebrated 1906–10 Liberal Cabinet, became Labour's Lord Chancellor. As Peter Hennessey has written: 'Twice a week the Haldane Committee would consume tea, muffins and cigarettes in Haldane's dining room at No. 28 Queen's Gate (his London home).' Among those questioning Cabinet ministers and senior civil servants were Jimmy Thomas and Beatrice Webb. 'I tell them that I am discovering the land of Whitehall *for the future Labour Cabinet*,' Beatrice Webb remarked. In 1918 Haldane's Report left a legacy in the corridors of power that endured until the 1980s. Celebrated for its comprehensive and coherent recommendations – including a streamlined and effective Cabinet at the heart of government – it had, however, already gathered dust by the time Haldane returned to power in 1924.[18]

In constructing his first Cabinet, Ramsay MacDonald chose moderate Labour politicians and trade unionists to broadly reflect the composition of his party. But he also included former Liberals and Conservative peers. 'Cartoonists and countesses were united in feeling that these men were safe and conformist,' another British Labour Prime Minister observed some fifty years later.[19]

Like other Labour figures, Beatrice and Sidney Webb remained in the dark about MacDonald's specific intentions except what they gleaned from Haldane. 'On Saturday we dined with the former [Haldane] – one of those little conflabs we have had now for over thirty years with this fellow conspirator. J.R.M. had consulted him about appointments and had persuaded him to become Lord Chancellor and Leader of the House of Lords... then on Monday Parmoor came in to tell us that he had consented to be Lord President of the Council and act as J.R.M.'s deputy on foreign affairs in the House of Lords.'[20] Sidney Webb, who had bombarded MacDonald in Lossiemouth with memoranda on the new administration, had not learnt of his own inclusion in the Cabinet – initially as Minister of Labour – until New Year's Eve. Even then, MacDonald first asked him 'not to speak of his office', and then moved him to the Board of Trade.[21]

What is patently obvious is that the future Labour ministers exercised little influence over MacDonald, apart from one or two individuals, such as the party secretary, Arthur Henderson, who dug his heels in for the Home Office. Brief details can be garnered about the formation of the first Labour government from the political autobiographies and accounts left by the central Labour figures.

Philip Snowden in his two-volume autobiography, published after the controversial fall of the second Labour government of 1929–31, provided a different slant on these early negotiations. He revealed serious misgivings that MacDonald possessed *carte blanche* in deciding appointments in the virtual isolation of his remote Lossiemouth retreat. Snowden recalled: 'Both Henderson and myself in these conversations expressed our resentment at MacDonald's secrecy, and thought he ought to be in London in regular consultation with his colleagues. Henderson thought that we ought to have sought from MacDonald that night at Webb's some indication of how he proposed to fill the particular offices.'[22]

In remarkable contrast, J. H. Thomas, Labour MP and former General Secretary of the National Union of Railwaymen, unabashedly claimed that he alone was the main architect, as MacDonald's chief ally, of the Labour administration in 1924. 'There have been many exaggerated stories about the formation of that Government, the bestowing of offices and the general composition of the Cabinet... the principal appointments were made in my private house at Dulwich where Ramsay and I had a long conference,' he wrote later. He recalled amusingly that they were not certain of all the posts to be filled and had to phone Thomas's son to consult *Whitaker's Almanac* for the information. However, Thomas's 'let me set forth the facts' revelation was hardly reliable testimony from a member of the 1924 Cabinet who mistakenly described Labour as the largest single party at Westminster after the 1923 general election.[23]

According to Blaxland, MacDonald was a frequent visitor to the Thomas home at Dulwich where Thomas's 17-year-old son, Leslie, over-heard conversations about likely Cabinet appointments. In this version, the youthful Leslie Thomas, later Conservative MP for Canterbury, was sent upstairs to fetch 'a *Hansard*' on the specific posts to be filled. He recalled that MacDonald, worried there was little ministerial talent within the Labour ranks, considered appointing outsiders; also that his father Jimmy might be destined for the Home Office.

MacDonald's exercise in assembling the first Labour government has received some scrutiny from historians. Fifty years ago, Richard Lyman, the American historian of the 1924 administration, did not have access to the private papers of MacDonald and his colleagues; though Lyman did benefit from the recollections of a number of Labour figures on the events of 1924, including the one surviving member of the first Labour Cabinet, Sir Charles Trevelyan. Lyman confirmed that MacDonald had ample time and a free hand to form his first government. Away at Lossiemouth, there was no attempt to introduce a reformed or different method of Cabinet appointments. 'Labour behaved in this major respect exactly like its Liberal and Conservative predecessors,' he observed.

Lyman admitted he did not know how MacDonald undertook his task of Cabinet making or how much advice he sought – though he believed General C. B. Thomson, who became Secretary for Air, was present at Lossiemouth as MacDonald's golf companion. In fact, the Labour leader was unaccompanied apart from his family. MacDonald never again played golf there – even when Prime Minister – after the Moray Golf Club had barred him from membership in 1916 over his courageous, but extremely unpopular stand against the Great War. On holiday, Lossiemouth's most famous son was reduced to solitary walks only on his favourite golf links. Lyman clearly acknowledged the influence of Lord Haldane.[24] But, unlike those who soon criticised MacDonald's social ambition and desire for recognition in upper-class society, he did not appreciate the significance of this early example of how the 'aristo-cratic embrace' may have influenced the Labour leader.[25]

There were three main phases to the formation of MacDonald's first Labour government – first a period of consultation after the election; then at Lossiemouth during the Christmas and New Year holiday when he sketched in a possible government; followed by his return to London when he confirmed his appointments as the new Parliament assembled. According to his diary, MacDonald began forming his Cabinet as early as 9 December 1923. In a walk on Hampstead Heath in the frosty night air, followed by dinner with J. H. Thomas, he contemplated that the lack of Labour talent would mean recruiting some specialist outsiders, despite probable mutterings within the party ranks. Also Snowden told Fred Jowett later of MacDonald's despair at the paucity of talent from which to choose his government.

MacDonald's thoughts on the realities of office as a future Labour Prime Minister had a longer history than indicated in his diary. During the post-war years, in attempting to give his party a broader national appeal beyond working-class voters, MacDonald contemplated eventually taking power as the leader of a future Labour government. In this capacity, he envisaged his administration could be based on extensive experience gained by Labour representatives in municipal affairs at the end of the nineteenth and beginning of the twentieth centuries.[26] From the 1870s partial democratisation of local government had widened opportunities for working men, and some women, to represent their local communities as well as enter the government bureaucracy. At the same time, the growth of trade unionism – particularly in mining areas – opened up career routes for union officials in local and national politics.

In municipal government, Labour had made great strides, which grew apace after 1919 in different parts of Britain. In East London, Labour had swept into power in Poplar, albeit the Labour councillors' six-week imprisonment during the infamous 'Poplar Rates Revolt' in 1921 earned MacDonald's public condemnation and Herbert Morrison's annoyance as Secretary of the London Labour Party. In 1924 this defiant Labour episode against the courts, the government and the Labour leadership cost the experienced campaigner, George Lansbury, the opportunity of a Cabinet post. In MacDonald's first Labour administration many of the ministers could claim some knowledge of local government as Labour councillors, county councillors, poor law guardians and magistrates – notably MacDonald himself as a former member of the London County Council; Clement Attlee, ex-mayor of Stepney; Fred Jowett, well-known Bradford councillor; and John Wheatley, leading socialist member of Glasgow City Council. However, in 1924 MacDonald was faced with a distinct lack of ministerial talent at the highest level. Only Henderson and Clynes within the Labour ranks had previously held government positions. Most of the new Labour MPs, even those with local government experience, had only entered the Commons in 1922.

A particular difficulty loomed on filling the armed services posts and appointments to the House of Lords. Not since the Tory government in 1852 after the death of Sir Robert Peel was such an inexperienced team to govern Britain as the new Labour ministry. As Prime Minister, MacDonald himself was unique among his predecessors over two centuries with no acquaintance with government office. He quickly realised that the recruitment of experienced non-Labour politicians would not only strengthen his ministerial team, but could broaden the appeal of his administration across class boundaries and beyond its natural heartlands. During the remaining weeks of December, MacDonald took soundings concerning taking office and policies to be pursued, as well as the difficult posts to be filled. As we have seen, Henry Massingham had asked Reginald McKenna to use his banking connections to ascertain the probable reaction in the City to an incoming Labour government. On 10 December, Massingham phoned the Labour leader with the encouraging news that there would be no financial panic among the London bankers if he took office.[27]

In Scotland during Christmas and New Year, MacDonald was absorbed in Cabinet making, though he recorded little detail in his diary except for 'loads of letters at Lossiemouth'. At that season of the year, his mind was preoccupied with memories of his late wife, Margaret, who had passed away so tragically in 1911. 'Times of sad reflections and gloomy thoughts' dominated the Labour leader's diary recollections.[28] It is idle to speculate on the influence his wife Margaret might have had on MacDonald's decisions in 1923–24 about taking office and likely appointments. Her early, untimely death was a devastating blow for the Labour leader that left him a lonely figure for the rest of his life. Margaret MacDonald had taken a keen interest in industrial and political questions and was actively involved in public life, especially the formation of the Women's Labour League and the women's suffrage movement. Also, she had played an important role in the early years of the Labour Party after its formation. Their London flat at 3 Lincoln's Inn Field, with one of the bedrooms overlooking the Holborn Empire theatre, had been more than the family home of the MacDonalds and their five surviving children. It served as the party's first central London office, where visitors constantly beat a path to its door. Ben Turner MP, textile workers' leader, attended meetings of the Labour Party Executive at Lincoln's Inn Field. 'I have sat upon the coal scuttle in MacDonald's room whilst we held our Executive deliberations,' he recalled with affection.[29]

Together, the MacDonalds shared a passion for foreign travel. Their world tours to Australia, New Zealand, the United States, Canada and

South Africa were reflected in the Labour leader's decision to retain the Foreign Office portfolio when he became Prime Minister in 1924. Back in London, Margaret MacDonald had hosted 'At Home' sessions – in effect creating a vibrant political salon for newcomers to rub shoulders with prominent socialists from Britain and abroad – over light refreshments every three weeks or so. Her death not only cruelly robbed MacDonald of his wife and the mother of their children, but he lost a steadfast and tranquil partner who shared abundantly in his political and public life. Lossiemouth was MacDonald's birthplace, but also the far-away retreat from the hurly-burly of the metropolitan politics specially chosen by Margaret and Ramsay MacDonald, to which the Labour leader continually escaped for the remainder of his life.[30]

Nevertheless, MacDonald, sketching in the form of the 1924 administration, was not in complete and splendid isolation at Lossiemouth, as has been suggested. According to Molly Hamilton, for a while American reporters besieged the Labour leader's cottage eager to uncover news of the new ministry. Besides family members, MacDonald had at least one visitor when John Bradbury, the leading British representative on the Reparations Commission and an important influence on the Dawes Report, journeyed to consult him at Lossiemouth. Sun Yat Sen's international appeal for assistance also got through to MacDonald's Scottish retreat, as did an invitation to address the Glasgow Independent Labour Party, which he promptly declined.[31]

However, on 23 December, MacDonald ventured out to nearby Elgin, to assist in starting a new branch of the Labour Party in Moray and Nairn. At this gathering, MacDonald made an important public speech about the prospect of Labour gaining high office. '[H]e was not quite sure yet that the Labour Party was going to get fair play . . . that between now and 5 January or 8 there was going to be a serious attempt made to wangle the Constitution,' he confessed. Despite his foreboding, MacDonald gave a rousing endorsement to Labour's claim to be the next government in Britain:

> The Labour Party, as he had declared, would take office if asked to do so, and if the circumstances arose. Why? Because they were agreed that the country would be all the better for the experience of a Labour Government because they believed that in international affairs the Labour Party would have more authority in establishing conditions of peace and justice than any other country. [Cheers.] They would take office because in dealing with unemployment they believed they had a programme, ideas, and a power that no other party possessed. They

believed that with regard to the great national problem of agriculture they were in a better position than either the Liberal or the Tory Party to advise on what would benefit agriculture without sacrificing the other interests of the State. Finally, the Labour Party would take office because it believed that until the financial position of the country was honestly faced there was absolutely no chance for a general revival of industry and commerce in this nation.[32]

Among MacDonald's surviving papers are his handwritten notes (most likely compiled at Lossiemouth for the 1924 administration) that indicate the Labour leader's rough draft of his first administration. Many of the posts had various names pencilled in, and crossed through, until he settled on a final choice. MacDonald privately noted the difficulties of Cabinet making. '...as if it is to be the most horrible job of my life. Am beginning to suspect human nature,' he admitted privately. As Secretary of State for India, MacDonald had pencilled in Trevelyan and Kimberley before he finally settled on the Fabian, Sydney Olivier, former Colonial Governor, who was elevated to the House of Lords to represent the government.[33]

On 7 January 1924 MacDonald returned by express train to London, with an important stop *en route* at Cloan, the Scottish home of Lord Haldane, the former Liberal War Minister and Lord Chancellor. As the Webbs discovered belatedly, the Labour leader had been in touch with Haldane repeatedly concerning his Cabinet appointments – even before MacDonald left London for Lossiemouth. Haldane saw himself cast in the role not only of Labour confidant but as the nation's deliverer, urged by Baldwin, Hankey and others to join a new Labour administration to pilot its through any troubled waters. 'In the evening he [MacDonald] offered me anything I chose if I would help him; the leadership of the House of Lords, the Chancellorship, Defence, Education and the carrying out of my plans...The press is in full cry and Williams [Haldane's butler] is keeping them off,' Haldane crowed after MacDonald first contacted him before Christmas. Haldane also told his mother that at Westminster the out-going Tory Lord Chancellor had observed gravely that 'it was my duty by taking office to try to save the state'.[34]

From Lossiemouth, MacDonald followed up his general proposition by offering Haldane specific posts, such as Education, and the Admiralty. 'India might also be available and that would help me get over the difficulty that all Secretaries of State must be in the Commons,' MacDonald declared. He ended with a final appeal to his new recruit: 'I have several awkward corners to get round.'[35] Haldane's reply set out the problems of forming a minority government including his proposal that MacDonald visit him at Cloan, his Scottish stately home in the Perthshire countryside, to discuss his own policy agenda for the Committee of Imperial Defence, Education and Judicial Reform. 'It is for the sake of the broad purpose that I should care to be of use in office ... [B]ut to office I have no personal wish to return. I have spent ten years of my life in Cabinets, and pomps and ceremonies and stipends are nothing to me. But I do care for my ideals having a chance, and to secure that chance there are things that have to be seen to,' he added.[36] A former member of Edward VII's circle, Haldane had been Secretary of State for War (December 1905–June 1912) and subsequently Asquith's Lord Chancellor (1912–May 1915). He had lost office in 1915 because of alleged pro-German sympathies. As an ex-Cabinet member, the intellectual Richard Burdon Haldane, who was educated at Gottingen and Dresden and 'held his cigars in a two-pronged silver fork', had judiciously considered the declining fortunes of his party before shifting to Labour. He was a valuable contact for the new Labour Prime Minister.[37]

What also brought MacDonald to Cloan was Haldane's word of warning that 'the management of the House of Lords will be a very delicate task indeed'.[38] For MacDonald, the appointment of Labour ministers to the House of Lords was a thorny issue, since the abolition of the heavily Conservative-dominated Upper Chamber that could impede socialist legislation was a formal party commitment. There was a significant difference of view between the Labour rank and file and party figures like MacDonald and Webb who might accept a second chamber – not based on the hereditary principle – in a modern British democracy. During the 1923 campaign, MacDonald hinted that an incoming Labour administration would take no action over their Lordships and believed he would be treated as fairly as a Conservative or Liberal administration. However, such seeming optimism did not remove the hurdles of ministerial appointments in the Upper House, where Labour was manifestly underrepresented and specific government posts had to be filled by peers.

As early as 10 December, as we have seen, MacDonald sought Haldane's assistance by hastily offering him various positions. Eventually the Labour leader was able to put together a government front bench in the Upper House. He solved in part the lack of Labour representation in the second chamber – and overcame party objections – by creating new Labour peers who had no son to continue the succession. Brigadier-General Thomson, Sir Sydney Olivier, former Governor of Jamaica, and the ex-Liberal MP, Sydney Arnold, were all persuaded to accept peerages.[39] In addition to Haldane, who suggested the Tory and former Viceroy of India, Lord Chelmsford, the Labour leader also added to his Cabinet the former Conservative and Christian pacifist Lord Parmoor, the father of Stafford Cripps. However, two Labour peers – Earl Kimberley and Earl Russell – did not join the government, nor did MacDonald secure his first choice, Sir John Sankey, as Lord Chancellor, once Haldane insisted on the post.[40] Five years later, when MacDonald again faced difficulties in the Upper House, Sankey eventually occupied this post in the second Labour government. A more difficult proposition in 1924 – Haldane warned him – would be the selection of the ministers for the armed services, owing to the possible opposition of the service chiefs to the appointment of former trade unionists. Chelmsford thereby became the First Lord of the Admiralty – to MacDonald's later regret – to ease any fears. The pacifist Stephen Walsh was eventually chosen for the War Office with Major Clement Attlee as his deputy.

During their important negotiations, Haldane declared that he wished to resume the Lord Chancellorship and to lead the Labour Party in the House of Lords. He had in mind easing the burden of official duties by agreeing later with the out-going Conservative Lord Chancellor, Lord Cave, that, in return for retaining his parliamentary residence in the Victoria Tower, Cave would continue to preside over judicial sittings of the House of Lords and Privy Council. Unencumbered by this judicial bureaucracy, Haldane proposed himself as Chairman of the Committee of Imperial Defence, presiding over the meetings of the Permanent Chiefs of the Staffs of the Navy, Army and Air Force, as well as supervising the superintendence of justice and the reorganisation of the magistracy in England and Wales.[41] In these circumstances, Haldane, rather than Lord Sankey, MacDonald's real preference, eventually became Lord Chancellor once more.

MacDonald handled these talks with consummate skill. Though his new political ally offered considerable advice about the Cabinet appointments drawn from outside the Labour Party ranks, the Labour leader kept him waiting several days, after they had both returned to London, before notifying him of his plans for the Lord Chancellorship. Not until 12 January could Haldane write proudly to his mother and sister in Scotland: 'Ramsay MacDonald was here yesterday. It is definitely arranged that I am to be L. Chancellor, on my own terms if he forms a Government. I shall be the senior peer, and shall take part in a leading fashion in all the important debates.'[42] It did not go unnoticed within the Labour ranks that at best he had only been a very recent convert to the cause and he never formally joined the Labour Party. Never-theless, Haldane had had more influence over the composition of the Labour Cabinet than the other members of 'Labour's Big Five' – Henderson, Snowden, Clynes and Thomas. When Thomas Jones met Haldane later at his London home in Queen Anne's Gate, he learnt of Haldane's significant role in securing the appointment of Cabinet members Parmoor and Chelmsford, from outside the Labour Party. 'Indeed, he had been most closely consulted as to the making of the Cabinet,' Jones observed sagely.[43]

One immediate repercussion was the scathing correspondence MacDonald received from Neil Maclean, socialist MP for Govan, protesting that the appointment of Parmoor and Chelmsford was 'contrary to the best interests of the Movement to have in a Labour Cabinet two peers whose politics have always been identified with the Tory Party, and requests the Prime Minister to ask Lords Parmoor and Chelmsford to resign from the Cabinet'.[44] Maclean declined the offer of the post of Junior Lord of the Treasury. 'The inclusion of Lords Parmoor and Chelmsford gives strength to the taunt that Labour is not fit to govern unless it has the assistance of men taken from other parties,' he told the Labour Chief Whip. However, Maclean also disclosed that, as a Scottish whip, he suspected that he had missed out on promotion to a parliamentary secretaryship, owing to his support earlier for suspended James Maxton and his fellow Clydeside members.[45]

During the 1923 general election, with the exception of the *Manchester Guardian*, MacDonald had been given a hostile press by the Liberal newspapers. However, the *Manchester Guardian* publicly advocated that the Liberals, who held the balance of power after the 1923 election, should support a minority Labour administration. As editor, C. P. Scott consistently encouraged MacDonald to take office, and met him on his return to London at MacDonald's Belsize Park home. At 9 Howitt Road, Scott noted that the Labour leader 'looked ragged and anxious'. He observed: 'I hoped he had enjoyed a rest at Lossiemouth. He said he would have done but for the postman. I said he would need about six secretaries. He said he had already got three and should have to engage a fourth. Between secretaries and political journeyings he had in one month spent ten years' savings . . . He did not expect to save anything in the first year of office (from his salary); in the second he might save "the price of a glass of whisky".'[46] MacDonald also told an unconvinced Scott that the Labour Party had been 'taken entirely by surprise and as they had not the least expectation of being called upon to take office, so they were quite unprepared for it'.[47]

In 1924 the new Prime Minister did not necessarily know all the members of his Cabinet such as Chelmsford and Parmoor, who became Lord President of the Council and later recalled that he had not met the Labour leader until the First World War. One of his first encounters occurred when MacDonald was smuggled on board the Channel ferry at the last minute because his anti-war views had become unpopular with seamen. An influential High Churchman, Parmoor received his invitation to join the Cabinet during Christmas and readily accepted office as he was in sympathy with Labour policy of international peace, arbitration and disarmament. 'The most vital and important immediate necessity is the reconstruction of Europe, with security for peace and industrial progress,' he replied on Christmas Day. Dr Burge, Bishop of Oxford, Parmoor's only confidant encouraged him to take up the opportunity: 'Now I think your influence in framing a wise and right international policy would be *unique*. You would encourage the better and more Christian spirits in continental countries to make themselves felt and heard more effectively – and you would do this better than anyone else. Then again your profound knowledge of constitutional law and practice would be of incalculable assistance to the first Labour Ministry in power.'[48] Part of the negotiation between Parmoor and MacDonald was that Parmoor shared responsibilities for arranging the government's business in the House. As Lord Chancellor Haldane explained to his sister Elisabeth: 'As I cannot sit on the Front Bench, Parmoor will be head there, as President of the Council.'[49]

Cabinet making reached its peak a few days before the announcement of the new government. On 21 January, MacDonald met some of the leading figures, including the future Labour Chief Whip, Ben Spoor, who had previously played little part in these proceedings. MacDonald noted in his diary: 'Consultation with Thomas, Henderson, Clynes, Spoor. Produced my proposals for ministers and Under Secys, etc., List generally approved after explanations of why and wherefore.' The meeting also confirmed one of the more interesting and eventually most successful Cabinet appointments, that of John Wheatley – although tense negotiations beset the selection of the Clydeside MP. MacDonald had written to Wheatley on 14 December about the post of Minister of Health, but then wanted to appoint Arthur Greenwood, a young member of the Labour Research Department, with Wheatley as his junior minister. The hostile attitude of the Clydeside parliamentary group forced MacDonald's hand when Wheatley declined MacDonald's offer of the Under Secretaryship. From the Cosmo Hotel, where Wheatley stayed while at Westminster, his fellow MPs made it clear that 'they would give him their support from the back benches'. MacDonald replied abruptly: 'The chief [of Health] has not been decided definitely. I wished to discuss that with you had you been more disposed to consider my proposal.'[50]

It had been a far from easy negotiation, as the Communist Willie Gallacher wrote in his memoirs – also the source of the nasty allegation that MacDonald deliberately tricked E. D. Morel, his former associate in the Union of Democratic Control (UDC), out of the Foreign Secretaryship that he coveted himself.[51] As noted MacDonald also believed he owed his relatively narrow victory over Clynes in the leadership contest two years before to the votes of James Maxton and the 'Red Clydesiders', the group of Scottish left-wing MPs, who had secured the vast majority of the parliamentary seats in the Glasgow area in 1922, but then caused the Labour leader considerable embarrassment with their unruly conduct and disdain for conventional parliamentary behaviour in the Commons. Relief tinged with some understandable anxiety was reflected in MacDonald's diary note: 'Wheatley finally fixed. Necessary to bring the Clyde in. Will he play straight . . . ?' With Wheatley's appointment, MacDonald gave the far Left nominal representation in his Cabinet while depriving the Clydeside group of one of their natural leaders. In fact, in the eyes of many seasoned observers, the Catholic socialist Wheatley, already greatly experienced in municipal government, was to outperform the new Prime Minister himself.

By this stage, MacDonald was almost ready to take up the harness of office: ' . . . Hurried dinner with Leach's party: Speech at 9.47. govt defeated & so I am to be P.M. The load will be heavy & I am so much alone,' he added in his diary.[52] At 57 years, MacDonald became Prime Minister and First Lord of the Treasury, though he had never held ministerial office or headed a trade union and, technically, had been leader of the Labour Party for only a year and a half after the post had been formally established in 1922. Though not strictly a pacifist, MacDonald was a co-founder with Clifford Allen, E. D. Morel, Charles Trevelyan and Norman Angell – with Arthur Ponsonby an early member – of the Union of Democratic Control, the body that brought together socialists and Liberals opposed to the British declaration of war in August 1914 to campaign for a post-war settlement during hostilities and after the War.[53]

MacDonald's own principled opposition to British participation in the Great War brought about his resignation of the party chairmanship in 1914 and made him a hated figure in many political circles – thereby contributing to his parliamentary defeats in 1918 and at the highly distasteful Woolwich by-election of 1921. Now, as Prime Minister, he had re-established his political career as the leading Labour figure. A significant number of the UDC were members of his 1924 government. His internationalist outlook meant that, despite misgivings in various governing circles, MacDonald was eventually determined to add the burden of the Foreign Secretaryship to those he carried as Prime Minister.

When Arthur Ponsonby journeyed to London on 10 December, he found that the majority feeling was that Labour should assume office if invited by the king. 'I was converted to this idea, provided it was not accompanied by any agreement with other parties of which there seemed to be no question,' he observed. But he also discovered from MacDonald, after a luncheon at the *New Leader* office, that he had pencilled in Jimmy Thomas as Foreign Secretary. A deeply worried Ponsonby then leaked the news to the ILP newspaper, that Thomas was destined for the Foreign Office. Trevelyan wrote to him that a pacifist was required at the Foreign Office and that the solution was for MacDonald to become Foreign Secretary as well as Prime Minister.[54] As a result, Ponsonby protested to MacDonald in the strongest terms: 'The incredible seems about to happen. We are actually to be allowed by an incredible combination of circumstances to have control of the F.O. and to begin to carry out some of the things we have been urging and preaching for years. To give this job to J.T. is simply to chuck the opportunity away.'[55]

The aristocratic socialist's intervention proved decisive. MacDonald, with his longstanding interest in foreign affairs, decided to take on the duties of Foreign Secretary as well as the premiership, a double burden that brought some concern from the King and criticism from other politicians. It was a decision that did not remain secret for long. Thomas Jones noted at a dinner conversation: 'Talk then turned to Foreign Affairs. JRM is to take the double office of Foreign Secretary, with Clynes as Leader of the House. This last he saw a great risk, as Clynes is so negligible a character. It would make JRM's absence at Conference abroad dangerous. I said that J. H. Thomas would be a better Leader of the House. He replied that Clynes was only five votes behind Ramsay for the leadership of the Party and therefore had a higher claim.'[56]

In the case of the inner Cabinet, two key appointments appeared straightforward. There seemed little doubt in political circles that Philip Snowden as Labour's Shadow Chancellor was destined for the Treasury.While MacDonald retired to 'The Hillocks' in Lossiemouth, Snowden went to Eden Lodge, the country house in Tilford, Surrey, bought by his wife Ethel from her profitable American lecture tours.

Arthur Henderson spent Christmas there as their house guest. On MacDonald's return to London, Snowden learnt from Henderson on 8 January 1924 that he was to be Chancellor of the Exchequer. Twelve days later, at a meeting of the likely new ministers, MacDonald confirmed Snowden's appointment by somewhat unceremoniously flinging him a pencilled note across the table.[57]

Despite his strong personal antipathy to MacDonald, Snowden had worked closely with him to build the Labour Party's national appeal as an alternative government in the early 1920s. When MacDonald became the party's first 'Leader and Chairman' in 1922, Snowden, although the pre-eminent Labour figure on economics and finance, was not a serious rival for the leadership. MacDonald had held the important position of party secretary, as well as treasurer (1900–15) and chairman (1911–14). The leadership instead was a close contest between Clynes and MacDonald, with Snowden voting openly for Clynes.[58]

J. R. Clynes became Lord Privy Seal and Leader of the House of Commons. Eventually it fell to him to propose the motion, 'The present advisers of His Majesty have not the confidence of this House', that was carried by 328 votes to 256, and led to the resignation of the Baldwin administration and the formation of the first Labour government. As Lord Privy Seal, Clynes had general duties and acted primarily as Deputy Leader of the House of Commons in charge of government business. Clynes revealed nothing of the circumstances of his selection and confined himself to the business of commenting on wearing old-fashioned court dress and the adverse costs of becoming a Labour minister. Though he included a list of the first Labour Cabinet in his two-volume autobiography, he provided far more detail about the various formal ceremonies and other occasions, such as kicking-off in big football matches and cup ties for Manchester teams, including Manchester United, during his first general election campaign in 1906.[59]

The appointment of Arthur Henderson, Party Secretary and the only Labour figure with previous Cabinet experience and a Labour member of the Privy Council, was the most difficult and the least straightforward, in part because he had lost his parliamentary seat at the general election. However, according to G. D. H. Cole, Henderson, who became Foreign Secretary in the second Labour government and eventually in 1935 was awarded the Nobel Prize for Peace, was relegated to the Home Office precisely because MacDonald wished to be Foreign Secretary as well as Prime Minister in 1924.[60] Henderson's defeat at Newcastle East in 1923 meant he had to decide, first, whether he would stand at a by-election or remain as the candidate for the north-east constituency.

During MacDonald's stay at Lossiemouth, Henderson wrote to him about the current political situation, including the selection of the Chairman and Deputy Chairman of the Committee of Ways and Means and possible names to fill the posts. MacDonald, who was well aware of Henderson's unhappiness at being outside the House of Commons, replied bemoaning the lack of candidates for government positions. 'We shall have to put in some of the offices men who are not only untried, but whose capacity to face the permanent officials is very doubtful,' he declared.[61] Notwithstanding, MacDonald proposed that Henderson did not seek a by-election to return to Westminster, but should remain outside Parliament to overhaul the Labour Party machinery for the next general election.

> I have tried a list of Ministers without you, and with you as Chairman of Ways and Means, and I must admit it enormously increases my difficulties. The only reason why I would ever think of a list without you is that I am terribly impressed with the importance of Eccleston Square. [Labour Party headquarters in Victoria]. I may be wrong, but for the life of me, I cannot see this Parliament lasting any time...
> We ought, therefore to have some smart and very much alive man at Eccleston Square driving with his own energy the whole machinery of the country, getting candidates fixed up and arranging for organisation and propaganda. The news that I hear of Wake [Labour Party national agent] is that he may be months before he can get back. We shall have to take this matter in hand and, that we may do it efficiently, we must be prepared to sacrifice something.[62]

Henderson, who returned to the Commons at the Burnley by-election in March 1924, rejected MacDonald's proposal outright and eventually took the Home Office, probably the least distinguished phase of his political career. Possibly MacDonald realised that the Labour Party would shortly be forced to contest another general election – the third in three years – and needed to be ready. However, in the final analysis, the verdict must be that MacDonald treated the loyal 'Uncle Arthur' shabbily.

The selection of Fred Jowett, a firebrand member of the ILP from Bradford and former critic of MacDonald, as the First Commissioner of Works with Cabinet rank was perhaps a surprising choice as he was a known opponent of the British Cabinet system. According to his biographer, Jowett had told MacDonald: 'I don't relish having no share in formulating the policy of the Government when I am expected automatically to vote for it.' MacDonald had replied that he did not intend to include Jowett in the Cabinet but the next day he was invited to join the "exalted twenty".[63]

At no point in his Cabinet making was MacDonald governed by the expectations of the trade union leaders, despite the special relationship the unions held in their own minds with the party they had founded in 1900 and bankrolled for nearly a quarter of a century. While the unions shared a common loyalty and commitment to the Labour Party, they were a diverse collection in terms of organisation, ethos and individual histories. Foremost in size and political representation was the Miners' Federation of Great Britain (MFGB) with a membership of 800,000. Though the MFGB sponsored 40 of the 190 MPs returned in the 1923 general election, the 1924 Labour Cabinet contained only three miners – William Adamson, Stephen Walsh and Vernon Hartshorn. In addition, three miners secured ministerial posts – Frank Hodges (Admiralty), W. Lunn (Board of Trade) and Jack Lawson (War Office). Better representation was enjoyed in the Whip's Office where Frank Hall continued a long career in parliamentary politics.[64]

One post of specific interest to the mining communities was nevertheless not filled by one of their representatives. Emanuel Shinwell's appointment as Minister of Mines was celebrated by a verse from Matthew Arnold, sent by his election agent Jamie Lamond, a fireman and amateur poet:

> Thundering and bursting
> In torrents, in waves –
> Carolling and shouting
> Over tombs, amid graves –
> See! On the cumber'd plain
> Clearing the stage,
> Scattering the past about,
> Comes the new age[65]

However, this paean of praise certainly did not reflect the views of the miners.

Shinwell recalled that MacDonald summoned him over in the parliamentary corridors to offer him the post, nominally under Sidney Webb at the Board of Trade but with executive powers and his own separate department. On Shinwell's suggestion that the post should be filled by a miner rather than himself, MacDonald responded: 'It would be wrong to put a man in the job who could not take an impartial view' – an indication that the Labour had little time for trade union experts in political office. Shinwell recalled discussing his appointment with close friends, including Duncan Graham and James Welsh, the miner poet. 'They said they thought the miners would be delighted to have me represent their industry. I gained the impression later that some of the South Wales MPs were unhappy that one of their number should not have got the job,' he added.[66]

The choice by the first-ever Labour Prime Minister, for the post of Minister of Mines, of someone who was not a former miner was deeply resented by the mining unions. Duncan Graham saw the appointment of Shinwell as a denial of the miners' natural right to have their representative in the Ministry of Mines and one that would deprive the Labour government of important support. 'Surely the part played by the Miners in the evolution of the Parliamentary Labour Party during the past quarter of a century – to go no further back – deserved better treatment from the hands of a Labour Prime Minister,' he complained. James Welsh wrote in similar terms to MacDonald that Shinwell's appointment 'has revolted the miners'.[67] Similarly, James Wilson, miners' MP, also penned an emphatic protest to the Labour leader: 'it has revolted the miners to place a man in that position who knows nothing about the industry. That has been our chief complaint for years against Liberal and Conservative administrations.... With the coming of Labour to office, it was expected that we'd be able to get an intelligent discussion on mining questions, with the Chief of the Department, instead of listening to permanent officials speaking through the figurehead of the government.... it will create indignation among... that section of the movement that forms its real back-bone, the miners.'[68]

The Labour leader's frank reply hinted at lurking doubts about Shinwell's suitability: 'I feel quite sure that Shinwell will justify himself at the Ministry of Mines. If he does not, we shall have to make a change.'[69] But Shinwell owed his selection to other factors: not only was he a loyal Labour associate but also identified with the strident Clydeside members, a parliamentary group underrepresented in the new administration.

Despite the advice he received from Haldane, MacDonald ran into considerable difficulties over the selection of his law officers, as there were few suitably qualified candidates within his party. Though the press speculated on his appointment, Henry Slesser, who became Solicitor-General, claimed he knew nothing of his selection until he was rung up by one of MacDonald's secretaries. 'The ignorance which Trollope expresses about the appointment of Bishops extends in my case to the selection of Ministers of State,' he later recalled. Slesser had lost his seat in the election and felt superseded by two King's Counsel, Patrick Hastings and Edward Hemmerde, who were among the Liberal defectors to the Labour Party after the First World War. 'I retired to the country, as I did usually on such occasions, and held converse with nobody,' Slesser remembered. But Sidney Webb pointed out that the hasty invitation to take silk from the Lord Chancellor was a preliminary step to his appointment as one of the government's law officers.[70] Similarly, his colleague, Sir Patrick Hastings, said little about the circumstances of his appointment seemingly determined by his profession. 'MacDonald appointed me Attorney-General. I don't know if I was glad or sorry,' he observed. [71]

A storm of Labour protest erupted over the appointment of a leading Conservative K. C., Hugh Pattinson Macmillan, as the Scottish Judge Advocate. The Scottish ILP complained bitterly against 'the dictatorial attitude of the Faculty of Advocates who ... are forcing Tory lawyers into a Labour Government with powers of interference not only in legal affairs but ... in local government'. Despite a hurried trip to Edinburgh, MacDonald lost his preferred candidate for the post, Rosslyn Mitchell, since the hostile Scottish Faculty of Advocates claimed he was ineligible as a solicitor. 'I wouldn't go through the past fortnight again for the throne itself,' Mitchell told the Labour leader.[72]

MacDonald's first Cabinet was almost as memorable for the few prominent Labour figures not included, as well as those who assumed ministerial office. At times, MacDonald felt besieged by those who clamoured for his patronage. However, the highly respected miners' leader, Robert Smillie, was probably the first to turn down the possibility of office. 'I had much rather seen two other elections, before Labour was called upon to form a government,' he wrote. In consolation, he added, 'If you are left with a free choice, I believe you have plenty of good material, from which to form a Cabinet.'[73]

According to Sidney Webb the most glaring omission was Labour's most popular class warrior, the Christian socialist George Lansbury, MP for Bow and Bromley. Lansbury had responded with enthusiasm when Henderson had sounded him out about a place in the Cabinet. As he told Henderson, for nearly 40 years he had been trying to help in the work of getting such a government elected.[74] But an adamant MacDonald had no truck with the East End socialist's brand of class war and refused to trust Lansbury with any large administrative office. 'Lansbury was always speaking so wildly and indiscreetly at meetings that he would injure the government,' retorted a fuming MacDonald after Lansbury's injudicious Shoreditch speech, in which he reproached George V about the fate of his ancestors, Charles I and James II, after meddling in party politics. Nor would MacDonald offer an alternative position of First Commissioner of Works, suggested by Webb – which MacDonald eventually did concede to Lansbury when forming his second Labour Cabinet. In 1924, Lansbury declined the relatively junior position of Minister of Transport, since it did not carry Cabinet rank and 'would, therefore, involve no participation in the formation of general policy or responsibility for that policy.'[75]

In fact, MacDonald, who had a meeting scheduled with Lansbury on Thursday 17 January at noon as part of his final negotiations to form a government, knew that the East End socialist would reject the offer, as he would suffer a loss of political independence.[76] Lansbury's reputation as a political dissenter over many years – SDF organiser in the 1890s, independent candidate at Middlesbrough in 1906, unflagging opponent of the National Insurance Bill in 1911, and maverick independent in resigning his parliamentary seat over 'Votes for Women', editor of the pacifist *Daily Herald* in the Great War, and chief advocate of 'Poplarism' had been a chronic discomfiture to MacDonald personally and a thorn in the side of the Labour Party leadership. However, MacDonald deliberately chose to keep the most popular class warrior outside the political tent rather than in it.

On 8 January, George Lansbury was on the platform at the packed rally at the Albert Hall alongside Ramsay MacDonald and most of the Labour members of the House of Commons to celebrate the election victory with speeches and Labour hymns. 'We will take office because we are to shirk no responsibilities which come to us in the course of the evolution of our movement,' MacDonald told the gathering. He added: 'We defy both the Liberals and the Tories to range themselves against us in that work.' Among the other principal speakers, Jimmy Thomas predicted that the Baldwin government would be defeated on the Thursday of the following week at 11.15 p.m.[77] On the same day as the Victory demonstration, the new Parliament assembled. Remarkably, the new Liberal MP for Stoke Newington, Dr G. E. Spero, arrived at 3 a.m. to secure his seat in the Commons even though the ceremonial election of the Speaker did not take place until the afternoon. On 21 January 1924 the Baldwin government was defeated 328 to 258 by the combined votes of the Labour and Liberal MPs on the Labour amendment to the Address in reply to the King's Speech – 'But it is our duty respectfully to submit to your Majesty that Your Majesty's present advisers have not the confidence of this House.'[78] Baldwin's resignation brought MacDonald to the Palace – first to be sworn in as a member of the Privy Council at 12.15 and again at 4.15 to see the King a second time to accept his invitation to form a government. George V, who was unhappy at the strains of the *Marsellaise* and the *Red Flag* at the Albert Hall Victory demonstration, soon voiced his fears about Lansbury's speech at Shoreditch Town Hall.[79] However, any Royal qualms about whether this band of class warriors would conform to the official solemnity of wearing official court dress were no doubt eased as the King met his new ministers. Following negotiations between Ben Spoor and Lord Stamfordham, the King's Private Secretary informed the Labour Chief Whip that: 'Messrs Moss Bros., 20 King Street, W.C.2. (Telephone No. Gerard 3759), which is I believe a well known and dependable firm . . . have in stock a few suits of Household, Second Class, Levee Dress from £30 complete. This comprises trousers, coat, cock-hat, and sword and is the regulation dress.'[80] Only two Cabinet ministers – John Wheatley and Fred Jowett – refused and attended Buckingham Palace in normal attire though, Beatrice Webb noted in her diary.

Only 24 years after the LRC had been founded and Keir Hardie and the Lib-Lab Richard Bell were returned as the first two LRC MPs at the 1900 general election, the first Labour ministry now stood seemingly at the portals of political power. Altogether there were 191 Labour MP's with around one-fifth serving as members of the first Labour administration. Later, with inevitable class pride, the Leader of the House, J. R Clynes, the former textile worker, famously recalled the occasion the new Cabinet ministers first gathered at Buckingham Palace to meet George V: 'As we stood waiting for his Majesty, amid the gold and crimson magnificence of the Palace, I could not help marvelling at the strange turn of fortune's wheel, which had bought MacDonald the starveling clerk, Thomas the engine driver (*sic*), Henderson the foundry labourer and Clynes the mill-hand to this pinnacle beside the man whose forebears had been kings for so many splendid generations. We were making history!'[81]

Nevertheless, Clynes's commentary was somewhat wide of the mark in terms of the social and political composition of the 1924 Cabinet. G. D. H. Cole declared that there were few surprises in MacDonald's main appointments in 1924, and this too is also difficult to believe.[82] The new Labour Cabinet of 20 was larger than the 14 ministers MacDonald originally anticipated. Seven members (five Liberals and two Conservatives) were from other parties, though six had switched to Labour after 1914. The seven trade unionists (or former unionists) in the Cabinet included three miners, as well as a single representative from each of the Ironfounders, Railwaymen, and the General and Municipal Workers.[83] After sponsoring 91 candidates at the 1923 election, of whom 45 were returned to Westminster, the ILP, as we have seen, claimed triumphantly that of the six who were in the Cabinet, MacDonald, Jowett and Wheatley sat on the ILP National Administrative Council. In addition, there were nine junior ministers from the ranks of the ILP.[84]

The principal Fabians in the Cabinet were Webb and Olivier, though around another eight ministers – including Cabinet members Henderson, Noel-Buxton and C. B. Thomson – had some association with the Fabian Society in their careers.[85] This assemblage was emblematic of the historic constellation of political forces that had founded the Labour Party over 20 years before. In counting their representatives in the new ministry, the ILP and the Fabian Society – with 230 members celebrating its fortieth birthday with due ceremony on 14 March 1924 – saw the advent of a socialist administration as an endorsement of their influence in British politics. In reality, it was the 'Big Five' – MacDonald, Snowden, Henderson, Thomas and Clynes – whose political values had been shaped in the mid-Victorian era of Gladstonian Liberal-Radicalism, who dominated the first Labour government. Notably, there was no place for a woman in the Cabinet, with Margaret Bondfield, also of the ILP and the Fabians, only securing junior office, and none for a representative of the Cooperative Movement. At the first Cabinet meeting in Downing Street, the ex-Lancashire weaver Clynes found himself alongside the 74-year old Haldane, as well as a past Tory Viceroy of India (Chelmsford), a middle-class Fabian and former civil servant (Sidney Webb) who had only entered Parliament at 65, not to mention a bevy of former Liberals, who had recently shifted their political allegiances to the Labour Party.

Overall, the new administration received a sympathetic reception at home and abroad. By common consent, MacDonald had handled a somewhat difficult task with a measure of sagacity. As the first-ever Labour Prime Minister, he had assembled a ministry to reconcile the demands and expectations of his party with the broader interests of the political nation. *The Times* welcomed the announcements of the new government appointments, acknowledging that MacDonald had cleverly woven his administration out of the complexities of the party that he led. 'The Government is now practically complete, and the public comments on its composition should satisfy its members that their future is in their own hands so far as the goodwill of the country is concerned,' the paper observed.[86]

There was also considerable delight in some sections of the press with MacDonald's decision to bring outsiders into the first Labour Cabinet. In this respect, there were laudatory words from the *Daily Graphic*: 'It must have required courage on composition of the administration brought his part to turn for aid to men like Lord Haldane, Lord Chelmsford and Lord Parmoor, who possess experience and a knowledge of practical administration which so many of his colleagues lack.'[87]

The *Manchester Guardian* commented: 'It is an interesting reflection that in the first Labour Cabinet there will be Lord Haldane, Lord Parmoor and Lord Chelmsford. This will be one of the things that will surprise continental socialists, who can hardly conceive of a Socialist Government taking office under such conditions and with such additions to its personnel.'[88] The *Morning Post* noted that only nine of the first Labour Cabinet had ever been manual workers. 'Taken as a whole, the new Cabinet may be described as one for show rather than wear. It has been designed partly to satisfy certain ambitions, but principally to demonstrate to the world that a Socialist Ministry is possible – that "Labour is fit to govern,"' the newspaper added.[89]

This sentiment was also shared further afield in governing circles. In the United States, with its isolationist stance towards the new League of Nations, Colonel House, American diplomat and close associate of Woodrow Wilson, took pleasure in the formation of the Labour administration, especially as MacDonald had also taken personal responsibility for the foreign affairs portfolio. 'Let us hope that [a Prime Minister]... has arisen in Great Britain capable of leading the world out of the ways of war into the paths of peace,' he declared.[90] From India, Lord Lytton wrote to Haldane that MacDonald 'had shown a discrimination amounting to genius in assigning the members of his government with which they were not previously familiar'. The reassured Viceroy added, 'I think I can trace your hand in most of the appointments.'[91]

In January 1924 the events in London, as the first Labour government was announced, received considerable attention in Australia and New Zealand. The *Sydney Morning Herald* provided biographical details of the new administration, including the reminiscences of British migrants in Sydney who had known the young Ramsay MacDonald as a pupil-teacher in Lossiemouth. Overall, the paper gave a cautious welcome to the new Ministry. 'Its duration depends on the goodwill of the Liberals. Mr. MacDonald had to determine between the wings of his supporters and the extreme Labour wing, and his choice ran to moderation, be the ultimate cost what it may,' the *Herald* observed.[92] Australia's largest selling newspaper, *The Sun*, noted that neither Ben

Spoor nor Josiah Wedgwood, two sympathisers with Indian nationalism, had been appointed to an office connected with the British colony. 'Mr. MacDonald has filled the Cabinet vacancies with remarkable cleverness. No one has been appointed to an office where he can put into force extremist views which he may hold,' was the paper's verdict of the new Premier.[93] In fact, Wedgwood had to settle for the Cabinet post of Chancellor of the Duchy of Lancaster. At the same time, the broad balance achieved in the new ministry, particularly with the appointment of Haldane, Parmoor and Chelmsford from outside the Labour ranks, was widely acknowledged. The *Lyttleton Times* declared that 'on the whole the Labour government will have a less alarming appearance in the eyes of sane folk than might be anticipated'.[94] For the Australian trade union movement, Labour's accession to office in capitalist Britain was a conspiracy by the Conservatives and Liberals to pass a poisoned chalice filled with unemployment and the problems of European unrest to the new administration. 'That is almost certainly why Ramsay MacDonald is now Prime Minister of Great Britain and at present is poking an inquisitive Scotch nose into the pigeon holes of the Foreign Office,' concluded the *Australian Worker*.[95]

On 22 January 1924, Ramsay MacDonald became Britain's Labour Prime Minister and First Lord of the Treasury as well as Foreign Secretary, a Scotsman from Lossiemouth who represented the Welsh mining constituency of Aberavon at Westminster, the home of the mother of Parliaments in Imperial London. An analysis of the social composition of the first Labour Cabinet reveals that eight of its 20 members were drawn from the middle classes with one-fifth of the Cabinet recruited from an upper-middle-class background, whereas 55 per cent of the Cabinet were former manual workers who had had only an elementary education.[96] However, 1924 was the year for Labour to allay any fears in Britain by broadening its appeal across class boundaries. Only six years after the Labour Party had adopted its new socialist constitution, MacDonald in 1924 was playing the long game in British politics. Gradualism was the strategy for the new Labour Prime Minister and his government.

4
Domestic Policies

On 12 December 1923, on the eve of the National Executive Committee meeting, Ramsay MacDonald dined at Sidney and Beatrice Webb's London home with Philip Snowden, J. H. Thomas, Arthur Henderson and J. R. Clynes. The Labour leader put before his future Cabinet colleagues his memorandum covering what they might achieve in government. As we have seen, even before taking office, MacDonald committed his future administration to a modest domestic programme of tackling unemployment, improving the housing stock, and widening educational opportunities in Britain. The minority 1924 government pursued limited social reform, rather than a socialist reconstruction of society. Despite some notable advances on different fronts, overall its performance disappointed many in women's groups and in the labour movement who had high hopes of the 1924 administration.

Within days of taking office, the new Labour administration faced its first major test, a series of industrial stoppages – including two national strikes that threatened the capital – organised by the powerful Transport and General Workers' Union (TGWU) led by the commanding figure of Ernest Bevin. MacDonald and his ministers viewed these national stoppages as an immediate challenge to their ability to govern in the national interest. On 22 January, as the Baldwin government was being toppled by Labour's vote of censure, the engine drivers, members of the Associated Society of Locomotive Engineers and Firemen (ASLEF), were on strike after a union ballot had rejected the National Wages Board's decision to lower rates for footplate and shunting staff. In a bitter inter-union dispute, the ASLEF action earned the hostility of their rival rail unions, the Railway Clerks and the larger rival National Union of Railwaymen (NUR).[1] Colonial Secretary J. H. Thomas, previously political secretary of the NUR until he entered the Labour Cabinet, had appealed with C. T. Cramp, the NUR general secretary, to stop the strike spreading to members of their union. Thomas warned that any NUR member refusing to work would be 'a blackleg to the signature of his accredited representatives, and a traitor' and called for loyalty 'not only to their Union, but to the great causes of Trade Unionism and Collective Bargaining'.[2] TUC intervention soon ended the rail strike by 69,000 train drivers and firemen, after 17 hours of talks in one day secured a compromise settlement, with gradual changes in mileage payments and the full rate for mainline drivers on shunting. The stoppage that lasted a week had little impact upon food and fuel supplies.

However, significant questions about the respective loyalties and relations between the Labour administration and the trade unions were now being raised, as well as questions of how far the government could intervene to protect the public interest in industrial struggles that were essentially between capital and labour. In the post-war years, British governments had coordinated the ministries and agencies of the state to deal with the challenge of swelling labour unrest and alleged revolutionary activity at home. Faced by a serious dock strike in 1923 Stanley Baldwin, in some secrecy, had appointed J. C. C. Davidson, Chancellor of the Duchy of Lancaster, as Chief Civil Commissioner responsible for shaking the dust off the strike-breaking arrangements originally established by Lloyd George to maintain essential services during the 1919 national rail stoppage, later confirmed in the 1920 Emergency Powers Act.[3] In opposition Labour protests at the actions of the Lloyd George coalition government brought a sharp response from the Premier that Labour ministers would do little in the future to preserve law and order in industrial disputes. Sir Eric Geddes became chairman of the re-named Supply and Transport Committee (STC) that drafted emergency plans and advised a conference of Cabinet ministers on handling domestic emergencies. During the early 1920s, the politicians involved with the STC had changed. However, as a policy-making agency of the Cabinet, the STC was staffed by broadly the same civil servants led by Sir John Anderson, the Permanent Under Secretary at the Home Office, who ran its various planning sub-committees.

When Labour took over from the Baldwin government the STC contingency plans were still largely in place.[4] In leaving office, the irony had not been lost on Davidson that a belligerent trade unionist minister in an incoming Labour administration could scupper his clandestine efforts to protect the Constitution against a Bolshevik-inspired revolution. In his memoirs he recalled his appeal to his successor at the Duchy Office, the maverick Josiah Wedgwood, not to undo his work in the national interest. Davidson added: 'When he [Wedgwood] returned the [emergency] plans he told me: "I haven't destroyed any of your plans. I haven't done a bloody thing about them." '[5] This was not entirely true. Wedgwood had attempted to adapt the plans to make them more suitable for Labour – but to little avail in the circumstances of a short-lived ministry. No sooner was the rail dispute over than a serious ten-day national dock strike loomed prominently. On 29 January a delegate conference in York voted for a national stoppage involving over 100,000 dockers for an extra 2s. per day (10p.), as well as the maintenance and guaranteed week recommended by the Shaw Inquiry in 1920. More favourable trade figures at the end of 1923 had encouraged union leaders to attempt to claw back cuts in wages and conditions imposed in the previous three years. The pugnacious Ernest Bevin moved smartly to demonstrate the industrial power of his mighty Transport and General Workers' Union, secured by amalgamation. After Tom Shaw the Minister of Labour's abortive meeting with both sides, the government was forced to implement emergency measures with the national dispute scheduled for 16 February.

Four days before, the Cabinet met to consider the looming national dock stoppage. Its special emergency sub-committee chaired by Arthur Henderson recommended that the STC be resuscitated with additional politicians and civil servants, including the apparently reluctant Wedgwood as the Chief Civil Commissioner. 'That post I had, naturally, because, Trades Union leaders disliked a job which might mean getting across with the Trades Unions [*sic*],' the impatient Wedgwood recalled.[6] In office, Labour ministers such as Henderson, Thomas and Shaw had little truck with British Communists and, notwithstanding any union loyalties, were prepared to face down national strikes – if necessary by resorting to the Emergency Powers Act (1920). In these circumstances, Wedgwood later privately warned the TGWU that the Government was prepared to use troops to keep essential supplies moving. But he also wanted a change in approach to industrial relations by the adoption of 'a plan more appropriate to a Labour Government' and by curtailing the customary secrecy surrounding internal emergencies. However, the docks dispute was referred to a court of inquiry and, pressed by the Labour government, the employers quickly agreed both to the dockers' wage demands and a joint investigation into decasualisation and maintenance. Open conflict between the Government and one of its major affiliated unions had been judiciously avoided.[7]

Nevertheless, extreme pressure had been exerted on the dockers' leaders that only a Labour administration could have got away with.

While on the union side there were optimistic expectations of a Labour government, Ernest Bevin later observed that he wished 'it had been a Tory Government, we would not have been frightened by their threats. We were bound to listen to the appeal of our own people.' In 1925, Ben Tillett, the dockers' leader, told the annual Labour Party Conference that he had never heard from Liberal or Tory 'the same menacing tones or the same expression of fear'.[8]

On 21 March further problems on the industrial front surfaced when Ernest Bevin brought out the London tram workers in a major strike for a wage increase of 8s. (40p.) per week, made before Labour took office. The new Labour ministry had inherited a complex public transport problem in the metropolis with the provision of trams, buses and underground under the divided control of three private companies, the London County Council and various municipal authorities with differing wage structures. The employers blamed the severe competition of the bus companies for their inability to finance tramwaymen's claim even if fares were raised. The Minister of Transport, Harry Gosling, intervened to postpone the strike for a few days but, at midnight on 21 March, the London public transport system was paralysed. Trams stopped running and 22,000 London General Omnibus employees came out in sympathetic support. The Court of Inquiry – set up by the Minister of Labour – produced an interim report within four days. It supported the workers' claim and proposed a single transport authority for London. 'His Majesty's Government intend to give effect to these recommendations and have given notice of such a Bill this afternoon,' Harry Gosling declared in Parliament.[9]

On 26 March, to press home this wage increase, Bevin announced that the railwaymen would halt the capital's underground service in support of the London tramwaymen at midnight on 28 March. A general power cut was also threatened when electricity workers at the Lots Road Station in Chelsea also downed tools. The seriousness of this industrial conflict as thousands of London commuters trudged through rain and misery brought the direct intervention of the Prime Minister who met both sides in the dispute. MacDonald warned Bevin that, if the dispute was extended, the government was bound to act – though the STC was divided over how essential services could be maintained without overt strike breaking. Bevin countered that the issues in the dispute had arisen before the formation of a Labour government. A joint meeting of the TUC General Council and the Labour Party National Executive condemned any resort to the Emergency Powers Act, urged the Government to take over London transport and to pay the men higher wages through the provision of a subsidy.[10]

The Parliamentary Labour Party endorsed this resolution on 28 March 1924.[11] The Labour government had reacted strongly against the actions of one of the most powerful trade unions and strongest supporters of the Labour Party. On 26 March Henderson chaired a meeting of the Emergency Committee which recommended proclaiming a state of emergency and the use of naval ratings in power stations – although it agreed to provide transport to work only for government employees. The next day, the Cabinet agreed a draft proclamation of emergency. This included the recruitment of special constables to protect any transport workers who continued to work and the use of naval ratings in power stations.[12] On 28 March the Privy Council approved the proclamation of a state of emergency, although the general dispute was settled before the proclamation was announced.[13] At 10.00 p.m. that day MacDonald announced the declaration of a state of emergency, but made it clear that negotiations were still continuing.[14] Nevertheless, Josiah Wedgwood also emphasized that the government was prepared to use troops to keep the essential food supplies moving.[15] The dispute was settled as the Court of Inquiry accepted the union's claim but stated that the employers could not afford to pay unless the government introduced legislation to co-ordinate London's fragmented public transport system.

The determination of the government to activate the STC and, if necessary, to use the Emergency Powers Act, despite earlier Labour objections, shocked many trade union leaders. As Sidney Webb reflected, the government was immune from 'turbulent strikers and foolish-speaking trade unionists' and was prepared to take on the Communists, who were blamed for much of the strike activity.[16] On 2 April, the Cabinet reviewed the industrial situation. Ministers recognised the economic causes of the unrest, but also believed that 'recent instances of sectional strikes, not recognised by trade unions concerned, among the shipyard workers of Southampton and the builders at the British Empire Exhibition at Wembley as symptoms of communist propaganda and agitation.'[17] In the end, Thomas helped to settle the industrial unrest at Wembley. On St George's Day, 23 April 1924, George V opened the extensive British Empire Exhibition, the symbol of his country's imperial glory, which Britain's first Labour government was destined to largely maintain. Of greater appeal, perhaps, to the British public was the new Wembley Stadium, the only part of the Exhibition to survive. For the remainder of the century, it became the official venue for the annual FA Cup Final, the showcase of the football season. In 1924 MacDonald's administration oversaw successful arrangements to deal with the chaos associated with the Stadium's opening at the 1923

Bolton v. West Ham Final, when 200,000 spectators invaded Wembley at the famous 'White Police Horse Final'.[18] According to Beatrice Webb, Henderson likened Britain in 1924 to Russia in 1917: 'The epidemic of labour revolts reminds him . . . of what was happening in Russia in 1917 against the Kerensky government.'[19]

On 2 April, the Cabinet decided that some members of the government would meet the TUC 'for an informal discussion on the industrial position', adding that 'it would deal with the representatives of the trades unions concerned, rather than the shop-stewards and others of their employees who at present were accustomed to represent the trade unions concerned'.[20] However, an Industrial Unrest Committee of the Cabinet that examined Communist activities found they were of little significance.

After the formalities at Westminster on 22 January, Parliament did not assemble until 12 February when Ramsay MacDonald made a general statement to the House of Commons on his administration's plans. At home looming industrial unrest was not the only problem facing the government from its own supporters. MacDonald declared: 'I am told also that the cancelling of a certain order by my Right Hon. Friend the Minister of Health (Mr Wheatley) was the signal that "the red flag was to be flown by every board of guardians from John O'Groats to Lands End". '[21]

One of John Wheatley's first acts as Minister of Health had been to rescind the so-called Mond Scale of 1922 on poor relief applied to the Labour guardians in the metropolitan borough of Poplar that Sir Alfred Mond and his successors had been reluctant to enforce. Following the six weeks imprisonment of the 30 Poplar Councillors, including George Lansbury, his son Edgar and daughter-in-law Minnie, the Poplar rates dispute had rumbled on. After the 30 councillors were released in October 1921, they continued to wage class war on an unjust and unreformed London rating system in their endeavour to improve the condition of the local poor and unemployed. But, as we have seen, the defiant action of this local Labour Party led by George Lansbury – with the possibility that 'Poplarism' might spread to other Labour councils – was a considerable embarrassment to MacDonald with his strategy of making Labour respectable for government.[22]

Wheatley's action in abolishing the Mond Scale – which affected large families and included a hated family means test – ended some of the tensions between the Poplar guardians and Whitehall officials. But it almost brought down the first Labour government as it provoked a hostile reaction in the House of Commons led by Asquith. In his opening statement, the Prime Minister had declared that everyone 'knows perfectly well that the [Mond] Order had ceased to operate . . . and had been again and again under consideration [for cancellation] in the Department concerned.' However, it took a masterly performance by Wheatley in the Commons debate over his action – assisted by Lansbury – that meant the Labour government survived its first crisis in Parliament.[23]

For the women's movement the advent of the first Labour government promised the possibility of a new era in progressing women's issues in post-war Britain after the post-war extension of the parliamentary franchise. The 1918 Representation of the People Act had enfranchised a majority of British women aged 30 and over, at the same time all adult men of 21 years and over gained the vote. In the nineteenth and early twentieth centuries, women had been active politically in a range of campaigns – notably for the suffrage – and played an increasingly significant part in political parties. They had become poor law guardians, councillors and county councillors – and after 1919 magistrates – in increasing numbers, but were still denied the parliamentary vote and entry to Parliament until after the First World War. In the 1920s, the male-dominated political parties therefore had to turn their attention to a new electorate that included women and to recruiting women members.

According to Arthur Henderson, in a foreword to *Women and the Labour Party* (1918), Labour had always promoted the interests of women on the 'grounds of sex equality'.[24] All the major parties were publicly committed to the principle of equal franchise reform, though Conservative MPs largely voted against further enfranchisement of women in 1919, 1920 and 1924. The Women's Labour League (WLL), founded in 1906 to promote the representation of women in Parliament and on municipal bodies, was fully integrated into the party structure in 1918. Women joined the party as individual members in greater numbers than men. The WLL branches became the bases of the new Women's Sections, which numbered 120,000 members by 1923.[25] Other changes gave women four seats on the party's National Executive Committee and the Standing Joint Committee of Industrial Women's Organisations (SJCIWO) acted as the party's women's advisory committee. The former full-time secretary of the Women's Labour League, Dr Marion Phillips, was appointed as the Labour Party's Chief Woman Officer and played a significant role in Labour politics in the 1920s in mediating between the conflicting interests of the party and different women's groups. In 1917 she had taken over the position of secretary of the SJCIWO that united women from the trade union, the cooperative movement and the Women's Labour League. With this new structure headed by the politically adept Marion Phillips, expectations were high that questions important to women would become a central feature of Labour Party's domestic policies.

The Women's Leader agreed in pointing to 'friend after friend' among the new Labour ministers prominent in the past in the division lobbies voting for women's franchise and social measures to benefit women and their families. The new Lord Chancellor, Haldane, was hailed as an unflagging supporter of women's enfranchisement since 1892, and noted for his recent attempts to open the legal profession to women and to admit them to Cambridge University.[26] 'But where is Margaret Bondfield?,' *The Women's Leader* asked on examining the composition of the new Labour Cabinet without any women ministers. 'It is conceivable that indirect sex-prejudice has determined this omission . . . a male Bureaucracy, distrustful of Labour dominance, doubly distrustful of female Labour dominance,' the journal complained bitterly.[27] A week later, the choice of Margaret Bondfield as Parliamentary Secretary to the Ministry of Labour, and her selection to represent Britain in Geneva at the Governing Body of the International Labour Office, soothed some of this disappointment among the ranks of the women's movement.[28]

However, Margaret Bondfield's appointment revealed the tensions for Labour women in the 1920s over divided loyalty to class and gender. Along with Dorothy Jewson and Susan Lawrence, she was one of three Labour woman MPs elected in December 1923. However, Labour was only the fourth party to successfully return women to Parliament – behind Sinn Fein (Countess Markeiwicz in 1918), Conservatives (Nancy Astor 1919 by-election) and the Liberals (Margaret Wintringham (1921 by-election). Of the 13 Labour women MPs elected between 1923 and 1931 – mainly from the middle and upper classes such as Susan Lawrence, Cynthia Curzon and Ethel Bentham – Margaret Bondfeld was unusually from a working-class background and had not attended university like Jenny Lee and Ellen Wilkinson. After her spell as a junior minister in the 1924 administration, she progressed to become the first woman Cabinet minister in 1929. Margaret Bondfield was an experienced trade union official, the Chief Woman Officer of the National Union of General and Municipal Workers and also the first woman elected to the TUC executive in 1918 and to its chair in 1923. At a time when trade union-sponsored MPs dominated the PLP, her valuable industrial experience helped overcome the barriers of securing a winnable seat at Northampton.[29] Yet her promotion of women's interests was often more muted in these industrial and political spheres, despite her pre-war career as a pioneering trade union figure in the Shop-workers' Union and the National Federation of Women Workers, prom-inent suffragist campaigner and member of the ILP. In 1924, however, she was quick to make her mark in Parliament with a challenging maiden speech on women's unemployment during Labour's censure vote on the Baldwin government.[30] In the main, her career trajectory became one that subordinated woman's interests within mainstream Labour politics, notably in her opposition to the proposals for the direct election of women to NEC and to making the women's conference a statutory conference of the Labour Party.[31]

In the post-war years Labour raised women's expectations with consistent support for various unsuccessful equal-franchise measures to give women the vote at 21, including backing the Women's Eman-cipation Bill (1919) that the Coalition Government defeated. Signific-antly, the Labour Party's 1923 election manifesto had pledged 'equal political and legal rights' for women but, in office, Labour agreed to adopt William Adamson's private member's equal-suffrage bill after the committee stage, only to fail to allot the necessary parliamentary time before the administration fell in October 1924.[32] In the early 1920s several women's groups – including the National Union of Societies for Equal Citizenship (NUSEC, formerly the NUWSS), the newly formed Six Point Group (1921) and the Consultative Committee of Women's Organisations, as well as exiting societies such as the Women's Freedom League – campaigned for political, social and economic equality. In fighting for women's rights beyond the vote, these single sex groups were in competition with the class-based and male-dominated Labour Party for the loyalty and support of women.

In 1924, as the new administration took office, extending the fran-chise was not the dominant question for Labour women, but instead the controversial matter of publicly funded information on birth control.[33] In Britain this contentious issue surfaced dramatically in 1922 over the celebrated case of E. S. Daniels, a health visitor in Edmonton, North London, dismissed for advising women at her clinic on how to obtain guidance about contraception. Labour and Cooperative women campaigned vigorously, but without success, for her reinstatement and a change in ruling of the Minister of Health, Sir Alfred Mond, banning maternity centres advising on birth control. The First World War had been a powerful agent of social change in first shifting attitudes on this largely forbidden subject that had received little public atten-tion. In 1915, the Women's Cooperative Guild's *Maternity: Letters from Working Women* gave one of the first public hints of the depth of misery, resentment and danger to health among women over frequent childbearing. The ground-breaking work of the scientist and eugenicist Marie Stopes, through her books, such as *Married Love* (1918), her libel case against Halliday Sutherland in 1923, and the opening of her family planning clinics, had also provided important momentum for the birth control movement.[34] Yet in a celebrated prosecution in 1922, the Glasgow anarchist Guy Aldred and his former partner, Rose Witcop, were convicted of printing the American writer, Margaret Sanger's pamphlet, *Family Limitation*. This 'obscene publication' was duly destroyed 'in the interests of the moral of society'.

In June 1923, Labour Women's Conference made birth control a pivotal issue for the Labour Party by passing a resolution in favour of the provision of full birth-control information for all social classes.[35] Six months later, the formation of the first Labour government offered the prospect of a change of official policy after the SJCIWO's previous abortive lobbying of the Ministry of Health. Within the labour movement, Dora Russell was representative of socialist birth control pioneers – including Rose Witcop, Frida Laski, Dorothy Jewson MP and Dorothy Thurtle, who wanted to confront male intransigence. She recalled that 'those of us who saw the issue as political began to feel that the obscurantist attitude might be overcome and that to achieve nation-wide permission to blend contraceptive advice with maternity care would be an immense boon to overburdened mothers.'[36]

However, Marion Phillips endeavoured to avoid direct conflict between the Women's Sections and the party once the Labour minority administration came to power. In February 1924 a compromise was reached based on the SJCIWO's sub-committee on birth control that promised 'further expert enquiry' into contraceptive methods by the Minister of Health, followed by a resolution on maternity before the annual conference.[37] Nevertheless, this did not stop the pro-birth control information group pushing ahead with more immediate demands. Aware that the March issue of the *Labour Woman* would contain pro-birth control information, Marion Phillips wrote an article advising that contraception was still controversial and that the health issue for individual women should be separated from the economic issue which should be examined by socialists, and because it could divide a Labour Party in which there were an increasing number of Catholic men and women.[38]

Famously, despite this appeal, a deputation of women, and some prominent men, met John Wheatley, the Minister of Health, in May 1924. Led by F. A. Broad, it included Dorothy Jewson, Dora Russell, H. G. Wells and Jenny Baker. Despite the appeal, Wheatley, an Irish-born practising Catholic and ILP-Clydeside MP, refused to take parliamentary action to reverse the Mond policy and would not consider administrative action.[39] The Women's Conference (National Conference of Labour Women), held on 13 and 14 May 1924, provided the opportunity for further discussion. Phillips attempted to stop any debate on the issue and placed pressure upon Dora Russell to withdraw her demand for a debate, stating that 'Sex should not be dragged into politics, you will split the Party from top to bottom.'[40] However, the appeal was to no avail. An addendum on birth control was added to a resolution on motherhood and passed by a large majority.[41] After the Women's Conference Dora Russell, Dorothy Jewson, Frida Laski and 200 delegates formed the Workers' Birth Control Group. It quickly gathered support amongst many of the Women's Sections throughout the country and at the 1925 Women's Conference, held at Birmingham in May 1925, got its previous resolution endorsed with only six votes against.[42] However, in 1925 the Labour Party Conference passed a resolution that birth control should not be made a party issue but remain a matter of individual conviction.[43]

If the Birth Control Society carried little influence with the Labour Party and found the first Labour government unresponsive, it is clear that this was not an isolated occurrence. In 1924 the new ministry was unable to take any significant action to resolve other issues raised by women's groups, such as the concerns voiced by the Association of Women Clerks and Secretaries at the dismissal of women clerks from the Civil Service to provide employment for ex-service men.[44]

During the inter-war years the state took little action on the significant problem of women's unemployment and instead relied heavily on voluntary bodies 'to fill the gaps' in social welfare provision. The Central Committee on Women's Training and Employment (CCWTE), established during the First World War, was the most influential organisation and from the early 1920s advocated the provision of domestic training for unemployed women.[45] A small number of mainly middle-class women associated with the CCWTE shaped official attitudes towards dealing with this social problem. Between 1920 and 1940 governments allocated grants of more than £1.3 million to the Central Committee to assist CCWTE programmes and more than 90,000 women received training for domestic employment through the organisation's Home Craft and Home Maker schemes, at an average of 4000 to 5000 per year.[46] Yet domestic work – badly paid, low status and uninsured – remained deeply unpopular with many women, even for those who received the benefit of training.[47]

Nevertheless, in 1924, in continuing this policy the first Labour government made available an annual grant of £76,703 19s. 11d. to fund CCWTE Home Craft and Home Maker schemes. Leading Labour figures – in particular Margaret Bondfield, Dr Marion Phillips and Susan Lawrence – were important members of the all-party Central Committee alongside such women as Violet Markham and Ivy Chamberlain. As early as January 1921 this group proposed that instead of the Central Committee's pioneer grants for higher education and study, alternative courses should be organised 'for training unemployed unskilled women from the age of 16 upwards', which would entail 'cookery, laundry, household management, home nursing, infant care, needlework'.[48] Margaret Bondfield and Marion Phillips, who were associated in 1931 with introduction of the Anomalies Act, which infamously deprived up to 200,000 married women of unemployment benefit, ensured that the first Labour government looked favourably on the role of the CCWTE.[49] Faced with an increasing number of unemployed female clerks, the Ministry of Labour also developed a myriad of training schemes, including midwifery, advance cookery and institutional housekeeping.[50]

In 1924 Marion Phillips became the main focus for enquiries from women's groups about Labour's policy towards domestic service. As a result of pressure from a number of Labour constituencies, as the Chief Women's Officer of the Labour Party's Women's Section, she lobbied and gave evidence to the Parliamentary Enquiry into the Conditions of Domestic Service in 1923 to limit working hours to eight hours per day and 54 hours per week.[51] Once the Labour government was in office she was also approached about the official licensing of domestic servants under the County Councils, but claimed such a course of action would be difficult for sometime, owing to 'unfortunately very large vested interests' and 'the legislative programme of the Government (that was) so very full'.[52] In the post-war years, the attitude of the state reflected the traditional view that a women's place was in the home. In the end, the first Labour government did little more than its predecessors on women's unemployment in farming out the problem to the voluntary organisations such as the CCWTE. In the 1920s the Labour Party backed this limited strategy of domestic training provided by voluntary bodies – a policy also continued during the second Labour government.[53]

During 1924 other important women's issues, such as the attempt to extend the franchise on the same basis as men, ran into the sand. The inter-war years were an important period for debates about women's rights particularly in relation to social and welfare policy concerning such issues as 'the endowment of motherhood'. Ever since the First World War there had been a campaign to provide cash benefits for women, along similar lines to the separation allowances paid directly to the wives of servicemen as in the war. The main advocate of family allowances, Eleanor Rathbone had co-founded the Family Endowment Society in 1917. After the Women's Conference of 1921, the Labour Party and the TUC formed an Advisory Committee on Motherhood and Child Endowment, but its report recommended a range of social provisions for women rather than cash benefits. The subject of benefits for women was keenly debated at the 1922 Women's Conference, where Marion Phillips played down prospects of cash payments to women. A second report from the Advisory Committee also advised caution in the making of cash payments and noted that 'Complete endowment is dependent upon the establishment of a new system of society based upon socialist principles and not possible in any effective form of capitalist society.'[54] In the absence of a working majority in the Commons, the 1924 Labour government chose to ignore the issue.[55] Some discussion for the need of pensions for widows and children took place, but relatively little progress was made. Indeed, the long-standing debate on the endowment of motherhood almost evaded the first Labour government. The 1922 Unemployment Insurance Act provided benefits only to women who could prove they were 'genuinely seeking full-time work', thereby barring many women from benefits. In 1924, such regulations disqualifying women from unemployment benefit were enforced more rigidly if, for instance, work as a domestic servant had been declined.[56]

Despite a lack of positive action by the Government, the Labour Party continued to appeal to women strongly throughout the period of the first Labour administration. The Women's Conference of 1924 demonstrated its interest in improved 'Care of Maternity'. Its leading figures extolled the virtues and opportunities of the moment. Dorothy Jewson wrote that 'As we come marching, we bring the Greater Days – The rising of Women means the rising of the race – No more the drudge and the idler – ten that toil where one reposes – But a sharing of life's glories: Bread and Roses, Bread and Roses' (in reference to the song of the American textile strike at Lawrence).[57] Florence Harrison Bell, Chairman of the 1924 Women's Conference, was even more direct. 'The Labour Party is engaged in trying to make a home for all the people. Because of that it makes a special appeal to women whose work, through the ages, it has been to make and keep homes against sometimes fearful odds,' she declared.

In 1924 the Labour Party had also made a great play about its Women's Day, in similar fashion to the event arranged by the Women's Sections in 1923. 'Last year the most successful were the outdoor demonstrations accompanied by processions of women with bands and banners....'[58] As a result of its success, the Executive Committee of the Labour Party agreed that further days of action would be organised for the weekends of the 7 and 8 June and 14 and 15 June 1924, including indoor and outdoor rallies addressed by both men and women 'on subjects of special interest to the women of the country'. Yet such appeals were precisely that and little was transmitted into positive action by the Labour government.

However, one important advance empowering the role of women in local government remains very much to the credit of the first Labour administration. Significant changes to the criminal justice system were implemented in 1924 concerning the nomination and appointment of lay magistrates responsible for the vast majority of criminal justice in England and Wales. Following the Sex Disqualification Act (1919), women were no longer barred from becoming magistrates, though conservatism, political influence and sex discrimination often limited any significant increase in their numbers until after the Second World War. As Lord Chancellor, Haldane started the reform of the system of advisory committees – responsible in England and Wales for the nomination of Justices of the Peace – by either a complete recon-struction of various committees with equal party representation or by making additional suitable appointments. The Chancellor's reorganisa-tion created increased opportunities for greater Labour representation on these advisory bodies, as well as the appointment of more working men and women to the magistracy.[59] This was a completely fresh approach in comparison to official resistance at the heart of government only a few years before. In 1920 the Chancellor of the Duchy of Lancaster, Lord Crawford had complained privately: 'I confess I do not at all like the idea of having to appoint women to the Advisory committees... In some cases it is difficult enough to get a woman competent to serve as a magistrate, and still more would it be difficult to find somebody who was competent to give opinions upon the appointment of men.'[60]

At the Duchy of Lancaster, the Chancellor, Josiah Wedgwood, used his power to appoint magistrates in Lancashire, to press resolutely – often against opposition – for the nomination of working men and, in partic-ular, women to serve on various benches, such as Blackpool, Warrington, Bury, Accrington, Nelson and elsewhere. In contacting local committees for appropriate names, his civil servants wrote: 'in considering women, Colonel Wedgwood emphasises the desirability, in the public interest, of appointing women in sympathy with Labour aspirations who are connected with educational and public work in the town.'[61] Wedgwood also endeavoured to increase the number of Labour representatives on the Lancashire advisory bodies with an archaic membership.[62] Magisterial appointments were a long-running battleground in centre–local relations, particularly when Labour was in office in the inter-war years. In 1930 complaints reached Oswald Mosley, the Chancellor of the Duchy of Lancaster. 'Labour is nowhere near its proportionate number' with only six JPs, including no women in Accrington he was told. 'Our people feel very strongly that the Advisory Committee ought to be strengthened by at least another Labour member,' Tom Snowden, the local MP declared.[63] Remarkably in 1924, owing to Wedgwood's persistence in demanding that women be nominated for the magistracy, Selina Cooper, the radical feminist, trade unionist and member of the ILP, was prominent among a group of women appointed to this important non-elective Crown post.

Other Labour measures included a commitment to reviving the countryside by providing grants to develop the Sugar Beet Industry.[64] There were also modifications in the rules about pensions. Indeed, the Labour Government did change the regulations to allow a single pensioner on 10s. (50p.) per week to earn 10s. per week from other employment and 15s. from thrift and benevolence before their pension would be reduced. In other words, a single pensioner, under certain conditions, could have a combined income of 35s (£1.75p) before his/her state pension would be reduced. The figures were doubled up for a married couple.[65] While these administrative changes appeared relatively minor compared to the major issues of tackling unemployment and housing, they were a significant aspect of domestic policy in the lives of the working-class electorate, which the Labour Government relied upon for its return to office.

During the inter-war years, mass unemployment was the major problem that confronted successive British governments in domestic politics. Britain no longer held its global lead as the workshop of the world. Her staple exporting industries – coal, iron and steel, textiles and shipbuilding – had crashed. The costs of the First World War had seriously eroded British income from late-Victorian investments overseas. After a short-lived post-war boom, around 10 per cent of the British adult population, known as 'the intractable million', were consistently registered unemployed in the 1920s – in the older industrial areas there were higher concentrations of workless.

Unemployment was the main challenge that faced Labour on taking office along with the hope and expectation in the Labour movement that a socialist administration would bring about positive change in the lives of ordinary people. In 1924 unemployment figures reached 20.4 per cent in the iron and steel industry and 28.3 per cent in shipbuilding, while 6.9 per cent of miners were unemployed. Labour had fought the 1923 election campaign arguing that the Tory tariff policy was not a remedy for unemployment. 'The Labour Party alone has a positive remedy for it.' However, schemes for electrification, transport development, land drainage and afforestation, however appealing, required local authority cooperation and national funding from the Treasury which was determined on curtailing public expenditure.

As Chancellor of the Exchequer in the two minority Labour governments of the inter-war years, Philip Snowden – in league with the Treasury – determined financial policy – based on an unyielding commitment to free trade and the need to return to the Gold Standard – with the result that the Labour government pursued deflationary economic policies. To Snowden public expenditure on socialist policies could be financed only out of a budget surplus. In effect, the Labour Chancellor's inflexible course of action severely curtailed the scope of the government's domestic programmes, particularly in relation to ways of tackling mass unemployment.

Both of Labour's performances in government – in 1924 and then in 1929–31 – disappointed its natural allies. In popular perceptions, the Labour Party, rather than its Conservative and Liberal opponents, was effectively regarded as the party of the unemployed. In 1924 various interest groups had high hopes of the incoming Labour administration, particularly in bringing a fresh approach to tackling unemployment. On 11 December, Beatrice Webb predicted that Labour would dash such expectations: 'What came out was that Snowden, who thinks he has the right to be Chancellor of the Exchequer, is chicken hearted and will try to cut down expenditure. He even demurred to a programme of public works for the unemployed. Where was the money to come from? he asked, with a Treasury clerk's intonation.'[66]

On becoming Shadow Chancellor, Snowden had declared: 'we shall always have the problems of unemployment with us under a system of competitive capitalism.'[67] Interestingly, in March 1923 he had moved the parliamentary resolution: 'this House declares that legislative effort should be directed to the gradual supersession [*sic*] of the capitalist system by an industrial and social order based upon the public ownership and democratic control of the instruments of production and distribution.' As he put it, he wished to draw attention to the shortcomings of capitalism. It created inequalities of wealth and unemployment whereas the significant advance of socialist ideas in Britain during the previous 20–30 years offered an alternative way to improve the living and working conditions of the majority of the population.[68] In government, his strategy was based on his belief that unemployment was a product of a capitalist society and would disappear when socialism was achieved.

Snowden was impeccably orthodox on economic matters – the need to return to the halcyon pre-war years based on international free trade and the world Gold Standard with the high pre-war parity of $4.86 to the £ sterling. The Labour Chancellor accepted that this financial strategy necessitated deflationary policies and balanced budgets to replace the deficits that had occurred during and immediately after the First World War. To reduce the National Debt that had increased inexorably from £650 millions to £6,000 millions by 1919 was a priority. In common with his predecessors, the Labour Chancellor committed himself to repayments of £50 million per annum through a Sinking Fund. This was pure *laissez-faire* capitalism that would have done justice in the 1920s to the most orthodox Chancellor. Diminishing debt in the context of balanced budgets would force interest rates down and thereby stimulate industrial activity. Underpinning all Snowden's policies was an intensely deep commitment, even almost a fetish, to free trade – matched by absolute horror of tariff protection.

His successor as Chancellor, Winston Churchill – with whom Snowden later fought some epic parliamentary duels – observed that 'the Treasury mind and the Snowden mind embraced each other with the fervour of two long-separated kindred lizards.'[69] At the root of Snowden's acceptance of the 'Treasury view' was his grounding in Gladstonian Liberalism that regarded borrowing as an evil and free trade as an essential ingredient in prosperity. From a Wesleyan Methodist tradition, Snowden's nineteenth-century Liberal Radical upbringing had imbued him with a strong belief in stable international relations as the basis of a thriving free trade world economy.[70] To his dismay the First World War had broken the progress of capitalism that would have eventually led to socialism. Snowden was thus eager to regain the normality of the pre-war years. Balanced budgets, the Gold Standard and free trade paved the way and had to be rightly applied for a socialist future. The fact that policies of sound capitalist finance might be anathema to socialism did not appear to occur to him. The Conservative MP Robert Boothby recalled the Labour's Chancellor's obsession with the shibboleths of nineteenth-century economics.[71] 'Economy, Free Trade, Gold – these were the keynotes of his political philosophy and deflation the path he trod with almost ghoulish enthusiasm.'[72]

Most of the Labour Party thinking appeared to accept that unemployment was inevitable under capitalism and that only socialism would solve the whole problem of poverty – of which unemployment was but a part. Like many other members of the Labour Party, Snowden rejected the more expansionary policies of David Lloyd George, John Maynard Keynes and other Liberals, which he regarded as palliatives, not solutions. The Liberal economist, J. A. Hobson, had suggested that the tendency for capital to over-save in slumps might be rectified by taxation, which would permit governments to restore the normal saving– spending ratios and help economic recovery. Such ideas were dismissed as mere 'reformist tinkering' that offered little to the unemployed, even in an expected transition period between capitalism and socialism.[73] Yet in the 1920s there was no substantial body of socialist opinion on how to deal with unemployment. Labour policy was based on the premise that every man had a right to work but that, since capitalist society could not guarantee that right, the first duty of a Labour government would be to provide humanely for the unemployed.

Snowden's Gladstonian convictions on balanced budgets rejected the idea of borrowing 'idle balances' during a depression. He was always reluctant to use budgets as an instrument for creating jobs for fear that it might stimulate inflation and ultimately bring about national financial disaster. Loyalty to Gladstonian economics always meant that Snowden was unlikely to accept fully even the most limited of the Labour Party responses to unemployment. His constant line of argument was that a prosperous capitalist economy was necessary to finance socialist policies and that there was a strict road to such prospects. Thus his priority was to encourage economic prosperity by adopting 'balanced budgets' and 'sound finance'. Snowden clarified this approach in 1920 when he published *Labour and National Finance*, which argued that under Labour all industries would be self-financing without reliance on Government subsidies.[74]

Only in three respects was Snowden's economic policy as Chancellor distinctive from that of other political parties. The first was his advocacy of a Capital Levy – an idea that first emerged in 1915. His plan was to regain the interest and profits – accumulating in the pockets of businessmen, financiers and industrialists from the rapid extension of war credits at high interest rates – by introducing a tax on fortunes of over £1000. He estimated a capital levy would yield £3000 millions and thus help to reduce the National Debt. Snowden maintained this could reduce normal taxation rates by £200 millions per year and that all but the richest sections of society would be better off. However, even before Snowden became Chancellor of the Exchequer, the scheme seemed less attractive than anticipated. Indeed, it had practically disappeared from Labour's pre-election statements in 1923, as Snowden later recalled, as it was not electorally popular.[75] MacDonald considered the Capital Levy had cost Labour 50 seats in the 1923 election. The abandonment of the proposal – to be replaced by a committee of businessmen, led by the cotton tycoon Lord Colwyn, to consider alternative ways of tackling the National Debt – was one of Labour's first financial pronouncements in office in February 1924.

The second distinctive feature was that Snowden presented Labour as the caring party prepared to provide better unemployment benefits and to improve the conditions for obtaining such benefits. But even this was a long way from the vision of the Budget 'as a means not only of raising revenue to meet unavoidable expenditure but as an instrument for reducing inequalities in distribution', which Snowden had outlined in his *Socialist Budget* (1907).[76]

Third, the Labour Party was committed to nationalisation or some form of public ownership – although Snowden was less enamoured of the idea than many of his Labour colleagues. In 1923 the Labour Manifesto failed to mention nationalisation since MacDonald and Snowden decided to put forward a non-controversial programme less likely to damage Labour's chances of a general election victory.

Snowden's economic and financial strategy reflected this blinkered vision. As Shadow Chancellor in 1923, he criticised the Conservative Budget, 'The Big Business Budget' for cutting the rates of super-tax when 'the first thing is to reduce the debt in a thorough manner'.[77] Indeed, in the same speech he argued that 'you cannot have a tax reduction on sound economic lines as long as the National Debt exists....'[78]

In 1924, Snowden moved to the Treasury during the annual scrutiny of expenditure estimates for the next financial year. Particular attention for 1924–25 was given to the Admiralty proposal to construct eight new cruisers at £1 million each, which led to much wrangling between austere Snowdon and the breezy Admiral of the Fleet, Earl Beatty. In the end, five cruisers were commissioned, but Treasury retrenchment halted the expansion of the naval base at Singapore. Cutting the estimates of the spending ministries and falling prices produced an unforeseen surplus of £48 million that the delighted Chancellor earmarked for reducing the National Debt.

On 29 April 1924, 15 years to the day since Lloyd George's famous 'People's Budget', as he recalled, Snowden who had never held ministerial office introduced the first budget ever presented by a British Labour government. He had not consulted the Cabinet who learnt the details on Budget day – MacDonald hastening back from Wales at literally the last minute.[79] In preparing his proposals, Snowden had an additional £40 million derived from increased revenue to distribute. He gave priority to reducing indirect taxation on food, rather than lowering income tax and supertax. In his so-called 'Housewife's Budget' almost £20 million was allocated to reducing the sugar tax from 2¾d. a pound to 1½d. a pound. Taxes on tea, coffee, cocoa and sweetened table waters were also cut, as well as a slight reduction on the cost of the telephone service and modification of the entertainments duty on cheaper seats. Snowden also repealed the inhabited house duty that eased the lot of professional families of moderate means and ended corporation profits tax that he deemed a disincentive to trade.[80]

At a cost of £3 million, Labour's free trade Chancellor next abolished the wartime McKenna Duties imposed in 1915 by a free trade Chancellor to restrict the purchase of cars, cycles, musical instruments, clocks and cinema films. Politically, despite sugaring the pill by spending £500,000 on removing the duty on motor vehicle licences, he earned the wrath of the growing British car industry that had flourished in the intervening years under the protection of the McKenna tariff. Snowden also took the opportunity of his budget speech to announce that the government was unable to endorse the preference resolutions at the Imperial Economic Conference. He blamed his Conservative predecessors for unfairly binding a future administration with a controversial matter such as tariff preference.

In this way, indirect taxation was cut by £29 million and direct taxation reduced by £14 million – actions that he famously described as 'the greatest step ever taken towards the Radical idea of the breakfast table'.[81] However, despite this appeal to the housewife, Snowden's main concern was to demonstrate his financial soundness and Labour's economic orthodoxy. A reduction of the National Debt was an essential precursor of industrial growth and real tax cuts. In the House of Commons he emphasised the significance of reducing the National Debt: 'I know a reduction of 1s. [5p.] in Income Tax is much more spectacular than paying off £50,000,000 of Debt. In the first case the relief is obvious, in the second it is indirect, but none the less real, and in fact more widespread and penetrating in its benefits. Improvement in national credit in turn regulates the rates at which money can be borrowed for industrial purposes.' He also emphasised the need for Britain to return to the Gold Standard. 'Moreover, in view of the great conversion schemes which we shall carry out in a not far distant future, the maintenance and improvement of British trade is a matter of vital importance.'[82]

Remarkably, Snowden's first budget was well received on all sides of the House of Commons. It drew general approval from the Liberals and the Conservatives, who applauded the tax cuts. The *Morning Post* cheerfully acknowledged the Chancellor's budget speech was 'a mellow and even genial performance'. 'We might have fancied ourselves listening to one of the bourgeoisie, of the grocer variety, descanting on the sacredness of capital.' The paper recalled that 'only a year or two ago Mr Snowden and his friends were declaring for the expropriation of all capital as an exploitation, and a truce-less war against our industrial system.' Yet, some harsh words were reserved for the removal of the McKenna duties – described as a 'menace to the motor industry' and Labour's refusal to honour trade preference that brought hostile reaction from Dominion representatives.[83] The *Daily Herald* believed that Snowden had produced a budget that would be popular all round. 'He holds with the Prime Minister that the chief business of the Government is to show that Labour can govern, and to lay the bases of an electoral success which will before long give our Party power as well as office.'[84]

At the same time it seems to have even confirmed Snowden's socialist respectability with some Labour MPs. While his commitment to tackling unemployment was real, owing to the enormous costs in a period of deflation as the Labour government endeavoured to display its economic orthodoxy he continued the policy of short-term public works that had developed since 1921.[85]

One of the Labour Cabinet's first decisions had been to set up a sub-committee on housing and unemployment, presided over by Sidney Webb, the President of the Board of Trade, that then split into two sub-committees – one on housing, chaired by John Wheatley, and the other on unemployment, with Thomas Shaw as chairman. Wheatley developed his own housing policy almost without any discussion with his sub-committee, but the unemployment sub-committee met frequently and submitted regular reports to the Cabinet that accomplished little. While public works schemes introduced in the early 1920s dominated the actions of the local authorities, the sub-committee relied on a revival of world trade based on free trade and the restoration of the Gold Standard.[86]

After meeting Sidney Webb, Thomas Jones remarked on Labour's dearth of ideas for the workless. 'We then talked of Unemployment, and it was rather disappointing to find Sidney Webb, the author of pamphlets innumerable on the cure of unemployment regardless of cost, now, as Chairman of the Unemployment Committee, reduced to prescribing a revival of trade as the one remedy left to us.'[87]

Nevertheless, Labour did have some prescriptions beyond the conventional nostrum of public works, first laid down by the Viscount St David's Committee in 1921. In April 1924 the government planned to create work through the electrification of the railways, though this approach was soon abandoned. Instead, a Cabinet unemployment policy committee, chaired by Snowden and including some of the Labour government's leading figures – Lord Haldane, Arthur Henderson, Sidney Webb, Tom Shaw and Harry Gosling – was established to examine the ideas developed by MacDonald in a speech made to the House of Commons on 29 May 1924.[88] Its main impact was to encourage the electrification of Britain. On 9 July the Cabinet approved proposals for electrical developments in Britain and, three weeks later, on 30 July, Snowden informed the House of Commons of a move to standardise electrical frequencies. The aim was the construction of a National Grid, financed from the Exchequer, to redistribute the nation's electrical output. In addition, the cost of electrical development in rural areas would be subsidised.[89] There was even discussion of mounting a feasibility study on the building of the Severn Barrage. Harry Gosling was instructed to prepare legislation on these issues for the autumn session of Parliament on 5 August.[90] At the same Cabinet meeting the Labour government decided to form a permanent economic committee to advise on the economy, a body that would be outside direct Treasury control.

On 30 July, however, Snowden reported that since February 1924 the Unemployment Grants Committee had approved 750 schemes to the value of £5.5 million and had under construction manual schemes to the value of £3.4 million. Besides drainage schemes, a £13.5 million road programme to which the Government would contribute £10.4 million was planned.[91] There is little doubt that many of the schemes announced on 30 July were bound to fall foul of the constraint on public expenditure if the Labour ministry had survived for a second year. Although the plan for the National Grid was developed, most of the remaining proposals ran into the sand with the fall of the administration.

Disquiet at Labour's unimaginative and limited approach to unemployment spread within Labour ranks. On 29 May the PLP condemned the Government's refusal to guarantee a loan to Russia and called for more initiatives, including an increase of trade with Russia using the Export Credits Act to indemnify firms from trading losses.[92]

Beyond this reproach, however, Labour members tended to fall in line with the need for electrification (including the setting up of electricity super-power stations) and afforestation projects – although there were some new ideas, such as the state inaugurating a scheme for making trunk roads and increasing grants for employment schemes of 75 per cent as against 25 per cent for the local authorities. On the 10 July these policies gained more support, but with a proviso that a minority Labour government would never have adopted. The PLP declared itself in favour of rejecting the London and Scottish Company Bills 'now before the House calculated to strengthen the grip of private monopoly in this important and growing industry' and advocated either 'the partial or complete nationalisation of the generating side of the industry coupled with municipal distribution' or legislation to strengthen 'public ownership and control of the existing electrification statutes'. This latter alternative included the proposal to form a Joint Electricity Authority with a majority of public representatives, plus various arrangements for controlling the industry in conjunction with local authorities. These might become the Joint Electricity Authority in their own areas with powers and responsibilities to improve production.[93]

The Labour administration was prepared to consider a variety of modernisation schemes in order to help tackle unemployment but, in the end, despite the views of the PLP, would not be drawn on the need to guarantee a loan for trading with Russia or a scheme to nationalise the electricity industry. Both the economic policy of Labour and its minority political position dictated a slower course of action.

Even if largely bereft of new ideas to solve the intractable problem of unemployment, Labour had always been more progressive about the relief of the workless. By 1924 two systems of unemployment provision existed, the contributory system and the uncovenanted system, or dole, which was provided for those out of benefit.

When Labour came to office in 1924 the government was naturally expected to improve conditions for the unemployed. The administration introduced an Unemployment Insurance Act that effectively created a statutory right to benefit, recognising only two kinds of benefit – standard and extended – to which all workers were entitled. The Act, introduced in April, amended the eligibility rules of the 1920 measure and extended the benefits from 26 to 41 weeks. Benefit levels for both men and women were increased. However, the new Act also introduced the 'genuinely seeking work' clause by which applicants had now to prove that they were actively seeking employment. There was a reaction amongst the Labour movement, particularly at this oppressive clause – the condition of extending unemployment benefit rights that the government believed would prevent abuse. But while there were clearly tensions between the first Labour government and some of its MPs, as well as the Labour Party in the constituencies, in the end party loyalty proved stronger than ideological and practical differences. This was demonstrated in the Labour Government's action at the Home Office.

On 28 February 1924, Arthur Henderson duly won the relatively safe Labour seat of Burnley in a parliamentary by-election with a majority of 7037 on a 5.4 per cent swing over the Conservative candidate, H. E. J. Camps.[94] While this victory secured his post as Home Secretary, Henderson achieved little in his time in one of the great offices of state. As Fred Leventhal has argued, Uncle Arthur – as he was known in Labour circles – took little interest in the day-to-day routine business of the Home Office over such questions as prisons and immigration, and was largely dependent on his adept Scottish Under Permanent Secretary, Sir John Anderson (later Lord Waverley), the future Governor of Bengal and wartime Cabinet minister.[95] As a leading figure in the 1924 administration, Henderson was reluctant to change policy and offended Labour's trade union supporters – thereby dashing any hope that Labour in office would offer them help.

Henderson's style and approach was no more evident than in his dealing with the case of those policemen dismissed by the Home Office for their part in the police strike of 1919. The Labour Party and the TUC had pledged that they would regain their jobs once Labour was in office, but on 7 April 1924 the Cabinet supported Henderson's recommendation not to reinstate men who had committed a serious breach of discipline and had contravened an agreement made by the Police Union representatives. 'My natural sympathies would be with the strikers,' Henderson advised but 'I could not assume the responsibility of suggesting, or even countenancing, the reinstatement of the dismissed strikers without most seriously compromising my position.'[96] On 12 April, Henderson notified the Labour MP, J. J. Hayes, the former secretary of the Police and Prison Officers' Union, of his decision. Hayes read this out to a rally of dismissed policemen on 11 May. The letter emphasised the practical difficulties blocking the route to reinstatement but included no further details.[97] But Hayes, on the instruction of his members, would not be fobbed off by Henderson's response and raised the issue with the National Executive of the Labour Party. The NEC remained deeply pledged on the question and reminded the Labour Party that it should have been consulted on the matter. This concern eventually resulted in the issue reappearing before the Cabinet on 14 May 'as a matter of urgency'. Although the Cabinet would have liked to have dropped it – on the grounds that a minority government could not take a decision – the Cabinet decided to appoint MacDonald, Parmoor and Henderson to meet Labour's NEC.[98]

At this meeting, Henderson stressed the practical difficulties and that special legislation would be required to help the dismissed men. Henderson was then empowered to offer other ways of helping the dismissed men and, if necessary, a Committee of Inquiry. In his Commons speech Henderson offered an inquiry, but expressed his distaste for a police strike, drawing 'a very wide distinction between an ordinary industrial dispute and a strike in what is a disciplinary service like the police force'. George Buchanan, the Clydeside MP, criticised Labour for its broken promises.[99]

Nevertheless, Henderson committed the government to a committee of inquiry that led to intense discussion between the Labour Party, the National Executive of the Labour Party and the PLP. The minutes of the PLP indicate the bitter nature of the debate. The report to the PLP of 29 May 1924 ranged over the whole case and the PLP expressed deep concern at the composition of the Committee of Inquiry: 'viz, two lawyers and only one Trade Union representative, and they felt that with such vague terms of reference, and with such a Committee, the dice would be loaded against the men'. Further, the Executive could not get any assurances that the attitude of the Department in the course of the enquiry would be sympathetic towards the men.[100] This contentious issue became sidetracked – as did the long-running case of John Syme, where Henderson brushed aside the harsh discipline that had been imposed on the dismissed Inspector. The findings of the committee of inquiry did not appear until December 1925 – over a year after the first Labour Government had left office – with a majority declaration against the reinstatement of the police strikers.

Henderson also exacerbated relations between the Government and the trade unions. In 1924 the Labour government's handling of industrial relations might have been harmonious – particularly considering his vast trade union experience and his leadership of Labour Party during the First World War when the unions took an increasingly prominent role. However, in June 1924, Haldane complained to Beatrice Webb that the trade union Cabinet ministers – Arthur Henderson, J. R. Clynes and Tom Shaw – were 'frightened of their own people'.[101] This may well have been true for, according to J. R. Clynes, 'an understanding had been arrived at by members of the government that its trade union members would keep to politics only and not take sides in industrial disputes.'[102]

While at 10 Downing Street, MacDonald kept his distance from the TUC – as did many of his ministers – and relations with the trade union movement were often strained since the government afforded the TUC no privileged treatment. Both Tom Shaw, the Minister of Labour, and Arthur Henderson, as Home Secretary, intervened in industrial relations with a total lack of sensitivity to the needs and beliefs of trade unionists. During the period of the first Labour government the number of industrial disputes increased, although the length of these stoppages was little more than in previous years and the number of days lost fell in line with a long-term downward trend. During this time, trade union membership increased slightly following a period of declining numbers.

Other issues also muddied relations between the first Labour government and its trade union supporters. At first glance the relations between the Miners' Federation of Great Britain (MFGB) and the Labour Government seemed positive, though, just a few days before Labour took office, the MFGB indicated to the coal owners their desire to end the old wages agreement. Negotiations began in March 1924 for an increase in the minimum wage originally agreed in 1921, which drew in both MacDonald and Emanuel Shinwell, Minister of Mines, after John Guest, a Yorkshire miners' MP, introduced a private members' bill to amend the 1912 Minimum Wage Act. Tensions developed quickly as Shinwell was an abrasive political figure not liked by some miners' leaders.[103]

The Parliamentary Labour Party was particularly concerned about Guest's Bill. When MacDonald addressed the PLP on 25 March 1924, his reply to the question of the bill to the House of Commons on the previous day was drafted on the basis that any detailed information of government intent 'could be disastrous to negotiations' between the coal owners and the coal miners.[104] Nevertheless, the topic was the subject of a special meeting of the PLP on 28 March presided over by Robert Smillie, the veteran miners' leader. The meeting demanded 'that the Government be urged to bring in a Minimum Wage Bill as quickly as speedily as possible'. This never occurred and instead the miners narrowly rejected the coal owners' offer of a small increase. The Buckmaster Inquiry examined the situation and the MFGB later accepted a small increase from the coal owners at the end of May 1924.[105]

This settlement was far from amicable for Labour. It resulted in some tense correspondence between the MFGB general secretary,

Arthur J. Cook, and W. Milne Bailey, Acting Secretary of the Joint Research and Information Department of the TUC [JRID] and the Labour Party, in the place of Henderson. Cook wrote to Henderson, as Secretary of that body, on 24 June, as follows: 'I was very dissatisfied with the department's efforts with respect to the Inquiry. After having written them as I did for help, I had to apply to the Labour Research Department, who provided me with very valuable matter for the Inquiry.'[106]

W. Milne Bailey replied suggesting that two months before the Inquiry, the services of JIRD 'were freely offered to the MFGB in their approaching dispute. No reply was made to that offer.' His department only began research when a letter, of the 15 April, received on 16 April, made a request for details of the wage rates of other industries on the day before the Inquiry began, when 'No useful action was possible at such short notice.'[107] Milne-Bailey stated that additional help had been offered but that no reply had been received and said that he would send copies of the correspondence to the secretaries of the TUC and the Labour Party to reveal his desire to help.

Tense relations between the miners and the Labour government continued over other matters. In particular, the MFGB leaders criticised the Labour government on the Dawes Plans for Reparations, which MacDonald regarded as a success in his pursuit of a permanent peace in Europe. The Communist-dominated Minority Movement claimed that the MFGB had spent £68,000 to secure a Labour government at the end of 1923 and had now 'been treated in a most contemptuous manner by Labour's figurehead'.[108] The MFGB complaint was that some of the changes in the reparation arrangements would flood the coal market and force British coal prices down, to the cost of the British miners. In fact, the worsening of the situation did not occur until Stanley Baldwin's Conservative government took office in November 1924 and subsequent events did eventually lead to the coal crisis of 1925 and the General Strike of 1926.

In other areas the first Labour government's industrial relations policy was less controversial, owing to its commitment to improve the working conditions of ordinary people. The administration demonstrated this in bringing forward its Agricultural Wages Bill, to set up a Central Wages Board and local committees to fix county wage rates. But this measure did not stipulate a minimum figure because of a difference of opinion among the unions concerned. However, the legislation was seriously modified by a Liberal amendment that took away the power of the Central Wages Board to revise the wage rates fixed by the local committees.

At the Home Office Arthur Henderson also had to deal with the vexatious issue of 'alien immigration'. Victorian Britain had been a political and economic haven for immigrants, refugees and revolutionaries, most famously Karl Marx who lived and studied in London for over 30 years. By the early twentieth century, alien immigration was subject to increasing government control and restriction on the right to entry into Britain. The landmark Aliens Act of 1905, and subsequent legislation in 1914 and 1919, began to close an open door for immigrants to Britain. As a result the Home Office had built up an extensive bureaucracy – still in place when Labour took office – in dealing with different migrant groups including Germans, Russian Jews and Chinese. In 1914 the Aliens Restriction Act was a hurried piece of legislation caused primarily by wartime spy mania and fear of enemy aliens. During the jingoism and xenophobia of the war years, 30,000 Germans, Austrians, Hungarians and Turks were expelled from Britain.

The Alien Immigration Act of 1905, concerned primarily with Jewish immigration from the Russian pogroms, and the Aliens (Restrictions) Act of 1914 had been the first significant attempts by British government to control immigration into Britain. However, the Aliens Restrictions (Amendment) Act of 1919 was perhaps the more significant act because Clause 1 extended the power of the Home Secretary to change the existing immigration controls by an Order in Council when changes became necessary. In 1920 all intending immigrants were compelled to either obtain a work permit or to demonstrate their financial independence before being allowed temporary residence in Britain.[109] Companies wanting to employ foreign labour had to apply to the Ministry of Labour, which would contact skilled workers living abroad and then issue temporary work permits. Once in Britain, these workers had to report to the police, could not change their place of work without permission, and had to remain law abiding.

Part of the general anxiety about allowing unrestricted entry into Britain was the fear that foreign labour would be used to undercut the wages of British labour, thereby increasing unemployment. Conflict between British workers and aliens became evident in the clashes between British seamen and foreign workers in Barry, Cardiff, Glasgow, Hull, London, Liverpool, Newport, South Shields and Salford in 1919.[110] As a result immigration controls were extended.[111]

Once Labour was in office, Henderson came under pressure to make changes to the 1919 Aliens Act, particularly from the Home Office Advisory Committee, part of the TUC's Joint Research and Information Department. The Advisory Committee pressed for an immediate

Home Office and Foreign Office enquiry into the administration of the Aliens Act and the issuing of passports and visa.[112] W. Milne Bailey, the advisory committee's assistant secretary, forwarded 42 copies of a memorandum on the Aliens Order to the Acting Secretary of the Labour Party, J. S. Middleton, to put before the Labour Party National Executive. On 29 July Middleton pressed Henderson for changes: 'The Home Office ought to grant to any alien who could support himself the right to stay in Britain, no alien should be deported because of political offences they had committed in their own countries.' He added that deportation should only be considered in the case of aliens tried and convicted of criminal offences.[113] An independent enquiry was also proposed into every deportation order.[114]

However, in a detailed reply, Henderson made a robust defence of Home Office policy, emphasising that alien migrants had to possess a passport, or similar documents, to land in Britain, as well as being physically and mentally fit and capable of supporting themselves. In addition, their employers had to hold a Ministry of Labour permit. According to the Home Secretary, deportation was rare without the recommendation of the courts – unless the 'alien is engaged in the white slave traffic'.[115] Henderson also rejected the idea of an independent enquiry as undermining the authority of Parliament and the Home Secretary. His concern was that any one could call themselves political refugees and that restrictions had to be administered in the interests of the country. While he promised to review the possibility of changes to the Alien Act after the parliamentary recess, there is little evidence that he did so before the fall of the Labour government. The Act remained the basis of British immigration law until 1971.

While tackling unemployment proved an intractable problem for British governments in the inter-war years, by comparison the provision of housing was a considerable success story in which the 1924 administration played a significant part. The total housing stock rose to over eleven and a half million homes after around four million houses were built and about half a million slums cleared during the 1920s and 1930s. Before Labour took office, two housing measures had followed Lloyd George's famous – but largely unfulfilled – pledge in 1918 of 'Homes Fit for Heroes'. The most noteworthy had been the Addison Act (1919) that granted subsidies for house building – until it fell foul of the 'Geddes Axe' economy cuts in June 1921. In 1923 the Chamberlain Housing Act, introduced by the Baldwin government, provided subsidies of £6 per house for 20 years to both local authorities and private builders. This measure also continued rent restrictions for a while, but offered no solution to severe labour shortages in a building trade devastated by the war. John Wheatley, the ILP-Clydeside MP, joined the opposition front bench specifically to expose inadequacies in the Tory housing programme, which favoured subsidising private builders rather than rented accommodation. 'Private enterprise is not in the future going to provide working-class houses [for rent] as it did before the War, but that the provision of working-class houses will in the future be a public enterprise,' he predicted.[116]

Housing policy had only a relatively brief mention in Labour's 1923 election manifesto, compared to the problem of tackling unemployment. The abolition of slums, an adequate supply of decent homes and rent control were the avowed pathways to a humane and civilised society.[117] As Minister of Health with responsibility for Housing, John Wheatley's scheme to subsidise local authority working-class homes for rent resulted in the 1924 Labour government's most significant domestic achievement. Wheatley was driven by an idealism born of his experience of the appalling working-class living conditions in Glasgow, where as a highly active ILP councillor for Shettleston, he became an acknowledged expert on housing. In 1914 his pamphlet *Eight Pound Cottages for Glasgow Citizens* made the case for functional low-cost, working-class homes constructed out of the profits of council tramways.[118] To revitalise the moribund building trade in Britain in 1924 and ease its chronic shortages of skilled labour, Wheatley secured the joint co-operation of both sides of the house construction industry – employers and unions – and fostered improved relations between local authorities and private builders.

In office Wheatley made a prompt start with Tom Shaw, the Minister of Labour, by consulting the most important employers and trade unions in the building trade and forming an industrial committee of 19 employers' representatives and 15 union members. The health minister took care to avoid any impression of direct government interference. Only one government official – a secretary from the Ministry of Labour – served on the joint committee, asked to 'report on the present position in the building industry, with regard to the carrying out of a full housing programme, having particular reference to the means of providing an adequate supply of labour and materials'. Within two months, on 10 April, the joint committee published its findings in a four-part report on General Purposes, Labour, Materials and Scottish problems. The report highlighted the key difficulties faced by an industry in decline for many years and the underlying causes of shortages in skilled labour. A sustained government programme over 15 years to build 2.5 million houses, starting at 50,000 and ultimately reaching 225,000 per annum was recommended. Changes to the system of apprenticeships, including lifting the maximum entry age from 16 to 20 and cutting training by one year were among other proposals to solve the acute shortages of bricklayers, masons, plumbers and other skilled trades. Wheatley told the Commons:

> In order to get the essential labour for the production of houses, it was necessary to stabilise the industry by the adoption of a long-term programme, and when the representatives of the men and the employers put me a proposal for a long-term building programme, I said, '. . . . If you are prepared to accept from the State a 15-years' building programme on condition that you deliver a certain number of houses every year, then I am prepared to consider entering into such an agreement.' They went into the matter very carefully, and ultimately we fixed and made an agreement on that basis.[119]

However, measures to improve the supply of building materials and the establishment of a statutory committee of building specialists were never realised. At the heart of the report, which the Labour administration adopted, was the 15-year housing programme with significant central funding and targeted proposals to remedy acute shortages in the workforce – but no direct government interference in the building industry.[120] Wheatley told the Commons on 26 March that Labour's housing plans did not amount to socialism. 'I wish this country were ready to receive a Socialist programme and we would show you how much easier it is to solve the housing problem . . . than trying to patch up the capitalist system . . . ,' he added.[121]

Instead, Wheatley's Housing Act tactfully adopted similar features to those of his predecessors – Addison and Chamberlain. Each local authority house built under Wheatley's scheme for letting at a fixed rent was subsidised at £9 per year in urban areas and £12 10s. per year in agricultural parishes for a period of 40 years to offset the interest charges on the capital raised for house construction. Government subsidies could also be obtained by private builders – but only for houses to let – emphasising that local authority rented housing was the basis of the first Labour government's housing policy.

Wheatley had initiated the most successful of the inter-war housing acts which, by 1934–35, when the subsidy scheme ended for new housing, had provided 520,298 houses at a cost of £41,088,113. The vast majority of these houses were built by local authorities for rent and some were still receiving subsidies until 1974. Wheatley left a legacy of large inter-war local authority housing estates throughout Britain, even though only 2486 houses were built under the Act in its first year, 1924–25.[122] The number of houses subsidised by the Wheatley Act increased enormously over the next few years, but fell well short of his original target of 200,000 per year for ten years.

After the Minister of Health's masterful performance earlier in the debate on the Poplar Order, Beatrice Webb had noted in her diary that 'Wheatley's brilliant speech in defence of his action [made him] a new star in the House of Commons dialectics, logical and humorous, with first-rate delivery.' 'He takes his place as a front-ranker in the game, a rival to Thomas for the leadership if J.R.M. breaks down,' she observed.[123] Wheatley's adroit handling of the Housing Act brought similar accolades. Despite some perceptive opposition in the Commons from E. D. Simon, the Liberal's housing expert, and 76 amendments at the committee stage that might have wrecked the measure, Wheatley successfully steered his proposals through Parliament. The Liberal MP, Charles Masterman, wrote in the *Nation*: 'the House has found a new favourite in Mr Wheatley. He has been the one conspicuous success in the new Parliament... he possesses a perfect Parliamentary manner; a pleasant voice, confident without arrogance, a quick power of repartee, a capacity for convincing statements, and above all, the saving grace of humour.' Yet, Haldane told the Webbs that 'Wheatley was a brilliant Parliamentarian but his administrative capacity remained to be tested.[124] Thomas Jones, the Assistant Cabinet Secretary, criticised Wheatley as being too compliant with the dictates of his civil servants: 'On Housing, the same watering down of expectations (as on unemployment) is taking place. Wheatley... is from the Clyde, but "Pale Pink" rather than "Turkey Red",' he noted in his diary. 'The officials, with the aid of Arthur Greenwood, are busily watering down this scheme also,' he added. In the event, whatever the deficiencies of Wheatley's Housing Act, it provided the foundations of local authority house building during the inter-war years. As Ian Wood has observed, Wheatley did not intend his measure to solve every aspect of the nation's housing problems. Furthermore, his housing strategy was handicapped by the failure to secure his Building Materials Bill – in part because of factors beyond his control – before the Labour administration fell.[125]

In conducting his Housing Bill through Parliament, Wheatley was particularly careful to consult the local authorities and to reassure them of no loss of autonomy. Throughout he made it clear that his scheme for the construction of working-class homes for letting was only part of the solution to the nation's complex housing problems. However, the Building Materials Bill – designed to prevent delays by suppliers of essential construction materials – ran into resistance from employers in the building trade and had not become law before the Labour administration went out of office in October 1924. The Attorney-General, Sir Patrick Hastings's injudicious speech, in which he described the Bill as a piece of socialism, followed by a building strike that hardened industrial relations, had stiffened opposition to the measure which delayed its parliamentary progress.

Wheatley's failure to solve the serious social problem of evictions – particularly prevalent in his city of Glasgow where rack renting by landlords under the 1920 Act resulted in over 24,000 cases for possession before the courts during January 1923 to February 1924 – was also in sharp contrast to the success he achieved with his major Housing Act. At the beginning of the Parliament, the Labour MP Benjamin Gardner had introduced a Private Member's Bill to put a stop to all evictions (except where the landlord took over the property for himself and provided alternative accommodation for the tenant) and to curtail rent increases. This measure received a second reading, but ran aground in committee. Wheatley wanted to take over Gardner's well-drafted Bill as a government measure, but MacDonald instructed him to bring forward amendments – which his Health Minister failed to do – to bring it in line with government policy. Finally, under pressure from his fellow Clydesiders, Wheatley hastily introduced an inadequately prepared government Prevention of Evictions Bill – only to lose the vote on the second reading. The Bill was assailed by its opponents particularly over the issue of clause 1 – which the minister had not shown to his law officers – on landlords and unemployed tenants. As Leader of the House, J. R. Clynes added to the parliamentary confusion by announcing a substitute clause – to assist unemployed tenants to pay their rent from public funds – which the Speaker ruled required a separate Bill or Money Resolution, and the bill was eventually talked out. The whole sorry saga continued when the Evictions Bill was reintroduced in April 1924, but suffered another defeat in the Commons. In the end the Government accepted a Liberal measure.[126]

As Gordon Brown has written, the establishment of a Scottish Parliament had been a long-standing commitment since the days of Keir Hardie's famous Mid-Lanark by-election in 1888. James Maxton, an out-and-out devolutionist, had signed the 1918 Labour Scottish manifesto pledging Scottish Home Rule, and was a founding member of the all-party Scottish Home Rule Association. A similar commitment had been prominent in the manifestos of most Scottish Labour MPs in the 1922 and 1923 elections. Maxton, Wheatley and their fellow Clyde-sider MPs also participated in the campaigning by the Scottish Home Rule Association, which reached its zenith between 1923 and 1924. The Clydesiders had been convinced by their parliamentary experience at Westminster of the necessity of a 'Parliament for Scotland and giving to that country a measure of Home Rule.'[127] James Maxton and Thomas Johnston, the former editor of the Glasgow *Forward*, addressed some of the largest public demonstrations in Scotland in support of the Govern-ment of Scotland Bill, introduced in May 1924 by George Buchanan with the backing of at least 56 Scottish MPs. The main proposal of the Private Member's Bill was to devolve most of the domestic Scottish business to a single-house assembly with some taxation powers supplemented by a central 'Imperial' subsidy (starting at £500,000 per year). Home Rule for Scotland was an issue of importance to the minority first Labour government. Of the 71 Scottish MPs returned to Westminster, the largest contingent was the 34 Labour members, vital to Labour's position in the Commons.

As with previous Home Rule proposals for Ireland, Buchanan's Private Member's Bill left untouched the position in any scheme for Home Rule of the Scottish MPs, who could still vote on English issues at Westmin-ster – until at least devolution for England and Wales had been agreed. Another weakness was that Home Rule for Scotland did not resolve the disparity in wealth between Scotland and England. In Parliament, Willie Adamson, Secretary of State for Scotland, indicated official approval of 'the general principle of the Bill', but after the Conservatives had talked out the second reading, the government – in the person of MacDonald himself in the Commons – refused parliamentary time for Buchanan's Government of Scotland Bill. The end of this debate witnessed another stormy parliamentary scene by the Clydesider group – leading to the Speaker's adjournment of the Commons, as the Scottish MPs challenged his refusal to allow James Maxton and Neil Maclean to keep the Bill alive by moving the parliamentary closure.[128] Despite further pressure, particularly by the Clydesiders in the 1920s, Scotland had to wait until the return of New Labour in 1997 for its own Parliament in Edinburgh.

In 1924 the former Liberal, Charles Trevelyan, became President of the Board of Education. He was an appropriate choice for the education portfolio – which he held again in the 1929–31 Labour Cabinet – with his previous experience as a junior Minister of Education in the Asquith government in 1908. Beatrice Webb considered Trevelyan, 'wonderfully well "self-advertised" as a go-ahead administrator'. 'He is quite fond of his job – far more determined and industrious than any of his recent predecessors,' she added.[129]

Like Arthur Ponsonby and Oswald Mosley, Charles P. Trevelyan was one of the upper-class politicians in Labour's ranks in the 1920s. He possessed a considerable pedigree in progressive politics. A product of Harrow and Cambridge, he was a member of an illustrious family and the heir to the Wallington Estate in Northumberland. His father, the historian George Otto Trevelyan, had been in government and his younger brother, G. M. Trevelyan, was another eminent historian. Charles Trevelyan had been a Liberal MP from 1899–1918 and resigned from the Asquith government in 1914 over British entry into the Great War to found the Union of Democratic Control with E. D. Morel, Norman Angell, Ramsay MacDonald and his close friend Arthur Ponsonby.

While a few Cabinet Ministers in 1924 – like the new President of the Board of Education, drawn from outside the working class – had passed through public school and university, the majority of the new Labour administration had attended only Victorian elementary schools and had entered employment at 14 or earlier. The members of the first Labour government not only reflected the significant divisions in British society over social class and educational prospects, but had first-hand practical experience of interrupted schooling and the realities of manual labour in industrial Britain.

Widening educational opportunities for ordinary people had been a long-standing concern of the Labour Party that went hand in hand with improving the general welfare of children. The one-time socialist Margaret Macmillan's pioneering work in Bradford and London was based on her famous adage that 'Education on an empty stomach was a waste of time.'[130] Labour had been closely identified with the demand for the state provision of school meals and medical inspections introduced by Liberal government legislation in 1906 and 1907.[131]

At the end of the Great War, the 1918 Fisher Education Act provided the basis for an expansion of educational discussion and the Young Report of 1920, which advocated the expansion of secondary education from 400,000 places to 2.25 million places. But the idea of extending secondary education to the working classes was aborted when the financial crisis of the early 1920s led to the 'Geddes Axe' on public expenditure, adversely affecting education expansion.

In 1924 Labour was not short of expert guidance on improving the educational prospects of the nation, since its Advisory Committee Education attracted intellectuals and specialists intent on educational reform. In 1922, R. H. Tawney produced a Labour Party pamphlet on education entitled *Secondary Education for All: A Policy for Labour* (officially the product of the Labour Party Advisory Committee on education) that was adopted as a key text.[132] Among its main proposals were the raising of the school-leaving age and the elimination of fee paying as part of an expansion of secondary education. On taking up his education portfolio, Charles Trevelyan had impressed the Webbs 'with his terseness in expressing concrete proposals', though his plans 'were largely derived from the influential R. H. Tawney'.[133] The key issue was how much change could be implemented within limited financial resources and strict Treasury control. Labour took office following a period of severe cut-backs, notably the 'Geddes Axe', in educational spending that had provoked teacher strikes in early 1923 under their Conservative predecessors. Trevelyan determined to end the cycle of educational economies by withdrawing the cost-cutting Circular 1190. 'I have, therefore, reversed the engines,' he claimed within two months of taking office. He also set about achieving a number of modest administrative changes: reduction of class sizes in elementary schools, efforts to reduce the number of unqualified teachers, improving dilapidated school buildings, raising the percentage of free school places in secondary schools from 25 per cent to 40 per cent and the restoration of state scholarships from state-aided schools to universities.[134] He told his wife Molly that 'the collective effect gave an impression of immense expenditure'.[135] The President of the Board of Education realised he had to steer between the Scylla of the local authorities who ran the state schools and the Charybdis of the Treasury determined to reduce government expenditure. 'All your proposals but one admit of great expansion,' Snowden advised Trevelyan. In such circumstances I rely on the watchfulness of my Department to safeguard me and my successors from future difficulties,' he added.[136]

Raising the school-leaving age to 15 – a major priority in 1924 – was not achieved until 1947 under the post-war Attlee government. In office, Trevelyan immediately attempted to press ahead with Labour's demand for 'secondary education for all' by asking Sir Henry Hadow, of the Consultative Committee of the Board of Education, to investigate the possibility of all children remaining at school until they were at least 15. The Hadow *Report on the Education of the Adolescent* appeared in 1926, well after the fall of the first Labour government. Despite having Tawney at its meetings, it produced recommendations – a change from elementary to secondary schools at the age of 11, based upon an 11-plus test which would sort out those pupils who would go to the new secondary modern and technical schools from those who would go to the existing grammar schools, based upon equality of opportunity. This prompted considerable voluntary reorganisation of schooling by some local education authorities in the late 1920s and the early 1930s, but the Hadow Report was neither Labour Party nor Labour government policy. The equality of opportunity for children imposed upon an unequal and class-based system simply meant inequality. Labour's demand for universal provision, effectively through a multilateral or comprehensive school, in which pupils could pursue their studies according to their abilities, was simply ignored in the years after the first Labour government and not achieved until the 1960s. On other fronts, also, Labour's education policies barely moved. There was pressure placed upon local authorities to use their existing powers to increase the number of children staying on at school, and a widening of scholarship provision, but this was merely window dressing and there was little in the way of substantial educational change during the lifetime of the first Labour government. In October 1924 the Labour Party Conference report summarised the educational aims and objectives of the first Labour Government:

> Labour's intention to give every child equality of opportunity in education has begun to be fulfilled in the drastic change of the policy of the preceding Government. The Labour Government has been investing in smaller classes, an increase in the number of qualified teachers, new schools, maintenance for poorer children, more free places in Secondary Education and Scholarships to the University; all practical steps towards the ideal of securing to all children the same choice of advanced education as the children of the rich.[137]

The fears of Thomas Jones that Trevelyan would not be able to achieve his goals were fully justified, his task was effectively an impossible one even for someone who achieved a reputation as an effective politician in the 1924 administration.

How then are we to assess the domestic achievements of the first Labour Government? Whatever judgement is made has to take account of the fact that the Government was in power for only nine and a half months and that its policy could barely be developed in such a period, much less implemented. During this time the Government was in a minority position at Westminster. In such a precarious political situation, the MacDonald ministry went boldly on. The administration's much-lauded achievement was the Wheatley Act, which stimulated the building of rented accommodation by local authorities for ten years and there was some movement in the need to promote schemes of electrification. But much else was disappointment. Some significant advances were made in education, health and other areas of social policy, but the first Labour government's handling of industrial relations and women's issues – with the exception of widening the composition of the magistracy – caused considerable frustration within the constituent ranks of the Labour Party. The economic constraints of Snowden's 'Gladstonian' economic policies made the introduction of costly unemployment schemes almost impossible. In the end, the 1924 Labour government did little to tackle unemployment in Britain and changed little in the lives of the country's population, even though its policies pointed in the direction of future change and improvement.

5
Minority Government

When Parliament assembled at Westminster in 1924, the new Labour administration did not command an absolute majority over the Conservative and Liberal opposition. Assuming office in these circumstances provided a timely opportunity to demonstrate a readiness for government, but one that was fraught with severe difficulties for an inexperienced administration that a Conservative–Liberal combination could easily turn out.[1] To all intents and purposes, during 1924 the minority Labour government was maintained in office for nearly ten months by Liberal votes at Westminster. In this sense, the 1924 MacDonald Government has gone down in history as a ministry that 'was in office, but not in power'. However, the notion that MacDonald and his ministers, who had little truck with socialism, actively relied on an alliance with the Liberals remains one of the myths of Labour history.

Throughout 1924, relations between the Labour and Liberal parties in Parliament and in the constituencies remained a central issue in British politics. Ostensibly, the conditions for a political alliance between Labour and Liberals seemed propitious. The two parties shared a fair amount of common ground on both domestic issues and foreign policy. Haldane, Trevelyan, Ponsonby and Buxton – members of the 1924 government – were, as we have seen, among prominent former Liberals who had shifted their political allegiance to Labour. Among the new backbenchers, E. D. Simon, Liberal MP for Manchester, Withington, and later to join the Labour Party, was heartened by 'the immense field of constructive work in which we could fruitfully co-operate . . . Foreign Affairs, Unemployment, Education and Housing are the most important.'[2]

Once Labour had taken office, C. P. Scott, editor of the *Manchester Guardian*, who had consistently championed Liberal backing for the new administration, interviewed both Ramsay MacDonald and Lloyd George, on the prospects for Liberal–Labour collaboration. MacDonald believed that his administration would last 'as long as we have work to do which does not bring us into direct conflict with the other parties'. The Labour leader appeared favourable to working on a day-to-day basis with the Liberals. 'I see no difficulty in the Whips – Liberal and Labour – coming to an understanding as happened when the Liberals and Irish were working together in Parnellite times. But I cannot accept a position of dependence on the Liberal Party.' Clearly the Liberals flaunting Labour's dependence upon them at Westminster irked the Labour leader. 'He showed a curious sensitiveness on this and spoke with feeling, as though this were a matter of deep importance. Probably it is the matter on which his own party feels most and on which he would be most exposed to attack,' Scott concluded at the end of his interview.[3]

In reality, the minority Labour administration did not govern by depending upon Liberal votes for its survival. Instead, from the outset, MacDonald resolved to tread a firm path of political independence and not to be turned out of office after an unexpected vote. On 12 February, addressing a packed House of Commons for two hours on his new administration's policy, he declared: 'We shall bring before this House proposals to deal with great national and international problems.' Though Labour enjoyed no parliamentary majority his government – which was to weather 11 defeats in the division lobbies during its 287 days – would only be ended after losing a vote of confidence.

To the chagrin of his Liberal opponents, many of whom would have welcomed some form of cooperation between their parties, the Labour leader rejected reviving a progressive alliance around his parliamentary programme, although he had been politically close to the pre-war Liberal government. He did not take up Harold Spender's proposal in 1924 for a Labour–Liberal concordat to secure 'a possible harvest of fruitful legislation', similar to the Liberals reforms of 1906–13.[4] MacDonald had a different project in mind – the destruction of the Liberal Party. The Labour leader was quite scathing about his opponents in the Liberal Party. 'Ups and downs. The quarrel, mostly personal and private, over the Liberal leadership succession, is really being badly conducted as such quarrels by small men always are. None of the claimants attend the H of C very regularly, but when they do they please themselves, vulgarly interrupt, cock their heads in the air, smile with superior airs – and have a good Liberal press next morning.'[5]

According to MacDonald, the only exception was Asquith whom he considered 'head and shoulders over them all', even though he had 'never hit it off with him'.[6] For both Stanley Baldwin and Ramsay MacDonald, the lesson of the 1923 election was that within a British political system, there was only room for two parties – moderate Labour and respectable Conservatism.[7] In the political uncertainty of December 1923, Asquith acquired the reputation, and later the blame, for being responsible 'for putting Labour in'.[8] His public declaration at the National Liberal Club (NLC) that he would not support the Baldwin ministry was a distinct change of tack from his original intention of ousting the Conservatives and then combining with them to turn out a demonstrably incompetent Labour ministry as a route to a possible Liberal government. Thomas Jones noted on 20 December 1923: 'Yesterday Asquith declared war on the (Conservative) Government at the National Liberal Club with the united blessing of L. G. and Sir John Simon . . . we shall have a Labour Government before the end of January . . . the idea is to give the Labour Party a fair chance for some months at any rate and then possibly bring the Liberals into power with a dissolution.'

Famously, as we have seen, Asquith had assured his fellow Liberals at the NLC meeting, 'if a Labour Government is ever to be tried in this country, as it will be sooner or later, it could hardly ever be tried under safer conditions', though he was somewhat wide of the mark. His patronising remark infuriated MacDonald, who was determined to demonstrate Labour's capability in government. The Liberal leader also miscalculated in believing his parliamentary party would hold the balance of power at Westminster.[9] A despondent Austen Chamberlain, the former Conservative leader, complained that Baldwin had lost the opportunity of a political arrangement with Asquith, thereby passing the initiative to MacDonald.[10]

However, Asquith's stance received a broad measure of support across a Liberal Party willing to back a moderate Labour regime. At a public meeting in the Victoria Baths at Manchester, addressed by local Liberal MPs, Charles Masterman surprisingly declared that 'all that remained now was to see how far the government would bring in Liberal measures or revolutionary measures. If it brings in Liberal measures, I shall support it, if it brings in revolutionary or socialist measures I shall oppose it.' His fellow Liberal, E. D. Simon, acknowledged Labour's moderateness: 'The only reason we have gone into Parliament is to try to get Liberal legislation passed, and personally it does not make much difference to me who does it, he added.'[11]

In 1924 there was no formal pact or informal understanding to maintain Labour in power. Asquith sought no *quid pro quo*, such as electoral reform, from MacDonald in return for any Liberal backing to end the Baldwin administration, or afterwards when MacDonald was in office. Lloyd George later complained to C. P. Scott, 'the real mistake of the past session had not been the putting of Labour into office but doing so without any understanding or conditions.'[12] In these circumstances, it was left to MacDonald to determine whether Labour would be cooperative or hostile towards the Liberals.

After Lloyd George fell from power as Prime Minister in 1922, his intrigues – including that he might at some point shift his affiliation to the Labour Party – were subject to much speculation in political circles. However, despite his initial eagerness to cooperate with Labour on a programme of radical legislation, his aim remained to work for a united Liberal Party under his leadership.[13] It was highly unlikely that MacDonald would have responded to any overtures from Lloyd George, since no politician was more distrusted by large sections of the Labour movement than 'the Welsh Wizard' who had lost his standing as the patron of Labour in the post-war years.[14]

While in Lossiemouth pondering his choice of Cabinet, Ramsay MacDonald talked to an American journalist, W. H. Crawford of *Collier's Weekly*. The interview was published in the United States, but only the *Liberal Magazine* in Britain appears to have reported it. Asked about the Liberals, the Labour leader pronounced the three-party system of government a disadvantage and that the British public would soon appreciate that the Labour Party was not controlled by the Bolsheviks, but believed in democratic parliamentary government. 'The time is coming quickly when there will be only two [parties] – the Conservatives, who represent capital, and the combined forces who favour a government by the people. I believe that they will see the wisdom of combining under the banner of the Labour Party rather than the half-hearted principles of the Liberals.'[15]

During Labour's first stint in office, the Liberal Party lacked the overall unity and discipline to have sustained any kind of concordat with Labour at Westminster. The implication of Liberal support was that the Liberal Whips had to keep a reserve of around 60 Liberal members at Westminster to prevent Labour being continually caught in a minority in the division lobbies. The internal divisions among the Liberals were apparent as soon as the Parliament gathered. On 21 January, 138 Liberal MPs solidly backed J. R. Clynes's motion of no confidence to bring down the Baldwin administration, but ten right-wing Liberals voted to keep the Conservatives in office – a significant core group around which other dissident Liberals could coalesce in the future.

During a weekend in April at Churt, Lloyd George's country estate, Thomas Jones discovered the former Premier's concern about Labour–Liberal relations in the country as well as at Westminster. Growing opposition among Liberals to the Labour government was evident among Lloyd George's constituents in Caernarfon Boroughs. 'It was absurd that the two parties should not understand and help each other in the present circumstances. The two Whips, Vivian Phillipps and Ben Spoor, were largely to blame for the present estrangement,' Thomas Jones noted.[16]

Earlier, Lloyd George's important speech on 22 April to a large gathering of his Welsh constituents at Llanfairfechan had marked a sharp turning point in his attitude to the Labour administration. Unstinting Liberal support in the Westminster lobbies had been repaid with Labour unfriendliness and ill will. 'Liberals are to be the oxen to drag the Labour wain over the rough roads of Parliament for two or three years, and at the end of the journey, when there is no further use for them, they are to be slaughtered. That is the idea of Labour cooperation [laughter],' he declared. The adoption of a Labour candidate in his own constituency produced an even stronger complaint about 'unmitigated hostility' shown to the Liberal Party in Parliament and beyond. 'Whilst Liberal members are voting for the Labour Government, Labour candidates have been put up against them throughout the constituencies, and Liberalism is being hunted, if possible, to death.'[17]

In the 1920s Liberal–Labour relations were distinctly different after the First World War had transformed British politics. The progressive alliance of Liberals and Labour (or rather, in ideological terms, New Liberal and moderate Labour) characterised the fact that Edwardian electoral politics no longer existed. Despite the temporary Liberal unity displayed in the 1923 election campaign, the deep split between Asquith and Lloyd George wrecked the party's electoral fortunes and divided the Liberals into feuding factions in the 1920s. But the fissures in the Liberal leadership between Asquith and Lloyd George and their supporters also extended deeper, beyond personalities into party policy, finance and basic philosophy. During the 1923 election, many of Lloyd George's former Liberal coalitionists had been defeated, including prominent figures such as Winston Churchill and Alfred Mond. However, Lloyd George did retain his important political fund built out of the proceeds of the sale of honours, while the Asquithian coffers remained virtually empty after two elections in as many years. This situation fuelled the Liberal Party rifts. Edward Grigg, Liberal MP, complained about divisions within the party leadership. 'There is no sign at present of any real understanding between Asquith and L. G. Asquith has been ill lately and has hardly been in the House of Commons at all.'[18] Hobhouse told Scott: 'I doubt if it (the Liberal Party) any longer stands for anything distinctive. My reasons are on the one side that moderate Labour – Labour in office – has on the whole represented essential Liberalism, not without mistakes and defects, but better than the organised party since Campbell-Bannerman's death. On the other side the Liberal Party, however you divide it up, never seems any better agreed on essentials.'[19]

These splits within the Liberal ranks were reflected in differing attitudes towards the Labour Government. On the party's progressive wing, Liberal MPs, such as J. M. Kenworthy, held common ground with the socialist administration through thick and thin. The Liberal member later recalled he had been prepared to support MacDonald over the Anglo-Soviet Treaties that threatened the survival of the administration: 'He need not have feared. William Jowitt, J. J. O'Neill and I had organised a "cave" of Liberal members who considered the Russian Treaty equitable and in the interests of trade and employment, and we had enough votes promised to give the Government a majority.' Kenworthy, who not surprisingly later joined the Labour ranks, also claimed he had 'an unofficial bargain made with [Arthur Henderson] which could have led to a Liberal–Labour alliance in the constituencies as well as at Westminster: 'From my place on the Liberal benches I gave steady support to the Labour Government on every matter of policy except this one of the new warship programme.'[20] On the other hand, the Liberal member for Leith, William Wedgwood Benn, who moved over to the Labour Party in 1927, reflected on the parliamentary debate on the Air Estimates in March 1924: 'A good day's work finishing very late. The Labour Party accept our help in the House, but, as I see from the local press, send down people to abuse us in the constituencies. I think we shall blow them out of the water when we attack...they are making no attempt to carry out the programme they advertised.'[21]

During the lifetime of the first Labour government there were nine by-elections between 1 February and 14 August (plus the uncontested one at Dover on 12 March) that provide some evidence of relations between the minority Labour administration and its political opponents. Some results were predictable, such as the City of London by-election on 1 February that yielded the expected Conservative victory in a Tory stronghold. But more significant was Burnley on 28 February, which brought Arthur Henderson back to Parliament for the fairly safe Labour seat. With no Liberal candidate, the Burnley Liberal Executive remained neutral. Henderson ran a moderate campaign – described by *The Times*

Table 1   1924 Labour government by-elections

Date	Constituency	Previous MP	Result
1 February	City of London	Conservative	Conservative
28 February	Burnley	Labour	Labour
12 March	Dover (uncontested)	Conservative	Conservative
19 March	Westminster, Abbey	Conservative	Conservative
22 May	Liverpool, W. Toxteth	Conservative	Labour gain
23 May	Glasgow, Kelvingrove	Conservative	Conservative
5 June	Oxford	Liberal	Conservative gain
9 July	Sussex, Lewes	Conservative	Conservative
31 July	Lincolnshire, Holland/Boston	Labour	Conservative gain
14 August	Carmarthenshire, Carmarthen	Liberal	Liberal

correspondent as 'the next best thing to a regulation Liberal'. He gained a pleasing victory by a margin of 7037 over his alarmist anti-socialist Conservative opponent, who had public support from the nominally Liberal Winston Churchill. For the Labour leadership, Henderson's success confirmed that the annihilation of the Liberal Party, rather than Liberal–Labour cooperation, was way forward. In the hope of attracting Liberal voters in future Burnleys, Labour launched candidates in rural seats and middle-class constituencies.[22]

While Liberal Head Office had discouraged the Burnley Liberals from contesting the seat, at Westminster Lloyd George – supported by the Conservatives – caused difficulties for MacDonald as Foreign Secretary by asking if Henderson's campaign speech – in which he called controversially for 'the inauguration of a new era of international co-operation and goodwill', including 'the revision of the Versailles Treaty with all expedition' – represented a change in government foreign policy. Inept handling of the parliamentary hullabaloo by an embarrassed MacDonald, at the time engaged in sensitive negotiations with the French Premier, only drew more press exposure of government divisions shortly before polling day in the by-election. It was left to Jim Middleton, the Assistant Labour Party Secretary, to defend Henderson on the grounds that he had used an old speech written by a party worker from the last election, in which Labour had called for an international conference on the Versailles Treaty and reparations. As Chris Wrigley has observed, tensions had surfaced again between the Prime Minister, angry at the intrusion on his personal domain of foreign policy, and his Home Secretary – the future Foreign Secretary and Nobel Peace Laureate – loyally committed to Labour Party conference decisions.[23]

On 19 March, Winston Churchill, standing as an Independent, narrowly lost in the Tory bastion of Abbey, Westminster, by only 43 votes to the official Conservative candidate. Most dramatically, the socialist candidate, Fenner Brockway, achieved a commendable result of more than 6000 votes, pushing Scott Duckers, the Liberal, into fourth place with fewer than 300 votes. The Westminster and Burnley results indicated that the minority government could survive and that the divided Liberal opposition was a spent electoral force.

In May 1924 two by-elections in Liverpool and Glasgow on successive days also cast an interesting light on Liberal–Labour Party fortunes, as well as the attitude of the Labour Government to Communist candidates. In Liverpool, until the Edge Hill by-election in 1923, Labour had never won a parliamentary seat in the city. On 22 May in the West Toxteth Division of Liverpool, in a straight fight against the Conservative candidate, a leading Orangeman and city councillor, the Labour victory was secured with a margin of 2471 votes. With no Liberal candidate in the field, the local association had advised their supporters to vote for Joseph Gibbins, the Labour nominee. This morale boosting result, at the time of Snowden's popular budget, represented a swing of 4.6 per cent – and was the party's only election gain during the period of the 1924 Labour government.

The following day, Labour lost the by-election at Glasgow, Kelvingrove, where the Conservative majority was increased to 4321 votes. The Labour candidate, Aitken Ferguson, who had been adopted by the Kelvingrove Labour Party, was a prominent Communist and former member of the Clyde Workers' Committee. His election agent was his fellow Communist, J. R. Campbell. A few months later, his bungled prosecution was to be famously responsible for the downfall of the Labour administration. Ferguson's creditable showing six months before in the general election – without official endorsement – had reduced the Conservative majority to 1004 votes. At first the NEC approved his candidature for the by-election by a substantial majority. However, alarm grew at Labour headquarters as Ferguson's unashamed and forthright Communist campaign was seen as a heaven-sent opportunity for Conservative denunciations of the Bolshevik revolutionary threat. Eventually no official support was forthcoming for the Scottish member of the Boilermakers' Union who also had to shoulder the blame for Labour's defeat. At Kelvingrove, the Liberal poll had collapsed with a cataclysmic 1372 votes – a harbinger of the party's performance in Scotland in the 1924 general election. This by-election result also had a wider significance – in terms of Labour's attitude to British communism at home. An official delegation (comprising C. T. Cramp, Will Lawther and Egerton Wake), sent from London to Glasgow to investigate the circumstances of Ferguson's candidature, advised a revision of the party's rules to protect Labour against Communist intrusion – thereby bringing further changes to Labour's constitution at the 1924 annual party conference.

Of the four remaining by-elections – Oxford, Lewes, Lincolnshire, Holland-with Boston and Carmarthen – the city of Oxford was a Liberal loss to the Conservatives – probably as a result of the Labour intervention. As Chris Cook has written, there was little to comfort the Liberals in these results, which reflected their poor organisation and divided leadership. At Lewes, where the Conservative increased his vote, the Liberals trailed in a poor third behind Labour.[24] The Holland by-election, fought by Hugh Dalton, later Labour Chancellor of the Exchequer in the post-war Attlee Government, was the only seat Labour lost – albeit narrowly by 12,907 to 12,101 – during the 1924 Labour Government. At 36, Dalton suffered his fourth successive election defeat in just over two years and complained bitterly about his Liberal opponents' 'indescribably dirty' campaign. After a stream of damnatory accusations – that Dalton was an extremist, a drunkard and had published a text-book for Communist Sunday Schools – the son of Canon Dalton at St George's Chapel, Windsor declared: 'There will be no health in our public life until they are exterminated as a Party.'[25] The Liberals, who did not contest the seat in 1923, finished in third place with a poorer performance than in the 1918 and 1922. At the last by-election at Carmarthen, where Labour came second, the Liberal candidate, Sir Alfred Mond, managed to hold on to the seat; but as in every other by-election during the 1924 Parliament, with a reduced share of the total votes cast than in 1923.[26]

Lack of unity in the Liberal ranks was also apparent in the party's performance in the House of Commons where those on the Right of the party might join the group of Liberals who had wished to maintain Baldwin in office. To prevent Liberal splits, firm leadership was required. According to C. P. Scott, Vivian Phillipps, with his close connections to Asquith's circle, was not an appropriate choice as the Liberal Chief Whip. On any form of Liberal–Labour cooperation he told Lloyd George: 'a great deal of course depend on the Whips . . . Vivian Phillipps, as Chief Whip, would be a serious obstacle.' The editor of the *Manchester Guardian* found the Liberal whips in general 'a poorish lot' with the exception of Lloyd George's son, Gwilym.

Speaking to East Anglian Conservatives at Lowestoft on 17 July 1924, Stanley Baldwin taunted the Liberals that they had 'voted to put the

Socialists in, and not only that . . . are still keeping them in day by day' – a policy that would lose them votes at the next election. To resounding cheers he declared: 'they will be between the upper and nether mill-stones' – the classic phrase that described the ailing Liberal Party increasingly trapped between their Labour and Conservative opponents. He added 'how can any elector believe that promise, if made at the next election, by any one of them, that a vote for the Liberals is a vote to keep the Socialists out?'[27]

Baldwin's speech was part of a public campaign – seven speeches in two weeks in May with three more in June 1924 – in Britain to restore Conservative Party fortunes in opposition during the months of the Labour minority government. He had almost brought about his downfall as Conservative leader by his decision to fight an election over his tariff policy when his party still had four more years in office. Earl Derby,the War Minister, observed: '[I]t saddens me to think that the Prime Minister should, within six months of taking office, bring us to this . . . It looks as if the Conservative Party has been smashed up for all time.'[28] With a net loss of 88 seats, the Tories had been in disarray on how to prevent the advent of a Labour government, but rumours that A. J. Balfour, Derby or Austen Chamberlain might replace Baldwin and form some kind of Conservative–Liberal coalition soon came to nought. During the 1923 election campaign, Baldwin's personal fortunes had reached a low ebb. Travelling with the Conservative leader, Thomas Jones noted the *Daily Herald* placard 'Baldwin's son on Premier's policy', a reference to Oliver Baldwin's public conversion to Socialism.[29]

In 1924 Baldwin used the months in opposition to restore the morale and unity of his party in preparation for a return to power. He met Balfour, the former Conservative leader, to talk over his position and that of those members of the late coalition government who had not been in office in 1923. Following careful diplomacy by Neville Chamberlain, his half-brother Austen and Baldwin were reconciled following a secret dinner meeting at Chamberlain's house. Lord Birkenhead was also brought back into the Shadow Cabinet, which Baldwin invited key figures to join in the interests of party unity. In reality, however, there was no alternative politician to head the Conservative Party than Stanley Baldwin. Between 1923 and 1926, he established his authority as party leader and was indisputably the Conservative's main electoral asset. With Ramsay MacDonald and Stanley Baldwin were the pre-eminent political figures in the inter-war years. At the first party meeting in February 1924, after Labour took office, the Conservatives endorsed Baldwin's position as Conservative leader and deftly dropped the tariff policy.

While briefly out of office, Baldwin took the opportunity to reshape the Conservative Party for the first time in nine years with an improved party organisation and policy that laid the basis for an eventual return to office as happened after similar defeats in 1945 and 1964. The re-organisation of party headquarters in 1924, mainly undertaken by Tory Central Office, was an important step forward, particularly as the party no longer had access to Civil Service facilities. Baldwin took a leading part, but others including Neville Chamberlain, Amery, Monsell and Davidson also made significant contributions.[30] Baldwin was directly involved in setting up a small Policy Secretariat to act as his private office, to review policy options and to draft a full-scale policy document. Colonel Lancelot Storr headed a new policy secretariat staffed with a number of able young Unionists, including Geoffrey Lloyd and Robert Boothby, soon to be the MP for Aberdeenshire East. Based at Central Office, alongside Baldwin's personal staff, the secretariat worked closely with them. Policy committees consisting of MPs and advisers were also established – each chaired by an appropriate shadow minister – to report directly to Baldwin and Austen Chamberlain. Neville Chamberlain compiled the secretariat's conclusions, which were published in June 1924 as *Looking Ahead: Unionist Principles and Aims*. This comprehensive Conservative policy review also became the party's manifesto for the October 1924 election and the basis for the Conservatives' second term in office under Baldwin's leadership during the next five years.[31]

However, equal attention was also placed upon improving other aspects of party organisation. A review of organisations went on within the party and changes occurred. The 1922 Committee was pressed forward to represent the views of faithful backbenchers. There were a number of new, more effective, appointments made. Herbert Blain in March 1924, a self-made businessman, replaced Sir Reginald Hall, who was a failure as the Principal Agent; Lord Linlithgow became Deputy Chairman; Joseph Ball was recruited from MI5 to look after propaganda – his connections with the secret service proving useful. The party's literature services were expanded and the number of agents appointed in 1924 almost doubled to 214, compared to the 117 in 1923.

By the summer of 1924, Baldwin's 'New Conservatism' was, according to John Ramsden, 'businesslike and organised, tough not in its adherence to old ideas but in its pragmatic realism'.[32] It emphasised the need to involve the whole of society in the new democratic era of manhood and womanhood suffrage, the right of people to belong, or not to belong, to trade unions, attempted to appeal to the common man, and sought conciliation rather than conflict. Indeed, in 1924, Baldwin's clarion call was that 'Socialism divides, Unionism unites'.[33] Englishness, the assumption of responsibility, and the duty of the people operating in an unfettered environment of free trade and *laissez faire* became its hallmark.

The Conservative Party had seized the opportunity to reorganise and to work out a more coherent set of new policies – the 'New Conservatism' – during its time in opposition. Tory Central Office helped to improve the party organisation throughout the country. It was, therefore, not surprising that Austen Chamberlain wrote in the *Evening News* of 30 July 1924: 'How has the Party fared since the disaster of last November? We must answer without hesitation that it has made good progress.' As a result of the various changes, the Conservatives at Westminster were now in a more confident position when it came to harrying the Labour government on the issues of the Irish Boundary Commission, the treaties with the Soviet Union, the decision to withdraw the Campbell prosecution, and in successfully contesting the 1924 general election.[34]

On the Labour side, party management fared little better, owing to the misfortune of Ben Spoor, the lacklustre Chief Whip, and the poor showing of J. R. Clynes as the Deputy Leader of the House of Commons during MacDonald's absences abroad. According to Beatrice Webb, Spoor's recurrent malaria sidelined him for most of the parliamentary session. For good measure, she believed his subordinates were little better. 'The dull headed miners (the senior Fred Hall, a notorious slacker) who are subordinate to him [Spoor], receive, but do not earn, over a £1,000 a year as Household Officers,' she observed harshly. Henderson, who found MacDonald distant, told her that 'No. 10 and No. 11 [residence of J. R. Clynes, the Deputy Leader of the House] see no more of each other than if they slept and ate a hundred miles apart.'[35]

Though the attitude of HM Opposition seemed crucial in deciding whether Labour might remain in office, neither the Liberals nor the Conservatives wanted the worry or the financial expense of a third general election in three years. Remarkably, Asquith's assault on the government during the first week of parliamentary business – over Wheatley's prompt decision to rescind the Poplar Order prescribing levels of poor relief – threatened the dismissal of the government he had helped into office. Beatrice Webb watched the Poplar debate from the gallery while Wheatley's masterful performance on the floor exposed Asquith's incompetence on the poor law and saved the day. 'The Liberals showed up badly, willing to wound but afraid to strike,' she observed on the opposition party's indecision.[36] Asquith had to back down, making it clear that his party was not ready for another general election. Instead, the Liberals trooped into the government lobby, once MacDonald had made clear his trenchant opposition to 'Poplarism'. As it happened, 13 Liberals nevertheless voted with the Conservatives.

At Westminster the fortunes of the minority Labour administration largely depended on whether or not the Liberal members continued to march into the government lobby, though increasingly it became apparent that the Labour leadership did nothing to encourage this support. The indecision within the Liberal ranks, on whether to support or oppose the Labour government, continued and was reflected in their voting behaviour at Westminster. On 21 February the Liberal Party split over voting on the construction of five new cruisers and two destroyers when 30 Liberal MPs voted with the Conservatives.

On 6 March, on the reduction of the levy on German imports from 26 per cent to 5 per cent, the Liberal leadership was divided and seven Liberal MPs voted with the Conservative opposition. The building of the cruisers was raised again in the House of Commons on 18 March, when the Liberal MP H. Seely moved an amendment to the Naval Estimates that the construction of the cruisers was not justified on the grounds of either creating employment or the defence of the Empire. Though defeated, the amendment was lost by 304 against to 114 votes for it, Parliament witnessed a backbench revolt of 18 Labour MPs – including George Lansbury, Ernest Thurtle and Ben Turner (while 45 Labour MPs were absent). However, on this occasion, being an issue of national defence, the Conservative opposition and 24 Liberals supported the minority government.

A major political row broke out over Labour's decision to abandon further development of the Singapore naval base. The Conservatives attacked Labour's proposals by moving an amendment to the naval estimates that attracted the support of nine Liberals. By contrast only one Liberal MP, J. M Kenworthy, voted against a Conservative motion denouncing the capital levy.

On 7 April the minority government faced another major reverse when its Rent Bill, including the issue of eviction orders, was lost by 221:212. However, it was the Liberals who were in disarray and as equally embarrassed as the Labour administration. In the division lobbies, 53 Liberals joined the government, 22 voted against the Bill and 83 abstained (including Asquith, Lloyd George and Phillipps, the Chief Whip). Liberal voting on this measure displayed utter confusion, brought about by the indecision of party leadership.

On the Labour side, despite support received from the majority of Liberal members, there was little thought of collaboration. On 2 May the Representation of the People Act (1918) Amendment Bill – brought in by the Liberal MP for Thornbury, A. Rendall – was defeated on a free vote by 238 : 144. Among those supporting the Bill that would have introduced a form of proportional representation in Britain, were 107 Liberals, 28 Labour and 8 Conservatives – including five Labour ministers. The killing of this measure – regarded later by Liberals as a sacred cow – was a tremendous blow to Liberal morale, doubly so after the Government, supported by the Parliamentary Labour Party, had refused to grant the Bill safe passage into law. Electoral reform was a vital issue for the Liberal Party and its defeat meant no opportunity for change before the next general election.

'Liberals again to the rescue' were the newspaper headlines on 30 May when the Labour administration faced its most serious crisis prior to the Campbell Case, which brought down the administration five months later. In the end the Government secured a relatively comfortable majority of 48 against the Conservative amendment to reduce the salary of the Minister of Labour, Tom Shaw, by £100 as a protest against the Government's failure to tackle unemployment. In a well-attended division of 556 MPs, 252 members voted for the Unionist motion and 300 against thereby avoiding the defeat of the Labour administration. In the end, 110 Liberals voted with the government, but only after Asquith's eleventh-hour intervention in the critical parliamentary debate gave the MacDonald administration a last-minute reprieve. Of those Liberals voting in the opposition lobby, Captain Freddie Guest sought to keep the rebel enclave together. 'There was grave danger of disintegration in the [Liberal] party because the policy of the party had come to a mere question of tactics and drift which would bring them into contempt,' he warned.[37]

The spreading confusion among the Liberals displayed in their voting on this issue was well observed by the Liberal member for Leith, William Wedgwood Benn: 'Policy at the present moment is very difficult. Mr A (Asquith) of course works in the background with Conferences with the Mausoleum, LLG will appear from time to time to force the party into stunts. Party meetings are difficult to hold, but without them, trouble will ensue. Brilliant nagging at the Government is all very well but seems to me to lead nowhere.'[38] Ultimately, declining Liberal morale propelled Benn into the Labour Party.

MacDonald decided to make this Conservative challenge on unemployment a matter of confidence that would bring about the resignation of the Government, if defeated. However, his minority administration

Table 2   1924 Labour government defeats in Parliament (in each case the lower figure represents the Labour government vote)

1.	13 March	207 : 234	Contested business to be taken after 11 p.m.
2.	7 April	212 : 221	Rent and Mortgage Restrictions Bill
3.	7 April	207 : 170	Amendment to Ways and Means Resolution (milk)
4.	16 June	189 : 126	London Traffic Bill
5.	23 June	315 : 175	Housing Bill
6.	24 June	168 : 195	London Traffic Bill.
7.	30 June	220 : 165	Finance Bill (Entertainment Duty)
8.	18 July	149 : 171	Unemployment Insurance Bill (Minister's powers)
9.	21 July	201 : 155	Housing (Financial Provisions) Bill
10	21 July	119 : 137	Housing (Financial Provisions) Bill (security of tenure)
11.	28 July	27 : 17	Agricultural Wages Bill (Liberal amendment)
12.	8 October	198 : 359	Censure Motion over withdrawal of criminal proceedings against the editor of *Workers' Weekly*
13.	8 October	364 : 198	Censure motion amendment (Select Committee of Inquiry concerning the withdrawal of proceedings)

remained on relatively safe ground. Privately, the Webbs did not fear the worst on this political tightrope after the creditable Labour performances in two recent by-elections. 'In view of the West Toxteth victory and the disappearance of the Liberal poll in the Glasgow Division, we doubt whether either of the Oppositions – specially not the Liberals – will dare to run us out,' Beatrice Webb observed.

Differences between the Liberal Party and the Labour government surfaced over on the Agricultural Wages Bill, introduced by Noel Buxton, Minister of Agriculture. The main point of his Bill, which had strong PLP support, was to increase wage levels for agricultural workers, without necessarily establishing a minimum wage, and to enforce improvement through a Central Board.[39] However, the Liberals hindered Buxton's efforts to pass the Agricultural Wages' Bill through Parliament during the standing committee stage, using F. D. Acland's amendment which was carried by 27 to 17 votes, and prevented the Central Board from overriding local committees and imposing county wage rates. Acland declared that the 'farmer regarded the Bill as an infernal nuisance, whether he paid food wages or not... They must establish all-round confidence in the local committees.'

R. I. Walker, General Secretary of the National Union of Agricultural Workers told the *Daily Herald* that the Liberals did not intend that the Central Board should have any power and that if an agricultural worker stood up for his rights, 'he is immediately victimised and hounded from the district; not only from his employment, but from his house, which generally belongs to the employer.'[40] Such conflict, of course, was simply a prelude to later divisions between Labour and the Liberals over the Russian Treaty and the Campbell Case.

Initially, a number of Liberals, including Lloyd George, had envisaged benefits from cooperation with Labour if their party sustained the new administration in office. After watching an Albert Hall concert from Lloyd George's box, Scott learned of the reaction of the Liberal leadership following the general election. With the coalition government finished, Lloyd George was determined that the Liberals should support the Labour government wholeheartedly in pursuit of radical reform. Similarly, the Liberal Chief Whip, Vivian Phillipps, also enthused about collaboration with Labour. 'With good will and consideration, not only in Parliament but in the constituencies, they could march together along way before their paths need diverge,' he declared.[41]

By the summer recess, Liberal opinion had a bitter edge. Vivian Phillipps told C. P. Scott: 'Frankly, I have been disappointed in the attitude of Ramsay MacDonald to our Party during the past six months. Not only does he appear not to seek our goodwill and co-operation but on several occasions it has seemed as if he went out of his way to make it as difficult as possible for us to back him.'[42] Lloyd George also reviewed Liberal relations with the Labour government with C. P. Scott, including his determination to bring about some kind of concordat by coercion:

> 'I confess,' he said, 'it never occurred to me that we could be treated as we were treated. I took for granted that the relations of two parties would be analogous to those between the Irish and Liberal parties in the home rule period... Later I tried to force an understanding and in July I proposed to hold up the Labour Party on the Unemployment question. MacDonald dared not then have dissolved; he was too keen about the London Conference and foreign affairs. But I was overruled and the party would not take the risk.'[43]

During 1924 other factors affected the longevity of the Labour government. As a minority administration, the ministry needed to retain the allegiance of its own 191 MPs as well as attracting Liberal votes at Westminster. Throughout the lifetime of the 1924 ministry, communications were greatly strained between the administration and its supporters. Serious difficulties arose from time to time in maintaining close links between the Labour government, the Parliamentary Labour Party (PLP) and the Labour Party in the country. In addition, the party conference was inclined to go its own way. In 1924 the *Daily Herald*, now edited by Hamilton Fyfe and with George Lansbury as its general manager, could be immensely critical of the Government, even though the Labour Party and the unions had owned the Labour daily since 1922. The government had to contend with a hostile Communist Party seeking to extend its influence over Labour – a potentially divisive development for relations between the Labour Government and its left-wing. Within the Labour movement in Britain, political expectations throughout the country were much higher than a minority Labour government could deliver.

On taking office, as we have seen, the incoming administration had set about strengthening its links with members of the PLP and proposed a joint committee to report on the organisation of the parliamentary party and its relations with the new administration.[44] The ballot resulted in a committee whose composition was overwhelmingly ILP – Robert Smillie, Fred Jowett, Jimmy Maxton, George Lansbury, John Scurr, D. Graham and R. C. Wallhead, though Jowett was subsequently replaced on becoming First Commissioner of Works. The Committee reported that some organisational mechanisms were already in place to keep the PLP, the Labour Party and the Government in touch with each other, by serving on one of the party's many advisory committees, or one of the parliamentary select or standing committees. Nonetheless, further changes were needed now that the Labour Party was in office. Committees of the party should consult the appropriate bodies if they were thinking of a course of action 'not hitherto considered by the Party'.[45] In particular, the committee recommended that the Executive Committee of the PLP should be increased to 12 elected members to deal with internal administration within the party and to liaise between the government and the party, as well as watching the progress of parliamentary business and nominating the party's representatives on parliamentary committees.[46] It was felt that if these arrangements were acted upon, 'they will pave the way to sympathetic and harmonious co-operation between Ministers and Private Members, and enable the Party to pull its full weight in the House of Commons.' The PLP accepted the report and the new diversified Executive broadly reflected the parliamentary party.[47]

Nevertheless, relations between those on the Labour front bench and the ranks of Labour members behind them remained a constant and abiding problem. MacDonald had continually to bestride the idealism of his party and the practicalities of office. 'My great concern at present is the failure of our backbenchers to respond to the new conditions. Some of the disappointed ones maintain a feud & are more hostile to us as though they were not of us,' the Labour Leader complained.[48] To buttress the links between the government and the party, each minister was asked to make himself available for a few hours in February to talk over issues with PLP members.[49] Charles Trevelyan, President of the Board of Education, indicated that he would hold 'frequent meetings with those Members especially interested in education, and stated that the first meeting would be held on Friday at 2 o'clock.'[50]

These various arrangements were intended to foster good relations and understanding between the PLP and the Labour government, since the members of the PLP formed the administration's only direct connection with the rank and file in the constituency parties. As fewer than a third of the Labour Party branches had MPs, there was clearly some unease about this gap in communications. In April, several members of the PLP 'emphasised the need for closer cooperation between the Members [of the PLP] and the Members of the Party'.[51] In February 1924, Ernest Thurtle, Labour MP for Shoreditch, put forward a motion to the PLP urging the 'Government not to proceed with the proposed construction of five new cruisers'. MacDonald dealt so effectively with this back-bench revolt that the motion secured only 12 votes.[52] In response to this and similar expressions of doubt, MacDonald wrote in his diary of the 'failure of our backbenchers to respond to the new conditions . . . the backbenchers think that there is nothing being done unless the H. of C. is talking'.[53]

The minutes of the PLP reveal continuing tensions between the government, the PLP and the Labour Party as a whole. In particular, there were numerous issues of conflict and concern over the need for more extensive schemes to deal with unemployment, the implementation of Labour Party policy and foreign relations. On 5 March 1924, there was a backbench revolt of 45 Labour MPs on the Trade Facilities Bill, which was passed only with the support of the Conservative and Liberal opposition. In the debate two leading ILP MPs, Tom Johnston, editor of the socialist *Forward*, and James Maxton, denounced government subsidies for private industry, which underpinned capitalism while there were no curbs on company dividends.[54]

On defence, W. H. Ayles and Ernest Thurtle moved a reduction in the size of the British Army. James Maxton supported the resolution by suggesting that any savings should go towards the social services.

Johnston was also a stern critic of the Labour administration's extremely disappointing performance on unemployment, which was reflected in widespread dissatisfaction during the parliamentary debate in May 1924. The NAC of the ILP pressed for the introduction of a 48-hour week for all workers and outside Parliament organised 41 conferences on a range of measures to assist the workless. On 28 March the PLP demanded that the Government should bring in a Minimum Wages Bill for miners, but to no avail.[55] In early May 1924, Tom Shaw spoke for the Cabinet Committee in an attempt to deflect criticism about inaction on unemployment by pointing to Government initiatives such as the Severn Barrage Scheme.[56] On 29 May, there was a special meeting to discuss the police, prison officers and unemployment.

The PLP took up the issue of the reinstatement of the police officers dismissed during the Police Strike of 1919. Jack Hayes, General Secretary of the Police and Prison Officers at the time, had been returned to Parliament in 1923 and was elected to the PLP Executive Committee in 1924. On this issue, the Government was forced to negotiate with its backbenchers through the medium of the PLP.[57] Despite his close understanding of the party, as already noted, Arthur Henderson had somewhat curtly turned down Hayes's request for reinstatement because of 'legal and practical difficulties'.[58] The PLP declared that Henderson's statement was 'directly contrary to Party policy' and that 'the dice would be loaded against the men' with an inquiry composed of two lawyers but only one trade union representative'.[59] In the event, though MacDonald was eventually drawn into the discussion with the PLP, the men were not reinstated.

On 29 May, the PLP also gave serious attention to the issue of unemployment in Britain and pressed the government to guarantee credit to Russia under the Export Credits Act and the Trade Facilities Act to help the purchase of a large number of engineering goods. The PLP also proposed that the Labour administration create work on the land through afforestation schemes, the building of trunk roads, the financing of local authority schemes (up to 75 per cent of the cost) and the establishment of electricity super-power stations. The government was also urged to proceed with the London electricity plan and the national electricity plan, as well as considering the nationalisation of electricity generation.[60]

The PLP also expressed some concern that the Government could not find the time to discuss the proposed motion of E. D. Morel, a member of the PLP Executive and leading figure in the Union of Democratic Control, on the parliamentary control of foreign relations – an issue the PLP raised again in May and June 1924 before it finally, if reluctantly, supported the government's stance of doing nothing.[61] 'Some of our backbenchers – the vain and empty-headed Neil Maclean, the asinine George Buchanan and the raucous voice of George Lansbury – as usual burble in proof of their majesty, but our benches as a whole gave fine support,' MacDonald noted during the critical exchanges in the Commons during the furore over the Campbell prosecution.[62] However, despite such serious tensions between the Labour government and the PLP, the backbench MPs in the House normally remained faithful supporters of the administration.

Throughout 1924 the *Daily Herald*, the main organ of the Labour movement, was highly critical of the performance of the Labour administration under MacDonald's leadership. In turn, MacDonald had never lost his distrust for the newspaper that two years before had supported his opponent, J. R. Clynes, in the contest for the Labour Party leadership. On 22 July, Rosa Rosenberg, MacDonald's secretary, told J. S. Middleton, the Assistant Secretary of the Labour Party, that the Prime Minister believed 'the *Daily Herald* is doing us much damage abroad . . . and that its work at home is more detrimental than helpful to the good spirit and unity of the Party; it is in fact becoming a Communist organ.'[63] Middleton suggested that the matter could be formally raised before the party's international sub-committee. 'I am bound to say, however, that I think probably an hours [*sic*] straight talk between the Prime Minister and Hamilton Fyfe would be more useful than a good deal of Committee deliberations,'he added [64] On 4 August, Rosenberg responded by suggesting that the Prime Minister 'had no objection to the suggestion'.[65]

By 11 August 1924, MacDonald complained to Henderson about the *Daily Herald*, particularly the leading article that day criticising two Labour ministers, Lord Thomson and William Leach. MacDonald viewed the newspaper as a constant source of dissension within Labour ranks and accused it of Communist sympathies. 'If Communists are to enjoy the luxury of a daily paper they ought to find the money & the patronage for themselves, and not play the cuckoo game. I cannot refrain from drawing your attention officially to it, as a culpable piece of disloyalty to the party & of damage to our common interests,' he complained.[66]

On 11 August 1924, the *Daily Herald*'s leading article – 'Two Moralities or One' – about the RAF bombing of Mesopotamia had resulted in some highly critical correspondence, including the charge that Leach had betrayed his pacifist principles and had become a 'contemptible creature through the pollution of power'.[67] In a lengthy article, Leach defended the decision to employ the RAF to prevent attacks by the border tribes of Iraq on a Mesopotamian villages. The minister added that even if a pacifist had replaced 'the weakling, turncoat, power-loving Leach', that person would have had to act in a similar manner. But, on the following day, the *Daily Herald* carried another article – 'Where the War Mind is Still at Work' – that was critical of MacDonald's leadership. 'As Foreign Minister he is a great success. But there are disadvantages in having no effective Prime Minister....No man could do all the work Mr. MacDonald has done in his special department and at the same time keep a sharp look-out on what colleagues were doing.'[68] Two days later, Lansbury hammered the administration in an article – 'Further Thought on Bombing' – pressing home the classic pacifist line that it was impossible to 'sow the seeds of civilisation by methods of violence'.[69]

The particular incident that had provoked these outpourings had occurred on 14 March 1924 when five bombing raids took place 130 miles south of Djalabi, near Basra, resulting in the deaths of 146 men and 127 women. There had, however, been other bombing raids between February and June 1924 that led to a major debate in the Commons on 10 July in which Lansbury closely questioned Leach.[70] The *Daily Herald* had continued to raise the issue, to MacDonald's anger, even though the newspaper had carried a detailed account of Leach's earlier defence of the bombings on 15 July, noting his concerns about the border tribes, 'who live by loot and fighting', slaughtering the people of Iraq and carrying off their cattle.

Although MacDonald's specific complaint was that two members of the government had been heavily criticised over the bombing of Iraq, the Labour Leader believed the *Daily Herald* was conducting a campaign against the government on behalf of the CPGB. However, the Iraq crisis was simply the final major engagement in the battle between the Labour government and Ramsay MacDonald, on the one hand, and the *Daily Herald* and Lansbury, on the other. It was, however, a battle that was to be expected given the long-standing conflict between the *Daily Herald* and the Labour leadership.

Despite the fact that the TUC and the Labour Party were effectively in control of the *Daily Herald* from 1922, both Lansbury and the paper remained stern critics of both MacDonald and the Labour government. Lansbury had, in fact, been opposed to Ramsay MacDonald in the leadership contest of 1922, but appealed for the Labour Party to give him 'the most loyal and hearty support' once he had beaten J. R. Clynes by 61 votes to 56.[71] Lansbury had objected to the cosy relationship that MacDonald had enjoyed with the Liberal Party during the period of the pre-war Liberal governments. As we have seen, MacDonald had only offered Lansbury the junior position of Minister of Transport, as he knew the East End socialist would not accept a post without Cabinet rank.[72] Lansbury therefore remained outside the Cabinet, a prominent member of the PLP and a constant thorn in the side of MacDonald's government. Lansbury's position at the head of the poll for the election of the PLP Executive Committee in December 1924 reflects his wide-spread popularity in a party disappointed by MacDonald's performance in office. He was openly sympathetic to the Soviet Union and members of his family were for a time members of the Communist Party.[73]

MacDonald accused the *Daily Herald* of reporting the activities of the CPGB rather than those of Labour. Indeed, it gave extensive coverage to William Gallacher's speech on 19 May in which he accused Labour of 'Treachery' for remaining in office. This had followed 'The Future of the Labour Government – A Call to the Workers', published in the *Worker's Weekly*, which had attacked 'the use of the forces of the state against the workers' in strikes.[74] On 20 May the *Daily Herald* also reported Tom Bell's charge that Labour had been 'utterly faithless and treacherous to the working class'.[75]

MacDonald's complaint to Henderson in August that the *Daily Herald* was an organ of the CPGB was simply a reiteration of the charges the Labour leader made in May and June, at the time of the *Daily Herald's* coverage of the CPGB conference. J. S. Middleton, Secretary of the Labour Party, had approached Lansbury who denied that the coverage of the CPGB conference was particularly extensive. Enclosing cuttings from the *Daily Herald*, Lansbury declared that 'from what you will see there is not a shadow of foundation for the statements which were made'.[76]

This conflict continued throughout the brief life of the first Labour government. As well as Lansbury's criticisms, there were other attacks from the Left. MacDonald thought that all such dissension was potentially damaging to Labour and fuel in the hands of Labour's journalistic and political enemies. On 1 August, MacDonald complained to Fenner Brockway, a journalist and politician closely connected with the ILP,

I have today received a letter from a friend who reports to me from time to time what is going on, and he tells me that a London Editor, exceedingly hostile to us and very much troubled by our success, remarked that we could not last much longer, that what our opponents could not do our friends inside were doing. The following words are given in quotation – 'The Bromley-Morel Revolt is what we have been waiting for. It could not have happened better.'[77]

Although the letter is vague in detail, it appears to have concerned Jack Bromley, the railway clerks' leader, and E. D. Morel, founder of the wartime Union of Democratic Control, of which MacDonald had been a prominent member, who were both critical of MacDonald's plans for security in Europe. It is clear that the issue was one of opposition to reparations and unease about the Dawes scheme. Morel, in particular, was hostile to the Inter-Allied Conference and the Dawes Plan and denounced the government for trying to 'square the circle' and fitting the facts to meet their diplomatic position.[78] He had been bitterly disappointed at missing out on office in the first Labour government and his views on foreign policy inevitably brought him into direct conflict with MacDonald. Even more internal conflict, as we shall see, followed the arrest of J. R. Campbell, the deputy editor of the *Workers' Weekly*, for the publication of an article, 'The Army and Industrial Disputes', under the Incitement to Mutiny Act. That action produced an avalanche of protest within the Labour Party.

While the relationship between Labour and the Liberals remained an important factor in 1924, the government's minority position did not hinder the administration as often as claimed. In a robust defence of the government's performance on unemployment, Margaret Bondfield claimed that 'no one outside a lunatic asylum would have assumed that the Labour Government could, in a house *in which we form a minority* . . . pass the (necessary) legislation . . . .' Pressed by her opponents 'to go and ask the country' for a majority, she retorted, 'It is open to the hon. Gentlemen to send us to the country whenever they think fit.'[79] However, whatever the difficulties of managing parliamentary business, the government was aware that their Conservative and Liberal opponents did not want a third general election in three years. However, equally important for the Labour government was internal unity or party loyalty. It is clear that the slow pace of Labour's legislative programme and many aspects of foreign policy placed the administration in conflict with a significant minority of Labour MPs and the party. This is not to doubt that the Labour Party, when put to the test, would prove itself loyal to MacDonald, but it suggests that he had more problems within his own party than he expected. Party wrangling influenced the Liberal decision to make a stand over the handling of the Campbell Case. MacDonald was certainly aware of his backbenchers in a government that did not have a working majority and could be outvoted in the House of Commons by two to one at any moment. It is equally clear that the Labour Party and PLP structures did not change sufficiently, or work well enough, to ease the difficulties created by the formation of the first Labour government. Significantly, this experience of office forced Labour to think anew about arrangements within the party when Labour again took office.

Illustration 1 Ramsay MacDonald at his home in Lossiemouth, Christmas 1923. *Source*: Labour Party Archives

Illustration 2 After an audience with the King: (from left to right) Ramsay MacDonald, J. H. Thomas, Arthur Henderson and J. R. Clynes outside Buckingham Palace. *Source*: Labour Party Archives

Illustration 3 Ramsay MacDonald arrives by taxi at 10 Downing Street.
Source: Labour Party Archives

Illustration 4 Immediately down to work: Ramsay MacDonald during his first
visit to Chequers, 1924. *Source*: Labour Party Archives

Illustration 5 'What would Grandmama have thought of a Labour Government!', Britain's First Labour Cabinet, January 1924. *Source*: Labour Party Archives

Illustration 6 Jimmy Thomas and John Wheatley step it out in Downing Street. *Source*: Labour Party Archives

Illustration 7 John Wheatley, Minister of Health. *Source*: Labour Party Archives

Illustration 8 The uncomfortable trappings of power: Ramsay MacDonald in court dress. *Source*: Labour Party Archives

Illustration 9 Philip and Ethel Snowden travel in style by train. *Source*: Labour Party Archives

Illustration 10 'Labour Marching On!', *Daily Herald* campaigns for Labour victory at the Party Conference, October 1924. *Source*: Labour Party Archives

THE LABOUR GOVERNMENT WINDS UP: THE PLATFORM AT THE LABOUR PARTY CONFERENCE, OCTOBER 1924, WITH THE PREMIER, THE RT. HON. J. RAMSAY MACDONALD, IN THE CHAIR.

L. P., I—240]

Illustration 11　The Labour government winds up: Ramsay MacDonald chairs the party conference, October 1924. *Source*: Labour Party Archives

6
Foreign and Imperial Policy

When Ramsay MacDonald became Foreign Secretary as well as Prime Minister – the only modern politician except for Lord Salisbury to combine both posts – George V worried in 1924 that the heavy weight of responsibilities and official duties that had taxed Salisbury would also overburden the Labour leader.[1] But MacDonald told the House of Commons that 'the position of this country in Europe had become so unsatisfactory that I believed that it would be a great advantage if, whoever was Prime Minister was also Foreign Secretary, in order to give the weight of office to any sort of policy that one might devise.'[2] However, anyone of either Arthur Henderson – who was to hold the post in the Second Labour Cabinet in 1929–31 – or E. D. Morel, J. H. Thomas or possibly Arthur Ponsonby, might have become a creditable Labour Secretary of State for Foreign Affairs. Free from burdensome Foreign Office duties, MacDonald as Prime Minister could still have brought the full *gravitas* of his office to bear on European affairs. Only a few years before, Lloyd George dominated the world stage – dynamic coalition Premier, triumphant war leader and British member of the 'Big Four' who negotiated the Versailles Treaty at the Paris Peace conference. The 'Welsh Wizard' not only overshadowed his Foreign Secretaries, Balfour and Curzon, but his famous 'Garden Suburb' at 10 Downing Street was regarded widely as an alternative Foreign Office.[3]

In 1924 Ramsay MacDonald had compelling reasons to ring-fence the Foreign Office for himself and to control his own destiny in foreign affairs. Ten years before, at great political and personal cost, he had taken a principled, brave, but controversial stand against the outbreak of the First World War by resigning the chairmanship of the Parliamentary Labour Party. MacDonald was not a total pacifist, but an Edwardian progressive who detested war and aggression in all its forms.[4]

As we have seen, in August 1914 he joined Charles Trevelyan, E. D. Morel, Norman Angell and Arthur Ponsonby in founding the influential Union of Democratic Control (UDC). Unlike the Fellowship of Reconciliation and the No Conscription Fellowship, the UDC was not another 'stop-the-war' organisation, but a group of Liberals, Radicals and intellectuals, such as Bertrand Russell, who opposed Britain's participation in the war and worked for a peaceful settlement of the conflict. Their key demands were expressed in four cardinal points: no transfer of territory without a plebiscite, parliamentary control of British foreign policy, and formation of an international council to maintain world peace, as well as comprehensive disarmament and the nationalisation of the armaments industries. By the early 1920s the UDC, with its expanded membership, had become a significant voice within the Labour ranks on international policy.[5]

Another important influence in the post-war years and beyond was Labour's Advisory Committee on International Questions (ACIQ), which provided an important forum for debates on Labour's foreign policy within the party. Amongst its key figures were Leonard Woolf, ACIQ secretary and author of the influential *International Government* (1916), Philip Noel-Baker and Noel Buxton, who produced detailed memoranda and papers. Arthur Henderson did not attend its meetings, but drew increasingly on the Committee's advice in moving Labour towards support for the League of Nations and a system of collective security during the 1920s. However, the ACIQ was less active during Ramsay MacDonald's stewardship of British foreign policy in 1924, though the Committee did contribute to the debate that led to rejection of the Draft Treaty of Mutual Assistance.[6] During the inter-war years, the non-partisan League of Nations Union (LNU) was the largest organisation in the British peace movement, though it had less influence during the lifetime of the 1924 Labour government. MacDonald, who was suspicious of the Liberal politicians in the LNU leadership, was unique among British Prime Ministers in refusing the position of Honorary President, as he was still offended by not being nominated earlier for the LNU Labour Committee.[7]

As an instinctive internationalist, the new Premier was essentially more committed to the pacification of Europe than to handling domestic affairs and regarded both spheres as intrinsically linked. Foreign affairs were of prime importance in the history of the 1924 administration as Labour assumed the responsibilities of governing the British Empire as well as Britain.[8] Like many of his Labour contemporaries, MacDonald came from a socialist and anti-imperialist tradition that viewed war as a barbaric result of conflicts between capitalist nations. A successful foreign policy would have a crucial effect in stimulating international free trade, thereby providing employment for the large numbers of the workless and contributing to the nation's general economic prosperity. In the post-war years MacDonald had been an impassioned believer in disarmament, though he remained highly critical of Lloyd George's diplomacy at the Washington Disarmament Conference in 1921 and the conduct of foreign policy pursued by the Bonar Law Government in 1922 in connection with Franco-German relations.

As Aneurin Bevan was to observe at the 1958 Labour Party Conference, 'foreign affairs and how to make war' were deemed the special prerogatives of the Tories rather than Labour.[9] MacDonald had started to chip away at this myth. As a member of the ILP, he was convinced the First World War was avoidable and had been the direct result of secret diplomacy by the governing elites in the belligerent countries. The prevention of further international conflict became a principal objective in his political career. In August 1923, he declared in the *New Leader* his plans for reform once in government: 'We intend to end the bureaucracy at Foreign Office.'[10] However, criticism from within the party was fuelled by the belief in some quarters that he did nothing of the kind.

As his deputy, MacDonald selected a fellow associate in the UDC, the aristocratic socialist Arthur Ponsonby. His diplomatic and political experience made him an appropriate choice that strengthened the new administration's claims of respectability and fitness to govern. Ponsonby's father had been Queen Victoria's Principal Private Secretary. He himself had served as a diplomat and in the Foreign Office, before entering politics to become Private Secretary to the Liberal Prime Minister, Henry Campbell-Bannerman, and had been a Liberal MP. 'My fate is sealed! I have just been called in to see MacDonald and he offered me the Und- Secretaryship [*sic*] . . . said he wanted my help & we would work together. On the whole it is the best thing I could hope for,' Ponsonby told his wife Dorothy.[11] But events turned out differently. At the Foreign Office Ponsonby became increasingly disenchanted with MacDonald's conduct of international policy.

In 1924 the first Labour government inherited an unstable European situation, and the distinct possibility of further international conflict. Tensions in Franco-German relations had intensified after five French divisions and one Belgian division of troops had occupied the heavily industrial Ruhr region a year before when Germany defaulted on reparation payments of timber and poles. In addition, a combined industrial commission of French and Belgian engineers and technicians (*Mission*

Interalliee de Controle des Usines et des Mines [MICUM]) took over strategic Ruhr mines and factories.[12]

MacDonald soon attempted to ease Franco-German rivalry by reassuring the French as to the immediate aim in British foreign policy. 'Have made up my mind as to policy. France must have another chance. I offer co-operation but she must be reasonable & cease her policy of selfish vanity. That is my first job. Armaments and such problems that are really consequences must wait,' MacDonald observed.[13]

After the First World War, France wanted guarantees of support from Britain and the United States against another German invasion, having suffered such incursions in 1870 and 1914. In the end neither country would be bound by a guarantee that could involve them in war. As a protection against a future German attack, France negotiated agreements with Eastern European states. Britain would not be drawn into a pact that could involve her in war should Germany attack France's East European allies. Instead Britain reluctantly guaranteed to help defend France in the event of a direct German attack. However, this was not enough for the French who, at the Paris peace conference, had originally wanted, but did not get, a neutral zone on the right bank of the Rhine and the formation of autonomous states on the left bank to provide a buffer against a future German invasion.

As a result, the French Government used the payment of reparations question to strengthen its post-war foothold in Germany. In 1923 Germany, faced with a reparations bill of about £6600 millions under the Treaty of Versailles, claimed that it was unable to pay. France therefore extended its occupation zone into the whole of the Rhineland, except for the British area. France also encouraged the formation of a separatist movement in the Rhineland but in turn was threatened by the counter-emergence of militant German nationalism. MacDonald and Snowden feared this Franco-German hostility would lead to another European war within ten or 20 years. 'It is no longer a local movement. It is the complete resuscitation of militarism in Europe. France has now taken the place we were told to believe that Germany was aspiring to fill,' MacDonald wrote to his friend Oswald Garrison Villard, editor of the New York journal, the *Nation*. According to Allen Hutt, MacDonald was convinced that 'Pursing the will-o-the wisp of reparations is the great curse of every country.' In 1923 at Leicester, the Labour leader declared: 'There will never be peace so long as the Versailles Treaty is in existence.'[14] Once in office, MacDonald and Snowden sought to settle international issues in differing ways, with MacDonald adopting the more pragmatic approach to the immediate issue of the payment of reparations.

At the end of 1923 the Reparation Commission, formed under the Treaty of Versailles, had established two expert committees to examine Germany's economic position and to recommend how she could meet her obligations under the Treaty of Versailles. About a week before the Labour government took office, the first committee under the chairmanship of General Dawes of the Chicago Central Bank examined ways of balancing the German budget and securing financial stability. A week later, the second committee, chaired by Reginald McKenna, began its investigation of the alleged flow of German capital abroad.

MacDonald could not act until the two committees reported. 'We are really marking time, waiting for the Report of the Experts,' Hankey told Smuts. He added that 'Ramsay MacDonald undoubtedly has an idea that somehow or other he is going to work up to a big Disarmament Conference. I am convinced he has no definite plan as yet.'[15] At this time the Labour leader realised that the political climate had to be improved and French fears allayed. On 26 January, MacDonald broke with Foreign Office conventions by writing openly and personally to Poincaré, the French Premier and Foreign Secretary, in the hope that Franco-British differences could be resolved by the 'strenuous action of goodwill'.[16] He received a positive reply and informed the Cabinet that he hoped for friendly relations with the French, but that he did have a policy of his own.[17]

A month later, MacDonald penned his famous letter to Poincaré in which he acknowledged the French need for security, but pointed out that the economic dislocation of European markets and the 'economic chaos' in Germany threatened British trade. Indeed, he stressed that the British people believed that France was determined to 'ruin Germany and dominate the Continent'. To avoid wearisome negotiations, MacDonald argued for a broad agreement that recognised the interests and needs of all.[18] The positive response in reports, letters and political opinion suggested the possibility of an improvement in Anglo-French relations. D'Abernon, British Ambassador in Berlin, who had warned MacDonald of the rise in the extreme Right in Germany if the European situation did not improve, reported: 'your letter to Poincaré has been well received here and is thought the strongest statement.'[19] A confident MacDonald wrote in his diary: 'M. Poincaré & I can agree. I hear the Experts will present a unanimous & satisfactory report. Then the chance will come. I may have trouble with some of our own people but not with the country; with the Liberal petty pinpricks but not with the H of C.'[20]

On 9 April the expert committees published their reports jointly. The Dawes Committee produced the more important report, that recognised Germany could not meet her obligations under the Treaty of Versailles unless her currency was stabilised and her budget balanced. Yet, this could not be achieved unless German economic unity was restored. Although the French occupation was outside the Committee's brief, it proposed that foreign troops ought not to impede Germany's economic activities. The Dawes Report therefore put forward a complicated procedure whereby Germany's reparations would rise from £50 million to £125 million over five years, although no instalments would be paid in the first year without a foreign loan of £40 million.[21] If the whole scheme worked, then the economy of Europe, and of central Europe in particular, would recover and help British economic interests.

Controversy surrounded the Dawes Report since it implicitly condemned the French occupation of the Ruhr and skated over the danger if Germany defaulted on her reparations by declaring that sanctions would be applied only in the instance of a 'flagrant failure' in payment. In addition, there was the worrying problem of obtaining security and guarantees for the £40 million foreign loan. These issues occupied MacDonald's mind for the next four months

International affairs moved rapidly from this point onwards. Britain accepted the Dawes proposals in their entirety. British ambassadors in Paris, Brussels, Rome, Berlin, Washington and Tokyo informed their host governments of the British acceptance; the Reparations Committee accepted the Dawes Report on 11 April and Germany did the same on 16 April.[22] This was combined with pressure upon France and Belgium to withdraw from the Rhineland in order to prevent Britain opening a wider discussion of its own complaints.

This international pressure worked. On 24–25 April, Belgium, and to some extent France, agreed to accept the Dawes Plan and end the occupation of the Ruhr as long as there were penalties for any German default on reparation payments, some of which the French wanted the British to introduce. There was a flurry of international diplomacy, which was partly affected by Poincaré's defeat in the French election of 11 May. Edouard Herriot, Radical Mayor of Lyons and less hostile to Germany, became the new French Premier and brought a fresh approach towards the negotiations. Whilst Poincaré feared the Germans but felt that France alone could contain them, Herriot sought British cooperation. At Chequers on 21 and 22 June MacDonald and Herriot mulled over the evacuation of the Ruhr, sanctions and the imposition of the

Dawes Plan by force or negotiation, as well as the question of French security. MacDonald obtained what he wanted on all the issues – except on the evacuation of the Ruhr. He had to concede Germany operation of the sections of the Dawes Plan and French control of some of the Rhineland railways to protect their troops. An additional problem was raising the foreign loans, upon which the agreement was based, but which American bankers doubted could be achieved. Otherwise, the negotiations went reasonably well. Herriot agreed to drop detailed discussion of the type of sanctions to be applied if Germany defaulted.

By the early months of 1924, MacDonald was winning support for his dual role of Prime Minister and Foreign Secretary. On 20 March, Thomas Jones, Assistant Secretary to the Cabinet, told Lord Astor and J. L. Garvin that 'the PM's position in the country is distinctly high.'[23] Lord Esher, admitted to Jones: 'It is no business of mine, but I think all this talk about the P.M. being *unable* to combine the F.O. with the P.M.-ship is twaddle.' He added: 'There *is* simply no Foreign Secretary available except the P.M. himself. So it is futile to look for one.'[24] Maurice Hankey informed Jan Smuts, the South African Premier, that MacDonald was 'an admirable Prime Minister, but I must qualify it by saying he would be if he could devote all his time to it. I am told he also has all the makings of a most admirable Foreign Secretary.'[25] Indeed, the insiders within the Civil Service believed that MacDonald, and also Jimmy Thomas at the Colonial Office, were doing well – unlike J. R. Clynes who was making a hash of his responsibilities as Leader of the House.

From the outset MacDonald's sure handling of his international role brought swift approval from Robert Cecil, stalwart of the League of Nations and former Conservative Under Secretary at the Foreign Office. He told Lady Cavendish: 'As for foreign affairs MacDonald appears to be carrying out the policy which I have always wanted. Great friendliness to France coupled with a real effort to make peace even though it costs us a good many concessions. He really is doing a great deal for the League as well.'[26] A few days later he dispatched a paean of praise about the Labour leader to Gertrude Bell, English archaeologist and influential 'oriental secretary' to the British High Commissioner in Iraq. 'He really does seem to understand that the business of the Foreign Office is to make agreements, not to score off foreign ministers, and if he can only remain in office for a few months, I do not ask for more, we may get foreign affairs relatively straight.'[27]

The Foreign Office quickly sent out the invitations to the Inter-Allied Conference in London that was to convene from 16 July. However, in the intervening three or four weeks between the Chequers meeting and the London Conference, there were many tense moments. The British Foreign Office declared that the Reparations Commission would not be empowered to declare Germany in default. In France Herriot faced a difficult situation where it was felt that he had abandoned vital French interests. Seeking support for his position from MacDonald, Herriot and MacDonald met in Paris on 8 and 9 July. However, all Herriot obtained there was a loose commitment to meetings and that Britain wanted 'the closest of alliances, that which is not written on paper'.[28]

Nevertheless, an Anglo-French memorandum was agreed which outlined the agenda with four main clauses to be discussed at the London Conference during the next six weeks. First, Herriot had successfully proposed that the Reparations Commission should not be weakened. It was also agreed that the American and British bankers subscribing to the loan would have some guarantees – including the presence of an American member on the Reparations Commission in an impartial capacity. If this arrangement failed, then an agent-general for reparations, an American citizen, would be called in. Second, it was agreed that if the Reparations Commission indicated that Germany had wilfully defaulted on payment then the governments concerned would operate to protect themselves. Third, the plan for the restoration of the economic stability of Germany was to be agreed at the inter-Allied Conference. Fourth, a special body was to be set up to advise the recipients of German reparations on their proper use. Nothing was proposed about the evacuation of the Ruhr, and the conflict between French security and German prosperity remained unresolved. On 10 July MacDonald communicated the basis of this agreement to Parliament when he made a full statement to the Commons in which he described the role of the American Reparation Agent-General:

> The view of the British Government is that this gentleman should act as arbitrator, and that, in the event of failure, they should get the unanimous decision from the Reparations Commission. The French Government wished for time to consider this, and bring the final decision on the point to the London Conference. To that we finally agreed.[29]

The Labour leader added that, in the meantime, the loans question – without which there could be no settlement – would be explored. However, serious problems still beset the whole issue of German reparations and threatened the fragile peace of Europe. MacDonald headed a government prepared to continue reparations in order to placate the

France and secure the withdrawal of French troops from the Ruhr. Indeed, as he informed the ILP Conference at York, held at Easter 1924: 'Here is Europe's chance. Put it into operation all at once. Finish the job and bring peace and security to the Continent.' He added that 'there are things in the Dawes Report that I do not like. But if I begin to raise this detail and that detail, France, Belgium and Germany would do the same.'[30]

As in domestic politics, MacDonald faced difficulties over foreign policy and defence – particularly for a more democratic conduct of international policy – from within his own party, especially from sections of the ILP and the radical members of Union of Democratic Control. In 1924, the ILP claimed an impressive representation within the new Labour administration as well as in the House of Commons. Besides the Prime Minister, five other members were in the new Cabinet – Snowden, Trevelyan, Jowett, Wheatley and Wedgwood. In addition, Ponsonby, Attlee, Shinwell, Graham, Spoor, Jones, Leach, Stewart and Muir held junior ministerial posts. Of the 91 ILP-sponsored candidates at the 1923 general election, 45 had been returned and the PLP numbered no fewer than 120 MPs among its 191 members at Westminster.[31] In opposition, Labour had condemned the post-war international order based on the Versailles Treaty and punitive German reparations. Parliamentary control of foreign policy, allied to a deep suspicion of Foreign Office mandarins, was a key demand of those who on the Left wished to sweep away the traditional basis of British foreign policy.

On 4 July, H. L. Lindsay, on behalf of the executive committee of the Parliamentary Labour Party, warned the Labour leader that many of his members had 'consistently opposed the policy of reparations' and that there were 'certain doubters' on the whole Dawes scheme.[32] Frustration had arisen within the ranks of the PLP at the failure of the government to respond positively to some of its requests on foreign policy. On 4 June the PLP Executive had passed a resolution expressing its 'deep regret that, in view of the unanimous support given by the Party to the request that time should be granted for the discussion of the motion on Parliamentary Control of Foreign Relations, the Government has not seen its way to accede to the request'. The Executive appealed to the Government to reconsider its decision, if necessary by prolonging the parliamentary session by one day.[33]

Within a matter of weeks, defence also caused some early dilemmas for the new Labour administration which was pledged to reduce armaments at the same time as defending Britain and the British Empire. Only ten years before, the new Prime Minister had been vilified for his pacifist opposition to the war. Even before Labour took office, Hankey had journeyed secretly one Saturday morning to MacDonald's Hampstead home to discover the attitude of his new master towards the Cabinet Secretariat and the Committee of Imperial Defence. He later recalled that MacDonald, 'pointing to his bookshelves, told me that General Smuts had said that he possessed one of the best military libraries in London.' Reassured of the Labour leader's 'every support in the C.I.D', Hankey took MacDonald on his first day in office to dinner at the United Services Club, where 'retired Colonels and Admirals of highly correct Tory politics... looked at us open mouthed, pausing twixt cup and lip as I filed down the room followed by the tall frock-coated figure of the new and sinister Labour Prime Minister.'[34]

However, after chairing the opening session of the CID MacDonald only attended two of the ensuing nine meetings, passing the chairmanship to the Lord Chancellor, Haldane. It also fell to the former Liberal Imperialist and War Minister to make the first Labour pronouncement on defence policy in Parliament. Once in office, the Labour government reviewed the decision of the Baldwin ministry to construct eight new cruisers that resulted in a Cabinet tussle between Snowden, opposed to armaments, and Lord Chelmsford on behalf of the Admiralty. The Parliamentary Secretary to the Admiralty, Charles Ammon, announced in the Commons a reduced programme of five cruisers and two destroyers. However, the argument that naval construction meant jobs at a time of mass unemployment did not quell the rumblings on the Labour backbenches. With Tory votes, the Government won by 304 to 114 on the Naval Estimates – though 14 Labour members went into the opposition lobby.

The armed services came under further scrutiny from the Labour Left and Lord Thomson had to defend the continuation of the development of the Royal Air Force started by his predecessor, Sir Samuel Hoare. Labour MPs put forward amendments during the debates on the Army Estimates. Ernest Thurtle, a former army officer, endeavoured to abolish the death penalty in court martial cases, while James Maxton proposed that appeals from courts martial should go to the Court of Criminal Appeal. Both were defeated by 207 votes to 193 and 193 votes to 120 respectively. A pacifist amendment virtually abolishing the army was overwhelmingly lost, Lansbury tabled another proposal that soldiers could contract out of service connected with industrial disputes which was beaten by 236 to 67 votes. However, the Government did abandon existing policy for a comprehensive project of defence construction in Singapore started by their Conservative predecessors, primarily because

Haldane – now chairman of the CID – wished to give priority to strength-ening Western European defences.[35]

In the final analysis, whilst the PLP generally remained loyal to MacDonald, it was always willing to challenge the authority of the Labour government at a time when it was by no means clear what the relationship between the Labour government, the PLP and the Labour Party should be. Such conflict was also inevitable given that MacDonald in government was prepared to play down his opposition to some issues, such as reparations, to gain a security agreement for Europe. It is also hardly surprising, then, that it was when George Lansbury was chairman of the PLP meeting that a resolution which was a direct challenge to MacDonald's control of foreign policy was passed, continuing a feud which, as already noted, was fuelled further by the bombings near Basra in Iraq.

In addition, MacDonald's speech to the House of Commons on the 14 July, anticipating the Inter-Allied Conference, revealed to the public the continuing conflict within the Labour Party as well as the hostility of the Conservatives. The *Daily Herald*, in reporting on the House of Commons debate on Monday 15 July, published the headlines 'France and Britain must be Friends', 'Mr. MacDonald Says the Pact Should be Pooled Security', and referred to 'Mr. Asquith's Approbation; Mr. Baldwin's Recrimination; Premier's Determination'.[36] It continued:

> After Mr. Asquith had given his benediction to the Conference and Mr. Baldwin had indulged in an unusually recriminatory speech, Mr. MacDonald briefly reviewed the situation. He brushed aside the personal attacks and declared his unswerving determination to secure a lasting peace in Europe. He urged that while the security given to France under the Versailles Treaty should be preserved, we should be exceedingly careful that she did not exceed the legal provisions of the Treaty. In the main he stressed the importance of two points: the accomplishment of complete unity between France and ourselves and the provision of security for investors in the £40,000,000 loan to Germany.[37]

A feature of the subsequent debate was the strong opposition shown by many Labour backbenchers to the continuance of the Reparations policy. A significant number of Labour backbenchers, including Lans-bury, who was still associated with the *Daily Herald*, were altogether opposed to the reparations payment demanded of Germany. One of the most unstinting critics of MacDonald's foreign policy was his former associate in the Union of Democratic Control, E. D. Morel, who harboured ambitions to be Foreign Secretary himself. Bitterly disappointed on his omission from office, Morel was openly critical of the Labour leadership, the direction of Labour foreign policy and the influence of the permanent officials.[38] He had conducted an unwavering campaign against the influence of foreign office officials for nearly 20 years from his leadership of the Congo Reform Association. Elected MP for Dundee in 1922, when he defeated Winston Churchill, Morel represented the section of the party who believed firmly that foreign affairs should be directly under the control of Parliament. This became one of his first demands of the Labour leadership once the Parliament assembled, to the extent that he personally wished to be responsible. Morel became highly critical of MacDonald's conduct of foreign affairs. The Prime Minister's friendly approach to the French, support for the continuation of German reparations, as well as his refusal to call a conference to revise the Versailles Treaty, were all roundly censured. 'Ramsay MacDonald was undisguisedly jealous of Morel. The latter mistrusted the former and was nervous about his frequent temptations to compromise or vacillate,' Ponsonby noted about his former associates in the UDC.[39]

The continuation of reparation payments and the parliamentary control of foreign affairs were to dominate the thinking of Labour backbenchers as the first Labour government failed to act on these two questions when confronted by the realities of the Inter-Allied Conference. MacDonald saw the discussions in London as a major opportunity to work for the continued peace of Europe that could not be wasted. However, the Labour leader obviously had to grapple with the difficult problem of reconciling German and French differences – a task made even thornier by Snowden's inflammatory actions, which frequently riled the French delegation.

MacDonald effectively ignored the challenges from the Conservative opposition and from within his own party to focus on the Inter-Allied Conference which commenced at 11 a.m. on 16 July in his room at the Foreign Office. He opened the conference with a speech in which he congratulated Britain's First World War Allies who were attempting to bring peace to Europe, but declared that the failure over reparations had led to the rise of militarism in Europe. His solution was for the Allies to accept the Dawes Plan, which he described as the only basis of a lasting peace in Europe.[40]

At this Conference three committees were formed – one to deal with the role of the Reparations Committee which would declare on German default and the security to be given to the subscribers of the loan; a second to settle the plan for the restoration of German economic unity; and a third to handle technical matters about how reparation payments could best be put to use. Snowden was appointed chairman of the first committee. Its brief covered many of the explosive issues that arose at the conference and, from the start, he refused to be rushed or browbeaten by the French, and remained adamant that his committee would decide matters. During these complicated negotiations, he deeply upset the French delegation with his pro-German stance and by pressing them to make concessions.

Snowden declared publicly that there was inadequate security for subscribers to the German loan. His behaviour angered the French, who felt it endangered the financial and reparation concessions proposed in the Dawes Scheme. Matters grew worse, particularly as he demanded the exact terms by which Germany would be deemed to be in 'flagrant failure' of her obligations and the precise timing of the French evacuation of the Ruhr. The Germans also wanted to know that the £40 million loan would be obtained before they accepted the Dawes Plan.[41]

On 8 August the Germans argued over the transfer committee set up to supervise the payment of German reparations to the recipients. The Inter-Allied Conference had agreed that any dispute between the German government and the transfer committee would be settled by an arbitrator, but the Germans felt that this would take away financial and economic powers and responsibilities from the German government. For the French, it was essential to the whole Inter-Allied agreement. Snowden entered the fray once again by supporting the Germans and arguing that foreign control over the German economy would be a 'menace to industrial interests'.[42]

On the same day MacDonald stressed the tensions between Snowden and the French: 'S has been terribly clumsy today & has negotiated like a drill sergeant giving orders. H[erriott] was furious & protested against one of us openly on opposing in a hostile way the findings of the Inter-Allied Conference.'[43] The conflict between Snowden and Herriot boiled over on to other matters such as the principles of arbitration and the time-scale for the withdrawal from the Ruhr. Crisis point was reached when Herriot threatened to withdraw the French delegation from the Conference.[44]

Matters were made worse by the fact that General Nollet, the French Chancellor, was as equally a wild card as Snowden. He seems to have been suspicious of Herriot and supported the French evacuation of the Ruhr over two years, which was totally unacceptable to MacDonald. On

7 August the Labour leader reflected in his diary: 'To reason with Nollet is impossible; he just goes off. I disconcerted him with my calm. 'You cannot break the Treaty for your convenience.'[45] On 8 October, Thomas Jones captured the unruly scene at 10 Downing Street involving General Nollet:

> Last night P.M., Herriot, Theunis, Hyman, at No. 10. Messenger let in General Nollet who rushed in and began a squabble with H [erriot] about evacuation of Ruhr and Rhineland territory, and wd not be ruled by L.of N [League of Nations], etc. P.M. tried to produce tranquillity and ultimately had to bring meeting to an end by pointing to pile of despatch boxes he had to deal with before bedtime. Later remembering that he wanted to know whether his daughter had accomplished the first stage of her journey he went downstairs to ask Messenger to phone, and was told that Frenchmen were wrangling in the Cabinet Room and that he was about to take them in some sustenance. When the P.M. went to bed at midnight they were still in the Cabinet Room.[46]

In this climate of distrust and internal wrangling, Herriot returned to France to consult with his Cabinet. MacDonald sent him a reminder that the Dawes Plan depended upon the evacuation of the Ruhr rather than Nollet's insistence on continued French occupation as a safeguard against future German aggression.

On 11 August, the Inter-Allied Conference was reconvened but quickly ran into troubled water again. Herriot announced that the French would restrict their occupation of the Ruhr to one year. The subject of arbitration between the Germans and the transfer committee provoked another round of Franco-German wrangling. Snowden's intervention once again on the German side upset Herriot. However, in the end, MacDonald managed to secure the formation of a special committee to consider the matter.[47]

Nevertheless, Snowden had deeply upset Herriot, who remonstrated that 'If Snowden tomorrow speaks against me & my country I shall with my delegation leave the Conference. Snowden is my enemy & the enemy of my country.' MacDonald moved quickly to stop Snowden writing to Herriot, on behalf of the government, for fear of wrecking the Conference. Early the next day, MacDonald took his Chancellor of the Exchequer to task over his errant behaviour. 'Your remarks yesterday have played havoc & the whole French delegation has been mischief-making the livelong day...I cannot persuade Herriot that your remark about his position on arbitration was anything but an attack upon his honour.... The effect has... made Herriot closed up like an oyster, and unless he is in a better frame tomorrow, I feel the Conference may fail.'[48] For good measure, MacDonald added that it would be folly to press forward with the Treasury's line on the improbability of raising the £40 million loan.

Despite these squabbles, on 15 August, Herriot agreed to the withdrawal of French forces from the Ruhr starting on the day of the final agreement – which Germany accepted after some discussion. In addition, MacDonald persuaded Herriot to include the French evacuation of the Dortmund district of the Ruhr. However, at the end of this day of successful negotiations, Snowden wrote to MacDonald threatening his resignation.[49]

On the next day, 16 August, Herriot was still in favour of a continuous withdrawal of French troops from the Ruhr. Nevertheless, MacDonald hoped that the British public would find the idea of a further year-long, though diminishing, French occupation more palatable. Snowden also continued to be difficult and MacDonald noted: 'Snowden absurdly mischievous. Raised every imaginable petty-fogging point, the underlying one being that we could trust the French in nothing. Gave him all the rope he took... in the end everyone was against him.'[50] Finally, the Germans accepted the French offer at 5.45 p.m.

In the end, despite its vicissitudes caused by Snowden's lack of diplomacy, on 16 August 1924 the Inter-Allied London Conference concluded with four agreements. Most important was the decision of Germany and the Reparations Commission to carry out those parts of the Dawes Report that applied exclusively to Germany. The other agreements outlined the procedures for implementing the Dawes Scheme, the preparation of a plan for German economic and financial development, as well as sanctions if Germany defaulted on her payment of reparations.

MacDonald pronounced the Conference a resounding success and saw it as the high point of the 1924 administration and his own political career. 'We are now offering the first really negotiated agreement since the war...', though he added the reservation: 'We have a long way to go before we reach the goal of European peace and security.'[51]

However, in Labour politics other disquieting events on the international scene clouded the announcement of agreements concluded by the Inter-Allied Conference. The Conference had coincided with the campaign conducted by the *Daily Herald*, under the management of George Lansbury, against the RAF bombings in Iraq. An indignant

MacDonald wrote on official Foreign Office notepaper to Arthur Henderson, as Secretary of the Labour Party, to complain about the 'leading article in today's *Daily Herald*' that attacked 'Lord Thompson (*sic*) & Mr. Leach' for their role in dealing with the RAF bombing near Basra.[52] The Inter-Allied Conference settlements also occurred soon after the arrest of John Campbell, assistant editor of the *Workers' Weekly*, in connection with a charge for incitement to mutiny. This incident eventually led to a vote of no-confidence that brought the downfall of the government and a general election that returned the Conservatives to office with Stanley Baldwin as Prime Minister.

Consequently, Labour recognition of MacDonald's valuable work at the Inter-Allied Conference was distinctly muted. Indeed there was widespread concern among the ranks of the PLP, since the outcome of the Inter-Allied Conference endorsed the continuation of reparations. The *Daily Herald* reflected this ambivalence over MacDonald's conduct of foreign affairs. On 14 August, the Labour paper included a piece entitled 'From the Workers' Point of View', commenting on the various contemporary political events:

> It has been an immense advantage to the country to have Ramsay MacDonald at the Foreign Office. When there was a possibility seven months ago of someone else going there, we urged strongly that Mr. MacDonald must take the post. The position we then took up has been fully justified. The Conference now coming to an end has, thanks to his efforts, brought very near the settlement for which Europe has been longing ever since war ended. As Foreign Secretary he is a great success. But there are disadvantages in having no effective Prime Minister.[53]

However, the article then declared that the handling of the Campbell case revealed that the Prime Minister had taken his eye off domestic events. 'No man could do all the work Mr. MacDonald has done in his special department and at the same time keep a sharp look-out on what his colleagues were doing,' the Labour daily concluded.

While the general press reaction was favourable to MacDonald's handling of international affairs, the Labour press was less enthusiastic than it should have been because of other developments during 1924. Mutterings were also heard from trade union leaders whose members felt they would be adversely affected by the continued reparation arrangements that flowed from the Inter-Allied Conference. Most aggrieved were the miners who, with William Adamson, Stephen Walsh and Vernon

Hartshorn in the 1924 Labour Cabinet, were annoyed at the threats that reparations paid in kind might offer to British coal production, still hoping to recover its pre-war production levels, and particularly its share of world trade. The Miners' Federation of Great Britain (MFGB) was clearly unhappy about this issue. Herbert Smith, the Yorkshire Miners' leader and President of the Federation, complained that the Labour government had adopted the Dawes Report without any consultation with them. 'We would not have expected it from the Tory or the Liberal Government,' he declared bitterly. For the Labour leader in 10 Downing Street, he added pointedly: 'I used to understand you, but I do not understand you now.'[54] Despite these misgivings, MacDonald had brought a fresh initiative to European diplomacy. However, in other parts of the world the Labour administration had little time or, faced with the realities of office, inclination to alter the policies of their predecessors.

In 1924 the Labour government became responsible for governing the British Empire, as well as Britain. The maintenance of British naval supremacy over global sea routes and the prevention of the domination of the European continent by any one major European power were now in the hands of ministers who had denounced armaments and the evils of imperialism. However, the First World War had destroyed a *Pax Britannica* that had sustained a worldwide empire. The British economy could no longer support the country's defence capability. Self-governing Dominions who had attained independent representation at Versailles and in the Assembly of the League of Nations were openly reluctant to be embroiled in another European war after the tragedy of the Dardanelles. In office, Labour faced the practical realities of continuing Britain's imperial foreign policy and defence strategy while being committed ideologically to open diplomacy, arms reduction and arbitration in international disputes. During the 1920s, Labour continued to support the British Empire while evolving a foreign policy based on the League of Nations and international collective security.

J. H. Thomas, general secretary of the National Union of Railwaymen, became the Secretary of State for the Colonies after MacDonald convinced him of its scope and significance. Thomas's new surroundings suited the former engine cleaner's growing penchant for the high life. His Whitehall office was the most magnificent of those occupied by the new administration, spacious enough for a cricket pitch and ostentatiously decorated, with portraits of celebrated British imperialists responsible for the greatest empire in the world on which the sun never set.

Stories abound about the new Secretary of State's proletarian credentials – often recounted by Thomas himself – as he took up the reins
from his predecessor, Lord Devonshire. 'I'm the new Secretary of State,'
Thomas told the porters on reception on his first day in charge of the
British Empire. 'Poor bloke; another shell shock case,' they surmised.
His opening staff briefing ended by declaring, 'Now, boys, let's have a
beer all round.' Thomas's staff found their new Cabinet Minister was
also accustomed to phoning his bookmaker and knocking out his pipe
on the marble office fireplace.[55]

On a more serious note, British coal miners blamed Jimmy Thomas for
'Black Friday' – the disastrous failure of the Triple Alliance (of miners,
railwaymen and transport workers) in April 1921 when he had refused
to allow his union to support the miners in a national lockout. A
decade later, Thomas was the only leading trade-union figure to join
MacDonald in the national government where his lamentable performance in dealing with unemployment led to a transfer to the Dominions
Office. In 1936 he was to resign over a budget leak. However, the carica-
tured picture of a minister seduced by a celebrated life-style of drinking
and gambling belied Thomas's considerable political reputation in the
1920s as a skilful union negotiator and a leading Labour figure – seen
by many as a possible successor to MacDonald.[56]

Sidney Webb took a particular interest in how the 1924 Labour
Cabinet functioned and behaved. 'The Cabinet found itself under a
constant pressure of business, even although it sat for three hours once
or twice a week, and was seldom troubled by MacDonald with foreign
affairs,' he noted. Foreign affairs remained mainly the province of the
Prime Minister who brought his colleagues up to date every few weeks
on European issues. Interestingly, the Cabinet gave greater attention to
imperial business, particularly in connection with India.[57]

As Secretary of State for India, Sidney Olivier, a founding member of
the Fabian Society in 1884 and one of the original Fabian essayists in
1889, was an obvious choice for the Cabinet post given his ample diplomatic experience that included his posts as acting Colonial Secretary
in British Honduras and Governor of Jamaica.[58] By accepting a peerage
in 1924, the new Lord Olivier strengthened Labour's slender representation in the House of Lords. His former Fabian collaborator, Annie
Besant, was a leading figure in the Congress Party in India, but the selection of Olivier exasperated Indian nationalists who favoured the overtly
sympathetic Josiah Wedgwood with his strong links with the Indian
subcontinent. According to Sidney Webb, Wedgwood was the cause of
occasional dissent within the Cabinet over Olivier's policy in India,

though a standing 'Indian Committee' (consisting of Olivier, Richards, Chelmsford, Trevelyan, Wedgwood and Webb) met frequently and even compiled telegrams Olivier sent to India.[59]

The First World War, in which large numbers of troops from the Empire had fought in the British armed forces, had transformed Indo-British relations and given rise to a militant upsurge of Indian nationalism. The Amritsar Massacre in April 1919, when Brigadier-General Dyer had ordered his troops to fire on a peaceful crowd in the holy city of the Sikhs killing almost 400 Indians and wounding more than 1000, sent bitter shock waves throughout the Empire.[60] The Congress Party founded in 1885 became the focus of those working for some form of Home Rule or independence for India. During the inter-war years the Indian National Congress pressed for an end to British rule; a demand that led to Mahatma Gandhi's campaign of civil disobedience in the 1920s and 1930s. However, during the First World War and the early 1920s, there were some minor concessions to those demanding moves to independence.

Many Labour leaders, such as James Keir Hardie and Ramsay MacDonald, had visited India before the First World War and viewed the chronic poverty as a product of British imperialism. They saw no way but to govern India through British rule for the foreseeable future. Indeed, MacDonald's book *The Awakening of India* (1910) had been fashioned by his experience of the subcontinent. He reasoned there was a need to give India 'wide liberty to govern herself in all her internal affairs'.[61] However, even within Labour circles there was still hesitancy about granting India full independence.

As Denis Judd has shown, during the inter-war years, India remained the symbolic jewel in the British Crown. There were powerful political, social and economic reasons that prevented the immediate granting of full independence. Despite a deteriorating position, the net balance in trade in 1924 still stood at £75 million in Britain's favour. Politically, ending British rule in India was tantamount to Britain losing her Empire and becoming 'straight away a third-rate power'. At home, many Conservative MPs were more concerned about the future of India than mass unemployment, principally Winston Churchill who was eventually to resign the Conservative whip in the 1930s on India, and not over rearmament and opposition to fascism.[62]

In opposition the Labour Party had been strongly anti-imperialist and in favour of national self-determination for subject peoples. Nevertheless, this did not extend to the granting of independence for India. Gandhi was released from prison in January 1924, but only after considerable public pressure after his serious illness. Instead, MacDonald and his ministers believed in the careful evolution towards self-government within the British Commonwealth that, commencing with the Morley-Minto Reforms (1909), had led to the Montagu-Chelmsford Report (1918) that formed the basis of the Government of India Act (1919). MacDonald made clear government policy in India from the outset:

> I can see no hope in India if it becomes the arena of a struggle between constitutionalism and revolution. No party in Great Britain will be cowed by threats of force or by policies designed to bring Government to a standstill; and if any sections in India are under the delusion that this is not so, events will sadly disappoint them. I would urge on all the best friends of India to come nearer to us rather than stand apart from us, to get at our reason and our good will.

As Secretary of State for India, Olivier found himself confronted by opponents who ranged from Indian Nationalists, and their sympathisers in the British Labour Party, who sought independence for India to the Tory grandees set on the preservation of the British Empire. He also became engaged in a lengthy constitutional struggle with Lord Reading, Viceroy and Governor-General of India 1921–26. Reading wished to secure the support of moderate Indian Nationalists, who were not part of the Swarajists Party, by holding out the prospect of constitutional reform before the statutory Commission scheduled for 1929. Olivier declared there would be no constitutional changes without his agreement, seeing that as a threat to his control, and proposed a limited enquiry into the operation of the Act of 1919. While Labour expressed sympathy for Indian aspirations, Olivier adopted a cautious approach to avoid opposition criticism of succumbing to the demands of the Swarajists, who had gained majorities in the Legislative Assembly, as well as in Bengal and the Central Provinces in the December 1923 elections. Ostensibly, Reading appeared more radical, although his motives probably had more to do with retaining the initiative in Indian politics than moving more rapidly towards self-government.[63]

MacDonald also advised his Secretary of State to handle the Viceroy with tact and diplomacy:

> I feel that I must strongly advise you not to be too rigid in your telegrams to the Viceroy, as I would like, on matters of internal policy, to make the Viceroy feel responsibility, and to introduce the same

relationship between the India Office and India as exists between the Colonial Office and the Dominions... You will probably unnerve him if you send too rigid departmental orders, and if he finds himself in a political fix he might threaten resignation.

The first Labour government did little to tackle the problems of India in its nine or so months in office. Despite MacDonald's view of internal independence within the Empire for the immediate future nothing was done concerning the 1919 Act resented by so many Indians. It was left to newspaper editors, such as J. L. Garvin of the *Observer*, to reflect that 'He thought it quite possible that within five years we might lose India, and with it, Goodbye to the British Empire. We took the wrong road when we took the road to diarchy. Lloyd George was much to blame because at that time he would back Greece instead of Turkey and the Moslems. The only solution was a federal one....'[64] Under the Labour government little change occurred in any direction, while in Europe MacDonald sought an alternative to the Draft Treaty of Mutual Assistance that his government had inherited.

In the troubled Middle East, the first Labour government did little to alter the policies of its Conservative predecessors in the provinces of the former Ottoman Empire that came under British rule in the early 1920s. The Treaty of Versailles had assigned Britain and France post-war responsibilities for the economic and political development of Palestine, Transjordan and Iraq (Britain) and Syria (France) under the Permanent Mandates Commission of the League of Nations at the San Remo conference in 1920. British rule – confirmed by the League of Nations in 1922 – meant relatively unrestricted administrative control over Palestine, where the former Liberal Cabinet minister, Sir Herbert Samuel, became High Commissioner between 1920 and 1925. Samuel had been influential in drafting the Balfour Declaration of 1917 that had promised support for the establishment of Jewish national home. However, to encourage the Arab revolt against Turkish forces during the First World War, the British had also promised the Hashemite Arabs backing in the Hussein–McMahon Correspondence for a united Arab country. These ambiguous undertakings about an independent Arabia helped to sow the bitter seeds for future Arab–Jewish conflict in the twentieth-century, while secret diplomacy determined the future spheres of influence exercised under the British and French mandates.

In Palestine, Britain had acquired the impossible task of supervising the free development of the majority indigenous Arab population, at the same time as helping to create the longed-for Jewish national home through substantial immigration and settlement. In 1922 the first census under the British mandate indicated that, of a population of over 700,000, nearly 600,000 were Muslims, about 80,000 Jewish, as well as around 70,000 Christians and other groups. Between 1917 and 1926 100,000 Jews and 6,000 non-Jewish migrated to Palestine between 1917 and 1926, eventually provoking Arab antagonism, community conflict and outbreaks of serious political violence. The demand for a Jewish homeland and the rising nationalism did much to make an even-handed and stable policy difficult, if not impossible, to achieve. The policy adopted by most inter-war British governments permitted Zionism to gain a hold in Palestine, although Samuel and his officials did occasionally upset the Zionists. Indeed, there was some concern about the Zionist experiment and Sir Gilbert Clayton, Chief Secretary at the Colonial Office, threw doubts on the whole idea of creating a Jewish national home, stating that 'In general a year in Palestine has made me regard the whole adventure with apprehension. We are pushing an alien and detested element into the very core of Islam, and the day will come when we shall be faced with the alternatives of holding it thereby by the sword or abandoning it to its fate.'[65]

While out of Parliament after 1918, MacDonald had undertaken a tour of the Middle East in the final months of 1921, visiting Egypt and Palestine where he took a specific interest in the emerging Jewish labour movement and the clash of cultures represented in Jewish–Arab relations. MacDonald's account of his experience in the region, published as *A Socialist in Palestine*, provides some significant insights into the influence of his travels on official Labour attitudes towards Jewish–Arab relations. He revealed considerable high regard for the Jewish socialists breaking new ground, who reminded him not only of his pioneering days in the British Independent Labour Party, but of the version of socialism he had published in his book *Socialism: Critical and Constructive*, shortly before embarking for the Middle East. However, as a prominent Labour politician, MacDonald was a pragmatist rather than an idealist on the contentious questions of the Arab–Jewish conflict, who advocated working towards eventual independence for the Jewish and Arab populations rather than immediate British withdrawal. Critical of British imperialism, he felt that the Balfour Declaration could be implemented – in establishing a Jewish home in Palestine – while recognising the promises British politicians had made to the Arab people. The influence of MacDonald's views – an expression of his internationalism – can be seen in Arthur Henderson's statement to the press in 1922 supporting continuation of the British mandate, 'to ensure the economic prosperity, political autonomy and spiritual freedom of both the Jews and Arabs in Palestine'. Essentially, in 1924 this was the policy Labour continued in office, including support for the work of the British High Commission in calming the political atmosphere in Palestine and attempting to win Arab support for the implementation of the Balfour Declaration.[66]

The natural inclination of the Labour government was to attempt to be even-handed in carrying out the Mandate. As a result it maintained the existing policies. As Bernard Wasserstein has written: 'When a Labour Government came to power in January 1924 it did not interfere with what was now established as a non-partisan national commitment. Only in the late 1930s, under the pressure of overwhelming international events did a British Government move decisively away from that policy.'[67] In the early 1920s the British Labour Party had a number of Jewish MPs and was subject to pressure from Paole Zion, the Jewish Labour Party, as well as the lobbying of Arab groups in Britain. Although the first Labour government sought to be equitable in its treatment of the Jews and Arabs, it was always a difficult position to sustain. By comparison, rising tensions and violence in Palestine confronted the second Labour government in 1929–31. Jews and non-Jews alike condemned the Passfield White Paper (1930), which attempted to restrict Jewish settlement and end Arab evictions. In Leeds the Jewish community expressed its concern to the local Labour Party at the second Labour government's suspension of Jewish immigration, 'as being against the spirit and letter of the Mandate, and the declared policy of the Labour Party'.[68] In contrast, in 1924 the first Labour government had tried to be more even-handed.

British relations with Egypt also changed little under the first Labour government. Egypt had been under some form of British administration from 1882 and had become a British protectorate during the Great War. There was an Egyptian revolt in favour of independence in March 1919. Lloyd George's Coalition Government failed to come to a settlement in 1920 but in 1922 the British government recognised Egypt's independence, subject to reservations about the defence of Egypt and the Suez Canal and the continuation of British administration in the Sudan. However, attempts to gain agreement with Egypt of these matters failed under both the Conservative government of Baldwin and MacDonald's Labour government and it is clear that British authority in Egypt was diminishing.

Two rounds of negotiations had failed before the first Labour government came to office. Since Ramsay MacDonald wanted a settlement with Egypt, a few exploratory meetings between British and Egyptian officials were held in Switzerland. However, violence broke out in Khartoum and in other parts of Sudan, and it is clear that Egypt was not going to give up its claims to the country. The Labour government rashly suggested that an agreement was near at hand, but Lord Parmoor stated to the House on 25 June 1924 that 'We shall never evacuate Sudan!' This made negotiations extremely difficult, and the tensions between the two countries were not helped by the mutiny of some Egyptian troops on 9 August and the appearance of a British cruiser off Alexandria on the same day.

Eventually, however, negotiations between Britain and Egypt were held in London between 15 September and 3 October 1924. Unfortunately, Inrahin Zaghlul, on behalf of the Egyptian Parliament, met Ramsay MacDonald in a set of ill-fated talks.[69] Subsequently, the rising tensions between Egypt and Britain over Sudan led to the murder of the British Governor-General of the Sudan, Sir Lee Stack, on 19 November 1924, shortly after the end of the first Labour government, whereupon Britain insisted upon the removal of Egyptian troops from the Sudan and tightened her control over the Sudan.[70] As in Palestine, the Labour government – in the brief period in office – continued along established lines and did little to shape, or reshape, British policies in the Middle East.

In Europe while the Dawes Report and the Inter-Allied Conference were clearly seen as a step towards peace on the continent, more problems arose from the Draft Treaty of Mutual Assistance put before the fourth session of the League of Nations Assembly in 1923 to ensure future European security by outlawing 'aggressive war'. While Herriot warmed to this proposal, seeing it as the basis of French security, the British Foreign Office was extremely hostile since it would commit Britain to an enormous increase in naval forces, well above and beyond the military needs of the Empire. Diplomatically, MacDonald told Herriot: '. . . I must assure myself of the support of the Dominions [which he did not have]'. 'As for the treaty of mutual guarantee, I must not hide from you the fact that all my experts of navy, army, air force and Foreign Office are opposed to it,' he added firmly.[71] Herriot's response was memorable: 'My country has a dagger pointed at its breast within an inch of its heart.' However, MacDonald was not prepared to offer any assurances in the fashion of the pre-1914 British governments, and stressed that even a succeeding right-wing British government was unlikely to provide cast-iron guarantees. He proposed to get the Dawes proposals out of the way first, and then visit Herriot in France to discuss matters of debts and security. In the end, MacDonald and Herriot simply agreed at Chequers to conduct a continuing negotiation between their two countries.

However, this was not the final word of the Labour government since MacDonald had promised Herriot he would look further at the issue of European security. He also agreed to attend the League of Nations Assembly in September with the French leader, when responses to the Draft Treaty on Mutual Assistance were to be considered. Despite personal doubts about his participation, MacDonald travelled to Geneva to deliver a memorable address, speaking to the Fifth Assembly of the League.

This was an important speech in which MacDonald reiterated that Britain was against the idea of military treaties, since they might mushroom out of control. He put forward the case for German membership of the League, advocated the need to discuss national security in relation to national armaments, and advocated a system of arbitration between nations. On his main point of arbitration, he told the delegates at Geneva:

> If we had the beginnings of arbitration...what a substantial step forward it would be! If large nations and the small represented here to-day would only... create the right commission, and inspire it with the determination that we had in London that no obstacle would baulk us, the success of the commission would be assured within a year, and the League of Nations would be able to summon the nations to a Conference and then, by careful handling... obtain a successful issue.[72]

Overall it was a brilliant speech and widely acclaimed – so much so that the *New Statesman* enthused that if MacDonald kept a diary, he might write of his visit to Geneva: 'I came, I saw, I conquered.'[73] By contrast, on the following day, Herriot's speech dampened the atmosphere by arguing that although arbitration was required, it needed to be linked with European security and disarmament. His concern that arbitration was not enough was fuelled by the fact that he had just heard that the German government was likely to repudiate the war guilt clause, the *raison d'être* for German reparations. In this political climate, as it appeared that there might be no agreement, MacDonald met the French delegates. He decided to 'Draft a resolution for the Assembly embodying the points of my speech (except German inclusion which had been jeopardised by the German statement about war guilt)'.[74]

The outcome was the Anglo-French resolution that proposed a disarmament conference in the immediate future and for the League of Nations to consider possible amendments to the Covenant, including whether the 'optional clause' of the statute of a permanent court of justice could be adopted. The Anglo-French resolution, aimed at preventing war, was accepted on 6 September, and three weeks later a 21-clause agreement, known as 'The Geneva Protocol', was put before the Assembly of the League of Nations. The fine detail of what became known officially as 'The Protocol for the Pacific Settlement of International Disputes' was drawn up by the various national delegations. Britain was represented by Arthur Henderson and Lord Parmoor, the former Conservative pacifist-lawyer who spoke for the Government on foreign affairs in the House of Lords. In the House of Commons, Henderson, who was largely responsible for promoting the scheme for collective security, urged:

> to deal with the war, to get rid of its root and branch... requires a scheme by which arbitration takes the place of war for the settlement of disputes; by which armaments... are limited and cut down to the lowest level on which we can agree; by which the sense of insecurity is removed through mutual understanding to support a state which is the victim of unlawful aggression.[75]

The Cabinet accepted the draft Protocol on 29 September. However, whilst other nations were able to sign up to it, the Cabinet agreed, because of the impending defeat of the government in the House of Commons, that Parmoor be instructed to state that the British delegation was 'prepared unhesitatingly, and with all the influence at its command, to recommend to the British government acceptance for signature and ratification of the proposed Protocol'.[76] This hesitancy by the British government was more to do with the divisions within the Labour Party than with the looming threat of parliamentary defeat.

The Geneva Protocol was accepted by the Assembly of the League of Nations on 2 October and unanimously recommended to the governments concerned. It was to be one of MacDonald's finest hours and he was loudly applauded whilst speaking in favour of the resolution. The Protocol offered an elaborate system of arbitration by force. Those nations refusing to submit to arbitration, or who refused to carry out the arbitrators' decision, were to be considered aggressors. The Council of the League of Nations could decide upon a range of sanctions with which to punish aggressors, as provided in Article 16 of the Covenant. The Protocol was to come into force once the disarmament conference (the Locarno Conference as it became) met in June 1925. In the end, the prospect of French disarmament led MacDonald to agree to Britain being drawn into the system of collective security. Brilliant as the arrangement was in satisfying both the needs of the British and the French, there were many concerns within Government and within Britain about the Protocol.

MacDonald and Snowden were in deep conflict over the Geneva Protocol. Snowden was worried that Britain appeared committed to a system of collective security, the like of which, had led to the First World War. There was also unease in the armed forces. Admiral Beatty expressed his strong reservations, at a meeting of the Committee of Imperial Defence on 28 July 1924, that the treaty being mooted might compulsorily pledge Britain to expensive mutual assistance.[77] On 27 September, Lord Chelmsford, First Lord of the Admiralty, circulated a memorandum warning that the Royal Navy would have to take naval action without the declaration of war if the Protocol committed Britain to the protection of the seaways. The Cabinet discussed the same point on 29 September.[78]

The Labour government was clearly divided. MacDonald, Parmoor and Henderson, who had helped him in the negotiations, supported the Protocol, but Lords Haldane and Chelmsford were against it, as were Snowden and Wedgwood. However, in the end, the discussion of the Geneva Protocol was eclipsed by the demise of the Labour government. The incoming Baldwin administration had no intention of being tied to any mutual protection arrangements that would commit Britain to an increase in her naval and military power and a reduction in the effectiveness of imperial defence. Finally, the Locarno Conference in 1925 saw the end of the Geneva Protocol.

Nevertheless, in the wake of the Labour government's defeat there was still some limited pressure from the former members of the Labour government. Henderson, in particular, stressed the need for the Protocol. He had spoken strongly for it in a major speech in his own constituency on 12 October, and after Labour left office, he continued to campaign for it.[79] On 25 January 1925, he persuaded the General Council of the TUC and the National Executive Committee of the Labour Party to urge that 'this country should do everything in its power to obtain the acceptance of the principles of the Protocol and the holding of the disarmament conference.'[80] Yet there was still rumbling discontent within the Labour ranks. Effectively, the Geneva Protocol was an idea that gained full acceptance from neither the MacDonald nor Baldwin administrations. Snowden attempted to heal the rift between MacDonald and himself three years later. He wrote to MacDonald that 'Now the protocol has been buried at Geneva I do not see any reason why we cannot agree upon an agreed policy for securing its fundamental aims and disarmament.'[81]

The Inter-Allied Conference and the Geneva Protocol both produced conflict between Snowden and MacDonald, the two most important figures in the government – prompting Snowden's threat to resign at one point. The division between Labour's two leading politicians was serious and exacerbated by the fact that from April 1924 MacDonald was holding early morning meetings with some, but not all, of his colleagues – thus creating the impression there as a more important inner circle of Labour ministers. The Snowden–MacDonald relationship was also worsened by the Russian loan negotiations.

One of the cardinal points of MacDonald's foreign policy was *rapprochement* with Soviet Russia. Before taking office, from Lossiemouth, MacDonald confided his policy on Russia to the editor of the *Nation*, H. W. Massingham, who was his intermediary with Rakovsky, the Russian chargé d'affaires, in London: 'I propose, as soon as I get back to town to continue conversations that I started just before the Election. I have no doubt at all of being able to fix the whole matter up. If you could do anything in the meantime to clear the way, I should be much obliged.' Indeed, an initial act of the Labour government was the establishment of formal diplomatic relations with the new Soviet regime, but the Labour leader wanted broader relationship between Britain and Soviet Russia that included settling compensation claims for British bondholders and the negotiation of commercial transactions.[82] Earlier MacDonald had expressed his pleasure at the amnesty granted in Russia by the Soviets to the Social Revolutionaries. As he took office he received an assurance from Rakovsky that the release of prisoners would follow the amnesty.[83] In February 1924 MacDonald told the Commons that there would soon be an Anglo-Soviet Conference in London to settle their outstanding differences.[84] In April he opened this conference with a firm speech, listing the differences between the British and Soviet systems of government, objecting to how the Communist Third International had misrepresented him, and forcefully pressing the interests of the Council of Anglo-Soviet Foreign Bondholders and the Association of British Creditors in Russia. He added that the guaranteed loan to Russia could only be negotiated when compensation had been secured to British subjects for their losses to Russia.[85] After the first meeting, Arthur Ponsonby was left by MacDonald with the main responsibility of leading the British negotiating team. His experience during these difficult talks over several weeks provides some acute insights into Ponsonby's deteriorating relations with MacDonald and his growing scepticism about his leadership.[86]

There were two major issues at the Anglo-Soviet Conference – the goal of settling the outstanding differences between Britain and the Soviet Union, and the economic need to conclude a commercial pact that would benefit British international trade. The desire to retrieve the position of British bondholders with claims on pre-revolutionary Russia that were repudiated by the Soviet regime had a high priority.

As the negotiations progressed, it soon became apparent that a commercial treaty would depend upon a British loan, probably backed by a government guarantee. In July, Ponsonby circulated his memorandum to the Cabinet, outlining a possible agreement based on a government guaranteed £30 million loan in return for two-thirds of it being spent on British manufactures and a satisfactory settlement of the bondholder issue. On 30 July, after discussing the Ponsonby memorandum, the Cabinet agreed to recommend this course of action to Parliament.[87]

Snowden's opposition in the Cabinet made the round-table discussion highly fraught. The Chancellor of the Exchequer accepted the desirability of a commercial treaty with Russia, and had opposed attempts to isolate Russia from the rest of the world, but he was not prepared to go along with the guaranteed loan of £30 million. The Russians had seized British property during the Bolshevik revolution without compensation being offered to British bondholders. Indeed, Snowden believed firmly that the Soviet regime would not pay compensation to British bondholders.

Nevertheless, Ponsonby was given the responsibility of negotiating with the Soviet delegation and preparing a formula that would meet the requirements of the Russians and be acceptable to Parliament. These were tricky and protracted discussions. Efforts were made to defuse Snowden's opposition in case it threatened Cabinet accord and parliamentary approval. After some particularly difficult negotiations, which broke down on 5 August over the precise wording of the article dealing with compensation for nationalised property, Ponsonby decided to come up with a compromise set of proposals. He wrote in his diary:

> I examined all of them, took Chapman's in my pocket, tore over to Downing Street, by a miracle met Snowden in the lobby, got him in a waiting room with a Treasury expert. A moment of hesitation, but he accepted.[88]

Ultimately, there were two treaties – one a commercial agreement and the other one, which promised further negotiations between the bondholders and the Russian government. Once the bondholders of at least half the outstanding capital value agreed to the terms of the Russian government, then the British Government would guarantee the loan.

The settlement was put before the House of Commons for 21 days, which ensured that it would not be ratified until after the parliamentary summer recess. By that time stiff opposition was developing. Conservative opponents of the treaty were joined by leading Liberals, including Simon, Runciman and Lloyd George. On 3 September the Liberals published a pamphlet, *The Sham Treaty*, which was followed on 8 September by a *Daily Chronicle* series of articles entitled 'In Darkest Russia'. Ponsonby put up a stout defence of the Treaty in reply to the criticisms, particularly about the loan to the Soviets. In an interview with the political correspondent of the *Manchester Guardian*, he emphasised the benefits to British trade and European peace that normal relations with Russia would bring.[89] He wrote optimistically to MacDonald about the splits in the Liberal ranks over the Treaty: 'Even Mond says nothing about a vote . . . LLG's pretence of "consulting" the party is pure bunkum . . . Asquith is silent . . . [T]o reject a Treaty would be unprecedented – a most serious step to take. At the general election which would follow they would be split finally and irretrievably . . . I think my interview with the *M.G.* did some good.'[90]

Eventually, on 22 September Asquith, the Liberal leader, wrote to *The Times* denouncing the treaties as 'crude experiments in nursery diplomacy', although he did allow that the treaties might be amended rather than rejected outright. Asquith was aware of the strong likelihood that the defeat of the Labour government would result in a third general election in three years, for which the Liberal Party was ill-prepared.

MacDonald believed in the Russian treaties and was not prepared to compromise. He felt that the Liberals were being less than honest in their tactics. On 26 September he noted: 'I am inclined to give the Liberals an election on it if they force it.'[91] On 27 September he made a speech at Derby in which he stated forcefully that the Russian treaties might become the basis of a general election:

> We shall take no words from the House of Commons or party leaders like 'I am in favour of trade with Russia and peace with Russia, but I am not going to accept the treaties' . . . An agreement with Russia on these lines, embodied in our two draft Treaties . . . is now an essential

part of the Labour Party's policy and if the House of Commons will not allow it, the House of Commons had better censure us. [loud cheers].[92]

On 1 October at a party meeting, the Liberals decided to oppose the loan guarantee and it looked certain that the Labour government would collapse.[93] Four days later, Austen Chamberlain, the Conservative Shadow Foreign Secretary, wrote to his sister Ida:

> Meanwhile . . . I take it that we are in for a general election. I think the Govt. will be beaten on Wednesday [on the Campbell Case] – I only wish that they would accept that defeat – then, if they last so long, beaten again on the Russian Treaty. They must resign or dissolve on the second, if not the first, defeat & then the deluge! I find myself absolutely unable to predict what will happen.[94]

As it happened it was the Campbell Case, not the Russian treaties that became the summer madness that led to the autumn general election.

Foreign policy was one of the most lauded achievements of the first Labour government. The Inter-Allied Conference and the Geneva Protocol seemed to offer the basis of the long-lasting European peace which MacDonald, Snowden and many of the leading Labour figures sought. However, little of it was of lasting consequence. The Geneva Protocol was allowed to flounder at Locarno owing to the attitude of the Foreign Office, the Dominions and the colonies that Britain should not be tied to the expensive business of strengthening the navy as part of a process of collective security. Foreign policy also divided the Labour Party in many ways. First, even internationalists such as MacDonald and Snowden were divided over the extent to which Britain should be tied into a system of collective security, likened in some respects to the secret treaties that brought Britain into the First World War. Second, there was deep concern over the continuation of reparations since many Labour activists felt that they were likely to be a continuing source of German grievance and the basis for future conflict. Third, there were those sections within Labour, the miners' leaders and the Clydeside section of the ILP, who were far more concerned with national issues. Nevertheless, the majority of the Labour Party fell in line with MacDonald and the government. The only aspect of his handling of foreign policy that drew widespread condemnation was the Zinoviev or 'Red Letter' scare, which occurred during the 1924 general election campaign.

7
Downfall

When Labour took office in January 1924, Beatrice Webb predicted that Ramsay MacDonald's minority administration would not last out the year.[1] However, G. D. H. Cole, who witnessed the vicissitudes of Labour in office as one of its first historians, believed that the Labour ministry was relatively secure – despite its precarious minority position. Nearly 25 years later, he recalled that 'up to the summer recess the Government, in view of the great difficulties under it which it had to work in Parliament, was on the whole doing reasonably well, except in its handling of Indian and Egyptian affairs'. By the summer recess as the politicians left Westminster, there were three main concerns confronting the administration – the Irish boundary dispute, the negotiations over the Anglo-Soviet Treaty, and the prosecution of J. R. Campbell, the editor of the *Workers' Weekly*. At the time, none seemed like gathering storms on the political horizon to sweep away the MacDonald administration.

The first Labour government ended when George V granted MacDonald's request for Parliament to be dissolved after his administration had lost a vote of no confidence on 8 October over the handling of the Campbell prosecution. The Conservatives won a sweeping victory in the ensuing general election – the third in three years – in which the 'Red Scare' of the Zinoviev Letter was prominent. On 4 November, MacDonald and his Cabinet formally resigned and Stanley Baldwin returned to 10 Downing Street as Prime Minister.

Nevertheless, during its short existence, the first Labour government had been defeated on ten previous occasions, none of which had led to its resignation. According to Charles Masterman, Liberal MP for Manchester (Rusholme) and an observer of the parliamentary scene, even the botched affair of the Campbell prosecution should not have brought down the Labour government.[2]

By October, after the summer recess, the parliamentary scene had changed dramatically. A combination of political circumstances, particularly the opposition parties' response to the Russian Treaties and the furore over the withdrawal of the Campbell prosecution, threatened the tenuous existence of the administration.

Predictions in the press of a Labour defeat at Westminster within a matter of weeks were privately shared by government ministers. Sidney Webb was not as deadly accurate as his wife, Beatrice, in forecasting the demise of the first Labour government. 'I have no inside news to tell you; but it is generally assumed that "our number is up": I am inclined to doubt whether we shall be defeated next Tuesday or Wednesday on the Communist prosecution motion,' he told her. 'On the whole I expect the defeat to take place on Thursday 30 October,' he predicted, only six days before Labour's actual fall. Though, for a good measure, the President of the Board of Trade added: 'If I am wrong, it might happen three or four weeks earlier.'[3]

After almost nine months, in what circumstances did the Labour government fall and how far was MacDonald responsible for mishandling the events that overtook his administration? Why did the opposition parties combine on 8 October to defeat a minority administration they had previously sustained in office from January 1924? Reflecting on Labour's defeat, Cole was clear on what had wrecked the party's first term in office. 'Then came the sad bungle of the Campbell prosecution, accompanied by signs that MacDonald was suffering from a bad attack of anti-bolshevism, which was aggravated instead of being corrected by the campaign carried on in the press and in Parliament against the Russian Treaties. If the Campbell episode was bad, that of the alleged "Red Letter", which occurred during the election campaign, was infinitely worse,' he declared.[4]

The story of the Campbell affair is generally well known in British history, but it is worth re-examining how, within a few weeks, this minor judicial prosecution became the *cause célèbre* that brought down the first Labour government after a short period in office.[5] At the end of July 1924, the Director of Public Prosecutions (DPP) drew the attention of the Attorney-General, Sir Patrick Hastings, to an article published in the 25 July issue of the *Workers' Weekly*, a relatively little known Communist publication. On its front page, the left-wing Glasgow paper had carried an 'Open Letter' with a plea to British soldiers not to shoot fellow workers.

This appeal cited examples of how the authorities had employed troops in industrial disputes – at Tonypandy in 1910–11 and against the miners in 1921 – as well as the gunboats used in 1912 by the Asquith government against the dockers and transport workers in Liverpool. The paper reminded its readers: 'Have you forgotten how the Labour government threatened to use the Naval men during the dockers' strike this year? How in the tramway strike the Government threatened to introduce the E.P.A. [Emergency Powers Act] which would have forced many of you to have shot your own brothers and fathers?' J. R. Campbell, the editor, hammered home his key message: 'Let it be known that neither in the class war nor in the military, will you turn your guns on your fellow workers.' This article on the *Workers' Weekly* front page soon led to his prosecution under the antiquated Sedition to Mutiny Act of 1797.[6]

In Parliament on 29 July the Conservative MP, Sir Frederick Hall, declared that he would put down a private notice question about the 'Open Letter' addressed by the Communist Party of Great Britain to soldiers and sailors that he considered seditious and treasonable. Rhys Davies, Under-Secretary of State at the Home Office, replied that the Home Secretary was considering whether any action was called for.[7] This initial parliamentary skirmish was followed on 29 and 30 July by further questions about the *Workers' Weekly* article.

At this point the Campbell case temporarily brought the Attorney-General's name to the centre of British politics. Sir Patrick Hastings was an outstanding criminal lawyer who had been appointed the Attorney-General in the 1924 government – a position that secured him a knighthood – although he was a relative newcomer and inexperienced in the world of Labour politics. In Beatrice Webb's diary he is spared no mercy from her acidic pen. She judged him as 'an unpleasant type of clever pleader and political *arriviste*, who jumped into the Labour Party just before the 1922 election, when it became clear the Labour Party was the alternative government and it had not a single lawyer of position attached to it . . . an unsavoury being: destitute of all the higher qualities of intellect and without any sincerely held public purpose'.[8]

In deciding to initiate the prosecution of Campbell, Hastings showed that he had little awareness of the political furore his action would cause on the Left, particularly within his own party. No sooner had he instructed the DPP to bring criminal proceedings against Campbell in Bow Street Magistrates Court than the prosecution of the editor was hurriedly withdrawn, following parliamentary questions, primarily by James Maxton and other left-wing MPs. In the House of Commons on 6 August 1924, John Scurr asked the Attorney-General the circumstances in which the police raided the offices of the *Workers' Weekly*, why the editor was arrested and why he was being prosecuted.

Hastings explained that the prosecution was brought under the Incitement to Mutiny Act of 1797 after the DPP had investigated the article published in the *Workers' Weekly* that constituted a breach of law. The raid took place under a warrant issued by the stipendiary magistrate. James Maxton intervened to ask if the Attorney-General had read the article that 'contains mainly a call to the troops not to allow themselves to be used in industrial disputes, and that point of view is shared by a large number of the Members sitting on these benches'. At the same time, George Buchanan, Jack Jones and George Lansbury, who intended to use the debate on the Appropriation Bill to air the matter, challenged the Speaker's ruling that it was *sub judice*.[9]

As Trevor Barnes has argued, Special Branch was closely involved in the decision to prosecute Campbell.[10] During the months of the first Labour government, Childs, Head of the Special Branch, continued to provide the Labour Cabinet with weekly reports on revolutionary groups, industrial disputes and British Communist connections with the new Russian regime. Though the Cabinet declined to circulate the reports, the Home Secretary, Arthur Henderson, found them valuable and his memorandum on the Communist Party of Great Britain was based largely on Special Branch intelligence. Specific attention was given in the Special Branch reports to the CPGB anti-war campaign of July and August 1923, including its international links. The CPGB campaign marked the tenth anniversary of the start of the Great War in 1914 with an intensive crusade against capitalism and global war.

While released on bail, Campbell did not hesitate to promote his paper's anti-war campaign and to seek assistance for his own plight. 'First step against Labour imperialism; the workers through their trade union branches, Trades Councils, and local Labour parties, must force the Government to abandon the prosecution of the *Workers' Weekly* and the Communist Party,' he appealed.[11] The *Workers' Weekly* printed a forthright declaration: 'The keynote of the campaign is that war is a continuation of capitalist policy, and they who would fight war must fight capitalism in the most uncompromising fashion...Until capitalism has been overthrown and replaced by the United Soviet States of Europe the workers are not guaranteed against a fresh outbreak of war.' The same issue carried details of various events around London at the start of the anti-war week, including an appearance of J. R. Campbell at the Trafalgar Square rally. The campaign speakers included prominent British Communists, Wal Hannington in Plymouth, Harry Pollitt in Liverpool, as well as various representatives from French and German

Communist Parties. The *Workers' Weekly* also published a pamphlet, *War and the Workers*.[12]

What also fuelled Special Branch's anxiety was Communist influence in the British Empire. The *Workers Weekly* had denounced Labour's imperialism in no uncertain terms: 'The Labour Party . . . is pursuing a policy of naked Imperialist brutality in India, Egypt and Iraq. It is pursuing a policy of Imperialist aggrandisements in Europe. In short, it is in spite of its pacifist protestations – or rather, assisted by them – preparing for a new war.'[13]

Special Branch warned MacDonald and his colleagues: 'Speakers at anti-war meetings openly advocated civil war.' On 26 June, Childs had also noted that extraordinary payments had been made to Campbell.[14] However, while Special Branch's surveillance on the revolutionary Left was steadfastly maintained, during its term of office virtually all the Cabinet remained ignorant of the existence of Tory plans for the Supply and Transport organisation that lay undisturbed until used during the General Strike of 1926.[15]

Recently released files in The National Archives throw interesting light on the activities of the authorities in the Campbell case and why the prosecution was mishandled. The authorities already knew of J. R. Campbell as a journalist who had previously edited another Glasgow socialist newspaper, the *Worker*. Special Branch discovered that in July 1924, he was in charge of *the Worker's Weekly* only in a temporary capacity, as editor Rajani Palme Dutt was in hospital.

Six detectives, led by Inspector Parker of Scotland Yard, raided the offices of the *Workers Weekly* in London. On discovering that Campbell was in charge of the newspaper, they had to secure a fresh warrant and could not arrest him until two hours later. However, the Secret Service then realised that the prosecution of Campbell was a maladroit move, since the Communist agitator possessed a distinguished war record.

'He is posing as a war hero and I rather wanted to get a look at his conduct sheet. I understand he is in receipt of a 60 per cent disability pension on account of having lost part of his foot from frost bite,' Major W. A. Alexander wrote to the Head of the Security Service, Major-General Sir Vernon Kell. His reply confirmed 'that it is quite correct that he has the Military Medal and that his conduct appears to have been good from the fact that he had a 1st class G. C. Badge granted to him.'[16] As the official file on Campbell confirms, he had been invalided out of the Royal Navy Volunteer Reserve after the amputation of all his toes on both feet and his Military Medal had been bestowed for bravery in the field.[17]

Parliament was in recess during August and September, but at a crucial meeting of the Cabinet on 6 August at 6 p.m., the Labour ministers discussed the Campbell Case for the first time. Thomas Jones, the Principal Assistant Secretary, stood in for Sir Maurice Hankey, the Cabinet Secretary, who was away on duty as the Secretary-General of the London Conference. While the official minutes are relatively brief, Jones's rough notes taken at the meeting – using his system of speedwriting – provide far more detail of the Cabinet discussion.

Interestingly, at first MacDonald claimed that he had found out about the prosecution by chance from Charles Ammon, Parliamentary Secretary to the Admiralty. Henderson then announced that the printers were not to be proceeded against since he had received their formal letter of apology. When the Attorney-General joined the Cabinet, he took full responsibility for initiating the prosecution. He then gave his Labour colleagues a way of retreat. Campbell, who was only the temporary acting editor, had also offered to write a letter of apology. It was this course of action that MacDonald and his colleagues agreed to take. They also decided that in future no public prosecution of a political character should be undertaken, without the knowledge of the Cabinet or the Prime Minister, and that the Attorney-General's suggestion to abandon the prosecution should be adopted.[18] However, this brief statement of the Cabinet's decision did not give the full picture of the 'considerable discussion' that had preceded it. Although the proposal to drop the prosecution had come from the Attorney-General, the Opposition parties were able later to censure the government for political interference in a judicial matter.

Within a week, the government announced the abandonment of the prosecution against Campbell. On 13 August the Treasury Counsel, Travers Humphreys, told the court that it had 'been represented' that the 'Open Letter' could not be construed as a specific attempt, maliciously and advisedly, to seduce members from their allegiance, but was a comment on the use of armed military force by the State for the suppression of industrial disputes. As a precedent, he cited the summing-up of Mr Justice Horridge in the case of Guy Bowman and Benjamin and Charles Buck at the Central Criminal Court in 1912 that, he submitted, constituted a valid defence.[19] Therefore, the DPP instructed that no evidence was to be offered in the Campbell prosecution. Furthermore, Campbell's excellent character and admirable military record – seriously wounded and awarded Military Medal – was also highlighted. In these circumstances all that remained was for William Fuller of Messrs R. Enver and Company, to request the return of seized books and papers on behalf of Campbell.

Triumphantly, the *Workers' Weekly* reported the collapse of the Crown prosecution with a banner headline – 'Working Class Agitation forces Government Surrender'[20] In addition, the CPGB made political capital of being deprived of the opportunity to call MacDonald and other Labour ministers as witnesses. Before the First World War, they had defended the Communist Tom Mann on a similar charge. The Treasury Counsel had not revealed who had made the representations referred to in court, thereby leaving the government open to the criticism that it was the prisoner of its own left-wing extremists.

At this delicate moment, Irish affairs intruded. Fifty years ago, Charles Mowat described the end of the Labour administration as 'sudden and messy'.[21] The timing of the political crisis, which soon overtook the Labour ministry, was determined by the Speaker's recall of Parliament on 30 September to resolve the Irish Boundary dispute. Article 12 of the Anglo-Irish Treaty of 1921 had empowered a commission to settle the border between the Irish Free State and the six counties of Northern Ireland. During September a cross-party parliamentary group had visited the boundary district and recommended that negotiations take place before any Boundary Commission was established. But the Northern Ireland government refused to nominate a representative to serve on the Commission – despite Baldwin's mediation with Sir James Craig, the Ulster Prime Minister at MacDonald's behest. With this *impasse* the Labour Cabinet referred the matter to the Judicial Committee of the Privy Council, who recommended that additional legislation was required to appoint a third commissioner. An early recall of Parliament was needed to pass a short Bill with all-party support to appoint a third commissioner.[22]

When Parliament reassembled, the Government faced a barrage of questions about the withdrawal of the Campbell prosecution. The Attorney-General explained 'I came to the conclusion that the words [in the *Workers' Weekly* article] were capable of a meaning which would constitute an offence provided that the person to be charged could be proved to be properly responsible within the strict wording of the Statute. I accordingly authorised the police to make enquiries and to institute proceedings.'

Hastings also pointed out that Campbell was not in the regular employment of the paper and was of excellent character. He added: 'His military record was exceptionally good. He had voluntarily enlisted for service at the beginning of the War. He had been severely wounded and thereby incapacitated for life, and had been decorated with the Military Medal for gallantry in the field'.[23]

On the same day, during Question Time, Sir Kingsley Wood asked the Prime Minister 'whether any directions were given by him, or with his sanction, to the Director of Public Prosecutions to withdraw the proceedings against Mr Campbell, the Editor of the *Workers' Weekly*, and whether he received any personal intimation that he would be personally required to give evidence on behalf of the Defendant at the hearing?'

The Prime Minister's reply – that he was not involved with the prosecution – was beyond belief. It is worth quoting in full since it demonstrates his direct responsibility in the mishandling of the Campbell affair. MacDonald told the House of Commons:

> I was not consulted regarding either the institution or the subsequent withdrawal of these proceedings. The first notice which came to my knowledge was in the Press. I never advised its withdrawal, but left the whole matter to the discretion of the Law Officers, where that discretion properly rests. I never received any intimation, nor even a hint, that I should be asked to give evidence. That also came to my attention when the falsehood appeared in the paper.[24]

MacDonalds's forthright denial of any responsibility came as a thunderbolt to his Cabinet officials. 'When I heard it, as I did in the House, a shiver went down my spine,' Tom Jones recalled on 15 October. In his diary he noted Hankey's statement that MacDonald's explanation was 'a bloody lie'.[25] During the summer, when the King had first heard about the Campbell affair, MacDonald had written from Lossiemouth to reassure him and to apportion blame elsewhere: 'I knew nothing about it until I saw it in the newspapers. Then I sent for the Attorney-General and the Public Prosecutor and gave them a bit of my mind.' The Prime Minister also stated that he had told them that 'as they had begun, they had to go through with it'.[26] In his view, only Campbell's offer of a written apology – which was never received – was an adequate reason to abandon the prosecution. However, Labour ministers feared that if the matter came to court, the Communists would have summoned MacDonald as a witness and subjected him to some 'awkward questions'. 'Nothing would have pleased me better... I would have said some things that might have added a month or two to the sentence,' the Labour Leader added defiantly. In the end, he blamed the botched Campbell prosecution on the inexperience of certain ministers and the inefficiency of departmental civil servants. MacDonald complained that 'in far too many departments there seems to have been a slackness of business administration.' He urged that 'department after department should be taken hold of by some men of business energy . . . [to] put an end to the muddling slackness that seems to prevail'.[27]

Jones's diary reveals that Maurice Hankey had gone to considerable lengths about the accuracy of the Cabinet minutes concerning the Campbell prosecution. On 2 October Hankey wrote to MacDonald about his parliamentary statement that he had neither been involved in the decision to withdraw the prosecution nor could recollect having been shown the Minute of the Cabinet meeting of 6 August. He explained to MacDonald that Jones had completed the draft Minutes but had written a note asking him to obtain the Prime Minister's approval. 'If he cannot look at all perhaps he would look at No. 5 (*Workers' Weekly*),' Jones had commented. Hankey's letter outlined their very busy schedules. Although he could not recall precisely, he reconstructed the different stages in the production of the Minutes. Hankey firmly believed he had put the draft Minute in front of the Prime Minister at the House of Commons when the Meeting of the Heads of Delegations concluded at 11 a.m. on 7 August. As he told Jones that MacDonald had challenged the official record, the Assistant Secretary to the Cabinet recorded a long note on 15 October on his involvement in the case of the *Workers' Weekly*.

Jones's diary also throws more light on the incident with a reference to Jimmy Thomas's reaction:

> On 3 October, J. H. Thomas sent for me and told me that the arrangement for the *Workers' Weekly* debate was that the Attorney-General and the Prime Minister would speak early in the debate, and he would wind up for the Government. Would I prepare a brief for him, and make special reference in it to the Curragh case, and to his own record as a strict Constitutionalist? I took advantage of the opportunity to show him the rough notes of the Cabinet Meeting of 6 August. He and Marsh read them together. He then turned to me, and, with the aid of the lurid language of which he is such a master, declared that unfortunately 'Mac' had gone beyond the truth and we had all got to try to pull things together. He himself did not want an election.[28]

As Gill Bennett has argued, a crucial factor in the downfall of the Labour Government was its ambiguous relations with the Soviet Union, particularly over the Anglo-Soviet Treaty negotiations. The Campbell episode illuminated the differing attitudes within the Labour Party towards the newly founded CPGB during the early 1920s. Many of the ILP shared common ground and wished to promote good understanding on the political Left, but some Labour MPs on the right of the party wanted no truck with the CPGB, who were considered to be a distinct disadvantage to Labour electoral fortunes.

Anglo-Soviet relations in 1924 provided Labour's opponents with an easy political target. While at home the Labour leadership displayed an increasingly hard line against British communism by excluding Communists as individual party members and as official Labour election candidates, a totally different stance was taken to Bolshevik Russia. On taking office, MacDonald's first act in international affairs was the *de jure* recognition of the Soviet Union. In March 1921, after the Krassin trade delegation had visited Britain during the previous year, the Lloyd George Coalition government had agreed a commercial treaty with the Bolshevik regime – a policy that the Labour administration in 1924 sought to continue. As Kenneth Morgan has shown, Lloyd George's pioneering approach among Western nations, despite truculent opposition from Churchill, Curzon and other ministers in his Coalition Cabinet, was a milestone in Anglo–Soviet relations. At a crucial time of rising unemployment in Britain, it was a bold and realistic attempt to open up the vast Russian market for British capital goods and manufactures – albeit the Treaty secured only £108 million in trade between 1921 and 1926 – as well as giving *de facto* recognition to the Bolshevik regime and the exchange of diplomatic representatives. However, Lloyd George's attempt to secure the full recognition of the Bolshevik regime for commercial and diplomatic purposes foundered in 1922 at the Genoa Conference when the Bolsheviks signed the Rapallo Treaty with the Weimar Republic.[29]

Nothing further was then achieved until Labour took office. The attitude of the Comintern in the early 1920s, particularly its campaign against British rule in India, made for uneasy relations with Conservative and Labour administrations. As Foreign Secretary, MacDonald saw the opportunity for a political success by restoring relations with the Soviet Union. An Anglo-Soviet trade agreement would resolve all outstanding issues between the two countries. Negotiations took place for four months in London between the arrival of the Krassin delegation in April and August 1924. After the inaugural meeting, addressed by Krassin and MacDonald, the British Premier – also occupied with the Allied Powers conference – delegated the conduct of the Anglo-Soviet talks to his Parliamentary Under-Secretary, Arthur Ponsonby, who felt increasing isolated from his Prime Minister during the lengthy negotiations.[30] He recalled: 'My chief job in the Foreign Office was the

Russian Treaties...MacDonald being engaged in a European Conference, left the whole matter to me unaided except for an army of officials, the leading ones being opposed to our policy. The intricacies of the question, the unaccountable methods of the Russians and the difficulty of getting MacDonald's attention were tremendous obstacles.'[31]

Two thorny issues dominated the negotiations that Ponsonby handled – securing Bolshevik recognition of debts incurred under the previous Tsarist regime to British bondholders and other creditors, and coping with the Soviet delegation's demands for a British loan as part of an Anglo-Soviet treaty. In 1924 British claimants using City organisations and Tory MPs lobbied the Labour administration consistently for a settlement. This created a hostile and contentious political mix for Labour's Russian policy, particularly after the Soviet delegation had arrived in London. The weeks dragged by as the conference faltered over the Russian demand for a British loan. Ponsonby granted a fortnight adjournment for Russians to explore raising funds in the City, but without success. He observed 'I have managed to head off a breakdown but...in a word everything depends upon the Russians getting a loan. My last card will be a government guarantee but I doubt if I can carry this [in the Cabinet].'[32] As the Parliamentary recess approached, *The Times* asked: 'What purpose, then, can this exhausted and discredited Conference now possibly serve?'[33]

After fruitless discussion with Montague Norman, the Governor of the Bank of England and Philip Snowden, Ponsonby drafted a Cabinet memorandum that was eventually considered in detail on 30 July – the only Cabinet meeting the Under-Secretary for Foreign Affairs attended. Ponsonby's correspondence with his wife, Dorothy, provides a fascinating insight into the divisions within the Cabinet over its Russian policy. He told her:

The discussion lasted about $1\frac{1}{2}$ hours & was at times heated. Haldane shook his head. Olivier bleated out some protest. Jos [Wedgwood] attacked most surprisingly violently. Uncle Arthur [Henderson] went for Snowden. Parmoor tried to smooth things over. Wheatley gave me excellent support going beyond detail to principle and policy. Sidney Webb came quite round & helped me. Thomson was very encouraging. Clynes supported & so did Charles [Trevelyan]. Walsh was very critical. J. R. M. became better & better & finally rounded the thing off in a decision which he put to the vote and 15 were in favour only 4 against [Snowden, Jos, Walsh, Haldane or Olivier].[34]

Despite the strong opposition of Philip Snowden – 'I cannot say how disagreeable he was – I found the greatest difficulty in keeping my temper,' Ponsonby wrote after an earlier tetchy meeting with the Chancellor of the Exchequer – the Cabinet had finally agreed two draft treaties.[35] Besides a commercial treaty, there was also to be a general treaty for negotiations with British bond holders which, if successful, would pave the way for *another* treaty for a government loan conditional settlement of outstanding claims.

On 5 August, as Ponsonby prepared to address Parliament, after a 20-hour marathon negotiation had reached stalemate, the talks had broken down, but on 6 August he announced in the Commons that a Treaty would be signed the next day – comprising both a Commercial Treaty and a General Treaty. According to E. D. Morel's front-page account of the events of 4–6 August in *Foreign Affairs*, the day had been saved by the dramatic intervention of four Labour MPs – Purcell, Wallhead, Morel himself and Lansbury – who provided a face-saving proposal.[36] These representations later exposed the administration to incessant sniping from the Tories and the Liberals that the Labour government was a prisoner of its left-wing extremists. However, as Raymond Jones has revealed, it was Ponsonby who had approached Morel and Lansbury as early as 31 July to influence the Russians. Moreover, on 6 August Sir S. Chapman (one of Ponsonby's team from the Board of Trade) had devised the formula on compensation for the owners of nationalised property that Ponsonby had rushed before MacDonald and Snowden for their agreement. This 'mere face saving device' then became Article 11 of the Treaty.[37]

The Commercial Treaty opened up trade for English goods and also guaranteed diplomatic immunity for some Soviet Union trade delegations. The second part was a General Treaty that renewed previous arrangements with the pre-Bolshevik regime and concluded a Fisheries agreement. Most controversially, the Treaty dealt with outstanding disputes over bonds and properties, which the new Soviet Union government agreed to honour once at least half the bondholders had agreed. In return, the Labour administration would provide the Russian government with a loan. This arrangement, which might in the future result in a substantive treaty, resulted in bitter denunciations by the Conservative opposition. 'Money for Murderers!' screamed the right-wing press. As a result of Conservative pressure, the government agreed, according to the Ponsonby rule, on a delay of 21 days between signature and ratification of the Treaty, which would not happen until after the summer parliamentary recess.

The position adopted by the leaders of three political parties over the Anglo-Soviet Treaty was a crucial factor in the downfall of the Labour government. By September 1924 the Conservative Party had recovered from its disheartening defeat in December 1923 and reorganised its party machinery. Having abandoned the protectionist manifesto, Baldwin had delivered ten major speeches on a renewed policy of Tory democracy and was ready to fight another general election.

Though at first divided over the Anglo-Soviet Treaty, most of the Liberals were either opposed to the idea of a loan or wanted amendments to the Treaty.[38] Originally sympathetic, Masterman declared: 'We did not guarantee loans to our Dominions, and he would not guarantee a loan to any country that kept giant conscript armies and instead of buying locomotives kept an armed terror on every border state on the west side of Russia. If when Parliament reassembles the Labour government would not accept amendments to the treaty, then the blood be on its own head.'[39]

Among the opposition leaders, no one was more opposed to the Russian Treaty than Lloyd George, particularly over the possibility of a British loan to the Bolsheviks – a total contrast, as we have seen, to his attitude to the appeasement of Russia when in office three years before. His career appeared over when the Unionists withdrew their support and his Coalition government came to an end in October 1922. Though he lived on until 1945, Lloyd George never held office again after he had fallen from power as Prime Minister. Nevertheless, he remained at the centre of British parliamentary politics in the 1920s and beyond.

Initially, as we have seen, the Liberal leadership had been divided over whether to maintain the Baldwin government in office or to combine with Labour to end the administration. Simon supported Asquith's view that the Liberals should combine with Labour to defeat Baldwin and in due course it could replace Labour and thereby form a new Liberal administration. Lloyd George did not agree, however, and eventually when the Liberals met, Asquith had decided only to turn out the Tory administration.[40] As the new Labour government settled into office Lloyd George soon became aware that his hope for Labour–Liberal cooperation for a radical programme was unfounded. MacDonald, who personally preferred Baldwin and the Conservatives to his Liberal opponents, took an independent stance. As the *Manchester Guardian* commented on 3 October, 'the Prime Minister, who can be so sweet to the foreigner from whom he differs most widely, has nothing but concealed dislike and exaggerated suspicion for those who in this country stand nearest to him in politics'.[41] No one was more detested among the Labour ranks than Lloyd George.[42] During 1924 his strategy was to work with the Tories in a temporary alliance to oust Labour from government so that he might replace Asquith as Liberal leader.

The advent of the Anglo-Soviet Treaty provided the opportunity for Lloyd George to advance his plans. At first there were divisions within the Liberal Party over the Russian Treaty. The Liberal *Westminster Gazette* took MacDonald's side arguing that 'the Prime Minister was well within his rights in insisting on signing the Treaty at once', although the *Daily Chronicle* declared 'the text of the two new Russian treaties thoroughly justifies Mr Lloyd George's description of them as a fake'.[43] In Parliament on 6 August, Lloyd George had attacked the commercial treaty as 'a fake...a contract in which the space for every essential figure is left blank', which he developed during September with a press statement over the fallacies of making a direct cash loan to the Bolshevik regime. Lloyd George approached Churchill – now back in the Conservative ranks – about the possibility of a Tory–Liberal combination to oust Labour from office. At the same time, Lloyd George, who controlled his own substantial election fund, knew that Liberal headquarters was desperately short of money and that Asquith's parliamentary seat at Paisley would likely be under threat in a general election.[44]

Not surprisingly, he wrote to his daughter, Megan: 'It looks now as if we are in for another General Election. I have done my best to precipitate it. Labour had its chance and with a little more wisdom and what the old Puritans sagely called "Grace of God" they could have remained in another three years and formed a working alliance with Liberalism that would have ensured a progressive administration of this country for 20 years. But they have lost their heads as men and women will from sudden elevation. Hence their fall.'[45]

On 1 October Beatrice Webb predicted the fall of the first Labour government, though she was not clear whether the Liberals would remove their support in the Commons over 'the silly little issue of the Campbell prosecution or rather the withdrawal of it' or challenge the government over the Russian treaty.[46] Nine days later she noted:

> The end of the tale of the Parliament of 1923–24 and of its Cabinet is soon told. The two Oppositions decided to kill the Government on the Campbell issue. Some say they drifted into their decision; others that the Russian Treaty proved [un]expectedly popular and that the Liberals, in particular, would have lost, not fourteen, but fifty, in the division lobbies if they had stuck to damning the Treaty. Anyhow, the Conservatives ran away from their direct censure, and beat the

Government by the meaner Liberal way of the Court of Enquiry
which the Cabinet could not accept without lowering its prestige a
few weeks before it was to be sent to the country on the Russian
issue [*sic*].[47]

The end of the Labour Government finally came when the administration lost a vote of confidence in the House of Commons on 8 October
1924. MacDonald had made it clear that in those circumstances he
would ask for the dissolution of Parliament from the King and seek a
new mandate at the general election. On 2 October he reported to the
King that the end of the Labour government was in sight. His opponents' attack over the withdrawal of the Campbell prosecution, followed
by the Liberal Party's resolution to reject the Russian Treaty, were part
of a general move to destroy the minority administration. Faced by
the threat of imminent defeat over the Campbell affair, or being put
out of office within a few weeks over the Russian Treaty, MacDonald
confessed to the King that he could continue no longer with the burdens
of the Foreign Office with a Damocles Sword above his head. 'It is quite
impossible for me to conduct these negotiations [with the Turks over
Iraq] with a sentence of death hanging over me for a month,' MacDonald
concluded.[48]

In March 1925, MacDonald discussed the fall of his Government
over the Campbell affair with C. P. Scott. He described it as 'an
extraordinary series of muddles' from the time that Hastings unneces-
sarily initiated the prosecution, the inaccuracy of the Cabinet minutes
that were inadvertently circulated among government departments,
as well as a compact among Lloyd George, Beaverbrook and Austen
Chamberlain during the summer to turn out his administration.[49]

Who therefore was to blame for Labour's defeat over the Campbell affair in October 1924? The Solicitor-General carefully distanced
himself from the Campbell case, explaining that criminal prosecutions were entirely a matter for the Attorney-General. Sir Henry Slesser
claimed he 'rarely read newspapers at all closely' and was not aware that
Campbell had been charged at Bow Street magistrates' court. Similarly,
the Solicitor-General had not heard of Campbell until on 4 August 'the
malcontents of the Mountain raised protest about him in Parliament.'[50]

He claimed his earliest contact was on 6 August when he went next
door to the Attorney-General's room at Westminster and expressed
his reservations about the prosecution on seeing the evidence about
Campbell. In his memoirs, Slesser emphasised his non-involvement
in 'the subsequent discussions between the Prime Minister, the

Attorney-General and the Home Secretary about the Campbell prosecution. I knew nothing; after the debate [on 6 August] I went home and had no further communications with anyone on the matter.'[51]

The conduct of parliamentary business, particularly when MacDonald was absent at meetings of the League of Nations at Geneva, was the responsibility of J. R. Clynes as Leader of the House. According to Clynes, who had plenty of first-hand experience of Labour's tribulations at Westminster, though the minority administration was actually defeated on several occasions in the House of Commons, there was no question of resignation unless it lost a vote of no confidence. Clynes's recollections brought a fresh perspective to why the first Labour government lost office. He believed that Labour's demise in 1924 was 'not because we were doing badly, but because our rivals feared that we had been doing too well!'

Clynes's explanation was that the withdrawal of the Campbell prosecution provided the pretext for the two opposition parties to combine against the government, lest Labour's performance in office should prove popular with the electorate. 'The fact was that, in the autumn of 1924 Baldwin and Asquith agreed that if Labour remained in office much longer, such a lot of obvious good would be done to the country that Labour would hold power for many years to come,' he believed. During the debate on the vote of censure proposed by Sir Robert Horne,[52] Clynes suspected a conspiracy between Lloyd George and Austen Chamberlain 'to go into the Lobby together and put Labour out'.

By contrast, Philip Snowden laid the blame directly at MacDonald's door. First, there was the matter of the sensational press revelations that Sir Arthur Grant, the head of the biscuit manufacturing firm, McVitie & Price, and an old family friend, had given MacDonald 30,000 shares in his company, as well as the donation of a Daimler motor car. The arrangement was that during his lifetime the Labour leader should enjoy the dividend income to run the car, with the shares eventually reverting to Grant or his heirs. Shortly after this scandal, Grant received a baronetcy in the Honours list. MacDonald's opponents frequently interrupted his parliamentary speeches with taunts of 'biscuits'.[53]

Also, Snowden had no doubt that MacDonald's 'inaccurate reply' about the Campbell prosecution to Sir Kingsley Wood had 'very unfortunate consequences'. In his autobiography, Snowden printed *verbatim* MacDonald's parliamentary answer and his apology later that he, 'went a little further than I ought to have gone . . . [and] implied that I had no cognisance of what was going on'. 'This incoherent, evasive and prevaricating reply staggered the House, and made his colleagues who were sitting on the bench hang their heads in shame,' Snowden added. But he did not stop there. Snowden made no comment on the manoeuvres of the opposition parties over the Conservative motion of censure and the Liberal amendment calling for a Select Committee of Enquiry. In the debate that followed, he exonerated Hastings: 'The Opposition were not in the least anxious to put the Attorney General in the pillory. They were concerned to discredit the Prime Minister and the Labour Government.' Similarly, the former Chancellor did his best in his auto-biography to damage the reputation of his former opponent with the testimony of others. After watching MacDonald's performance in the Commons, John Wheatley whispered to Snowden: 'I never knew a man who could succeed so well, even if he is telling the truth, in giving the impression that he is not doing so.' Snowden observed that after the Prime Minister's speech, 'the fate of the Government was sealed'.[54]

In his memoirs, Tom Johnston noted that the prosecution of Campbell was withdrawn after the Attorney-General discovered the Scottish Communist had been decorated for gallantry during the Great War. But, in Johnston's view, there was a more compelling reason. He firmly believed that had the prosecution had been continued, the CPGB would have subpoenaed Ramsay MacDonald as a witness since, in 1912, the Prime Minister had defended Tom Mann when he had been accused of incitement to mutiny in similar circumstances.[55]

In the middle of the Campbell case MacDonald sent for his Minister of Mines, Emanuel Shinwell. 'I found him in the large drawing room at No. 10. He was pacing up and down in a welter of indecision and excitement. Finally he turned to me and said that he 'intended to resign,' Shinwell recalled. He explained that if the Government instituted an inquiry as demanded by the Liberal amendment to the Tory vote of censure, it would provide a way out of the dilemma. However, Shinwell believed that MacDonald was more worried about the criticism of Labour backbenchers and the government's hapless minority position than the Campbell Case. When the government lost the vote of censure by 364 to 198 votes, Shinwell declared: 'The first Labour Government was over, buried by its leader – a man who could no longer stand the criticism from his own side. It was not the Campbell affair that brought him down.'[56]

Haldane said little about the Campbell incident except that the mishandling of the prosecution, 'put a weapon into the hands of the adversary with which he could belabour us'. More serious was the Russian Treaty and loan, which was attacked by Labour's oppon-ents in Parliament.[57] G. D. H. Cole recalled over 20 years later that the Russian loan was the main reason for the fall of the 1924 administration since it provided the spur for the two opposition parties to combine against the government. In addition, the withdrawal of the Campbell prosecution then became the occasion for the government's annihilation. MacDonald declared that defeat over either the Liberal amendment or the Tory vote of censure would be followed by the dissolution of Parliament and the third general election in almost three years.[58]

More recently, Andrew Thorpe has provided a different perspective – that the Campbell case afforded MacDonald a timely opportunity to leave office. The Prime Minister was exhausted from the heavy workload of dual office and sensitive to opposition criticism that Alexander Grant had received a baronetcy in exchange for the £30,000 loan. 'This was as good a time as any to bow out,' Thorpe believed.[59]

In 1957 Richard Lyman provided the first comprehensive account of the downfall of the Labour government, in which he examined the Campbell case and the effect of the Zinoviev Letter during the 1924 election campaign. Lyman commented that the Campbell prosecution was abandoned when the DPP realised that the Scottish Communist was 'a man of excellent character with an admirable military record'. The Treasury Counsel on 12 August 1924 also told the court that the article in *Workers' Weekly* 'was a comment upon armed military force being used by the state to repress industrial disputes'. According to Lyman, there was little press reaction to the withdrawal of the prosecution at the time with the attention given to the negotiation of the Russian Treaty. Not until a month later when Parliament reassembled, did the opposition parties press the government over its reasons for not continuing with the prosecution. Lyman also described the nature of the opposition attack and Asquith's difficulty in restraining his party. The Liberals eventually agreed to demand a select committee of enquiry rather than the vote of censure favoured by the Tories. In particular, he rejected the view that MacDonald welcomed the row of the Campbell case since it provided him with the opportunity to bring his minority government to an end. He dismissed the testimony of MacDonald's former colleagues, Snowden and Shinwell, as well as the Clydesider David Kirkwood, who believed MacDonald had caused the problem as an escape route from his political problems.

According to Beaverbrook, the Labour government fell as a result of political manoeuvres among the leaders of the main parties at Westminster, rather than any time-honoured political strategy. His account of the last days of the administration places the blame squarely on a series of blunders and accidents, principally by MacDonald, Baldwin and Lloyd George. Convinced that his administration would have been defeated over the Russian Treaty, MacDonald chose to stand his ground on the withdrawal of the Campbell prosecution. Beaverbrook was convinced that the government would have lasted longer if MacDonald had avoided this earlier crisis, as the Zinoviev Letter would have removed the Russian Treaty. On 30 September, MacDonald declined Baldwin's offer to postpone the Campbell debate until 18 November, thereby creating the seeds of an unnecessary crisis. 'The Conservative tried to keep the Socialist in, and the Socialist insisted on being turned out!' Beaverbrook observed. What happened next still might not have meant the end of the government, as the Conservatives put down a vote of censure and the Liberals opted for an amendment requesting a select committee of enquiry. If the voting had gone along party lines, both would have been defeated with the government still intact, since the Conservatives were not prepared to support the Liberal amendment.

Lloyd George was totally opposed to the Russian Treaty, especially the proposal of a loan of £30 million, and attempted to persuade the Conservatives to abandon their motion of censure and support the Liberal amendment. According to Beaverbrook, Lloyd George therefore met Austen Chamberlain at Lord Birkenhead's house to persuade the Conservatives to take a stand against the government. In turn, Chamberlain secured Asquith's assurance that he would not abandon the Liberal demand for an enquiry.[60] On 8 October, Sir Robert Horne moved the vote of censure that claimed that, owing to the influence of its left-wing MPs, the government had 'interfered with the course of justice' by dropping the Campbell prosecution. Sir John Simon moved for the Liberal amendment for the appointment of a Select Committee to inquire into the Campbell affair. It was left to Baldwin to announce in the debate that the Conservatives would vote for the Liberal amendment.

Even while this crucial debate was in progress, the Cabinet had met at 8.45 p.m. in the House of Commons to confirm that 'in regard to the Parliamentary position as it had developed up to that moment . . . in the "*Workers' Weekly*" prosecution . . . [that it would] . . . continue to oppose the Motion and the Amendment'.[61] As the censure motion and the amendment were both matters of confidence, Baldwin's announcement sounded the death knell of the government. In winding up for Labour, J. H. Thomas censured the Conservatives' action as 'a mean and contemptible party manoeuvre', but to no avail. The Speaker put the question 'That the words proposed be left out stand part of the question' and the Liberal amendment was carried – Ayes 198 to Noes 359. The amended motion asking for a select committee of inquiry was then put and, although remarkably 14 Liberals and two Conservatives went into the same lobby with the Labour MPs, the result of 364 votes to 198 meant the defeat of the first Labour government. The Cabinet met briefly at 11.30 p.m. to note that MacDonald would see the King at Buckingham Palace the next morning at 10.00 a.m. to seek the immediate dissolution of Parliament.[62]

George V reluctantly granted the dissolution even though it brought about another general election within less than a year. He observed: 'I am sorry that the appeal to the electorate cannot be made upon a more vital issue than that [the Campbell prosecution] raised last evening in the House of Commons. Further, there is the possible contingency that the General election may return to Parliament the three political parties in numbers similar to the present House of Commons.' However, there was no other course of action, as he already knew that neither Baldwin nor Asquith would take office or form a coalition government.[63]

While MacDonald had been defiant during the annual party conference in October, the Labour election manifesto had a defensive tone. It emphasised what the administration would have accomplished had it remained in office. Only an unassuming list of achievements were included – the Wheatley Housing Act, Snowden's free trade budget, and educational reforms in domestic politics, as well as MacDonald's success on the European scene. If returned to office, Labour promised only another moderate programme. It included the reorganisation of the mining industry, a national electricity generating system, the taxation of land values, and the establishment of a royal commission on the licensing laws.

Labour came under attack from the Conservatives principally over the Russian Treaties and the failure to find any remedies for unemployment at home. Instead, their opponents pledged a range of measures including agricultural rates relief, improvements in education and national insurance in return for a majority in the next Parliament. Characteristically, free trade and temperance, as well as education pensions and national insurance, were prominent pledges in the Liberal manifesto, though this somewhat old-fashioned approach heralded a lacklustre campaign in which only 340 candidates took the field.[64]

The centrepiece of the Labour campaign was MacDonald's speaking tours across Britain. The Labour leader undertook a punishing schedule that soon left him totally exhausted, physically and mentally. On 13 October he addressed a sizeable crowd at Euston Railway Station before travelling to Rugby, Crewe and Glasgow for large rallies later in the day. By 17 October he had toured Scotland, the North East, Yorkshire, Lancashire, the Potteries and the Midlands, addressing

considerable crowds at innumerable venues. MacDonald then journeyed by car to his Welsh constituency of Aberavon. Arriving next
at Cardiff he finally lost his voice completely, although this did not
prevent him addressing large gatherings at Barry, Bridgend and Kenfig
Hill later on the same day. Back in his constituency for the weekend,
he was again surrounded by surging crowds who brought his motor-car
to a standstill in the main street of Aberavon. Nevertheless, after the
weekend, MacDonald embarked on a second nationwide tour that took
in Leicester and a number of other cities. Such non-stop and unrelenting
campaigning was hardly the action of a politician who had deliberately
brought his first spell of political office to an untimely end.

For the first time, radio made an appearance in a British general
election campaign. On 13 October, MacDonald's speech was broadcast
from Glasgow, but his colourful observations on a public stage about
an opposition plot to engineer Labour's downfall withered in comparison for those listening on their rudimentary crystal sets to Baldwin's
urbane performance on the radio two days later. The leader of the opposition speaking from the BBC 2LO studio displayed a mastery of the new
medium by meticulous preparation and cultured delivery. Remarkably,
while he addressed the invisible millions at home, Mrs Baldwin sat in
the studio knitting in front of her husband to create the appropriate
ambience for Baldwin's broadcast.[65]

MacDonald attacked the opposition parties for bringing down the
Labour government. In turn, his opponents turned their fire on the
Anglo-Soviet Treaty, which prepared the ground for the shock news of
the Zinoviev Letter during the last week of the campaign. The 1924
general election will always be remembered for the notorious Zinoviev
Letter – revealed four days before polling day by the *Daily Mail*. On
its front page, the newspaper carried the sensational headline: 'Civil
War Plot by Socialists' Masters: Moscow Orders To Our Reds: Great Plot
Disclosed.'[66] On 9 October the Foreign Office received a copy of a letter
supposedly written by Gregori Zinoviev, the President of the Comintern,
to the Arthur MacManus, the British Communist and representative on
the Comintern Executive. The infamous 'Zinoviev Letter' called on the
CPGB to stir up insurrection and revolution in Britain. In Labour legend
it has always been roundly condemned as a timely 'Red Scare', used by
Labour's opponents in the Tory press (especially the *Daily Mail*), Conservative Central Office and members (or former members) of MI6 (Secret
Intelligence Service) to bring down the government and restore the Tory
Party to office. All of these groups had a hatred of Russian Communism
and were highly suspicious of the Labour governments' recognition

of the Soviet regime and its endeavours to promote commercial links between Russia and Britain.

In 1924 the Special Intelligence Service submitted copies of the Zinoviev Letter to Sir Eyre Crowe and J. D. Gregory at the Foreign Office and also forwarded it to four other Ministries. While the Foreign Office officials apparently believed that the Zinoviev Letter was genuine, they were divided over whether it should be published and a protest made to the Soviet government. At the Northern Department, William Strang provided a long and detailed minute, but only once he knew that Crowe was adamant that the letter had to be published. Even so, as it would upset Anglo-Soviet relations, Strang advised against publication, a view shared by Gregory.[67] Gorodetsky suggests that 'both MacDonald and Crowe are to be blamed in the different stages of dealing with the letter'.[68] MacDonald received the letter in Manchester while on his punishing election campaign and drafted a minute for Crowe, though he warned that the authenticity of the letter had to be established. In fact, MacDonald never approved the dispatch of the protest note sent by the Foreign Office to Rakovsky, the Soviet chargé d'affaires in London.

The first repercussion of the Zinoviev Letter during the 1924 election was that it highlighted the central question of Anglo-Soviet relations, thereby preventing MacDonald from limiting the Labour campaign to the relatively minor issue of the withdrawn Campbell prosecution. Famously, on first hearing of the Zinoviev Letter, Jimmy Thomas declared: 'We're sunk' – in reference to Labour's chances of returning to office after the election. Labour's opponents – particularly the Conservatives – used every opportunity to exploit the issue of the danger of communism in a most bitterly fought election campaign.

In Labour folklore the Zinoviev Letter gained notoriety by discrediting its first administration during the 1924 election campaign when an anti-communism atmosphere was rife. Since then, the episode of the Zinoviev Letter has been the subject of constant conspiracy theories surrounding its authenticity. At the time, the Labour Cabinet considered it a forgery. An inquiry by the Baldwin Government in 1928 pronounced the Zinoviev Letter genuine, including the testimony of the businessman, Donald im Thurn, who claimed to have secured the original letter from British Communists via a Russian businessman. In 1967 an investigation by *The Sunday Times'* Insight team that uncovered an alleged plot by forgers, led to a three-year enquiry (1970) by Millicent Bagot, a retired MI5 official. Her report was not published, but 'remained the definitive internal account of the Zinoviev Letter' until Nigel West and Oleg Tsarev's book, *The Crown Jewels* (1998), based on the newly opened KGB archives prompted Robin Cook, the Foreign Secretary in the New Labour Government, to commission a fresh official investigation.

Three-quarters of a century after the fall of the first Labour government, the Foreign and Commonwealth Office published a 126-page report on the Zinoviev Letter. On 3 February 1999, Cook announced that Gill Bennett had compiled the report after an extensive 12-month investigation into every available source including MI5 and MI6 archives, as well as American and Russian records. Such a comprehensive investigation still could not identify the authors of the Zinoviev Letter, the architects of the notorious 'Red Scare'. A 'best guess' was that White Russian Intelligence Services employed a forgery ring in the Baltic countries and links with 'certain members' of British Intelligence to circulate the fictitious letter. Whereas a number of MI5 and MI6 officers, such as Stewart Menzies, a future Head of MI6, had plotted against the 1924 Labour government, the Bennett Report concluded there was no evidence of a general Foreign Office conspiracy against the Bolsheviks and MacDonald's administration.[69] However, according to Jonathan Pile, the Bennett Report failed to disclose significant operational details from MI6 that could throw important light on the role of British Intelligence either in ordering the Zinoviev Letter or perhaps being deceived by White Russian forgers. Also, Major Joseph Ball of MI5 had played a crucial role as a link with Thurn, who died in 1930 in mysterious circumstances, and later in covering up the plot surrounding the Zinoviev Letter.[70] From 1927, Ball worked in Conservative Party Central Office where he supplied confidential reports on the Second Labour Government based on intelligence from informants within Labour circles.[71] If it ever existed, the original Zinoviev Letter has never been produced – only copies or copies of copies of the document have been published. The story of the Zinoviev Letter – and its effects on the first Labour government – have echoed down the generations to the more recent allegations of the conspiracy to destabilise and undermine Harold Wilson's Labour government in the mid 1970s.[72]

After a short-lived spell in office, Labour had lost the 1924 general election, though the party had fielded more candidates than in any previous contest in its history – 514 compared to 427 in 1923. As a result, only 40 parliamentary seats had been lost. Remarkably, Labour had polled a million *more* votes on a turnout of 77.0 per cent of the electorate than in December 1923. Of the total votes cast, Labour secured 5,489,087 – as against 4,439,780 in 1923 – while the Liberal share of the vote fell disastrously from 4,301,481 in 1923 to 2,928,737.

In fact, it was the Liberal Party that was roundly beaten in the 1924 general election. The *Daily Herald* pointed to the 'Tory electoral avalanche, which has swept away practically the whole of the Liberal Party'. Symbolic of the Liberal rout was the Labour lawyer Rosslyn Mitchell's defeat of Asquith at Paisley. The Liberal leader had made his last speech in the Commons on the Campbell Case and was never to return. Eventually he took the Earldom of Oxford and Asquith, a title that Lady Salisbury likened to 'a suburban villa calling itself Versailles'.

The 1924 general election was a triumph for Stanley Baldwin and the Conservatives. His party had run virtually the same number of candidates – 534 compared to 536 – but increased its vote from 5,514,541 in 1923 to 7,854,523. The Conservative leader returned to 10 Downing Street with a commanding victory. When the new House of Commons assembled, 419 MPs represented the largest total in the Conservative Party's history – in contrast to 12 months before when Baldwin surveyed their worst electoral performance since the Tory calamity of 1906. Though defeated in the 'Red Letter' campaign, Labour in 1924 had established itself as a party of government, whereas the decimated Liberal Party was never to assume office again in twentieth-century Britain.

8
Political Aftermath

On 29 October, despite polling an additional million votes, Labour suffered a decisive defeat in the general election that took Stanley Baldwin, not Ramsay MacDonald, back to 10 Downing Street. Philip Snowden admitted to Fred Jowett, the only Cabinet minister to lose his seat, 'I am terribly distressed at the whole business of this General Election. I get no satisfaction from the increased Labour vote.' Snowden added later that MacDonald had 'thrown away the greatest opportunity whichever came to a party and has landed us with five years of Tory government.[1] Ethel Snowden, away on a Canadian lecture tour, attracted the attention of the British press when she confirmed her husband's disenchantment with MacDonald: 'The British Labour Party has been the victim of the worst leadership of modern times,' she told her audience in Winnipeg.[2]

When the Cabinet gathered on 31 October, MacDonald entered the Cabinet Room just before 10.30 a.m. 'pale and serious, as if not certain what his reception was going to be.'[3] Thomas Jones, who was deputising for Maurice Hankey, recalled that in the circumstances the Cabinet attempted to 'maintain a cheerful countenance'. The main item of business was a heated discussion of the election, the impact of the Zinoviev Letter, and the role of the Foreign Office. Remarkably, no FO official alerted MacDonald to the press revelations, which had not reached him until the Friday night in South Wales via a *Daily News* correspondent. Ill prepared, he didn't comment publicly until three days later after he had met J. D. Gregory on the Monday. 'I felt like a man sewn in a sack and thrown into the sea,' MacDonald remarked.[4] The post-mortem finally led to the establishment of a committee consisting of Haldane, Parmoor, Henderson and MacDonald to investigate the authenticity of the Zinoviev letter. After examining the role of Scotland Yard, the War

Office and Sir Eyre Crowe at the Foreign Office, the Committee's report that there was no conclusive evidence on the question of authenticity was circulated at the final Cabinet meeting on 4 November and a public communiqué issued. Amid the allegations and rebuttals over the last 80 years, as we have noted, the original Zinoviev Letter has never been produced for inspection.

According to the Webbs, the Labour Cabinet went its separate ways from its last meeting 'amid kindly words from one another'. Yet after nearly ten months in office, MacDonald, however, remained an elusive mystery. 'We certainly did not expect and cannot explain either the brilliant success of his handling of the Franco-German situation or the shocking fiasco of the last phase of his Premiership – culminating in the complete collapse of any Cabinet leadership in the General Election,' Beatrice Webb confessed.[5]

In the new House of Commons there was a significant change in the fortunes of the three parties. The Conservatives had achieved a major victory. In the new House of Commons they now had 413 MPs – an increase of 155 members – whereas the loss of 40 seats reduced the Labour contingent to 151 MPs. However, this defeat confirmed Labour as still being the progressive force in British politics. In 1924 the Liberals, who fielded only 340 candidates compared to 453 in 1923, were reduced to a rump of 40 MPs at Westminster after losing 118 seats. The Liberal vote had plummeted dramatically from 4,301,481 to 2,928,737 (from 29.7 per cent to 17.8 per cent of the total votes cast), including the defeat of Asquith, the party leader, at Paisley. In the wake of this disastrous set of results, the Liberal Party began to collapse throughout the country.

By comparison, despite losing 42 seats – Labour had 191 MPs at the general election and two by-election successes in 1924 – the party's vote had increased from 4,439,780 in 1923 to 5,489,087 (rising from 30.7 per cent to 33.3 per cent of the total votes cast).[6] As David Dutton has written, Labour and Conservatives were now the beneficiaries of two-party politics that consigned the Liberals to third place in the British electoral system. The outlook for the Liberals was depressing as the party was challenged successfully by Labour in industrial areas and by the Conservatives in rural constituencies.[7] The Conservative vote had increased from 5,514,541 (38.0 per cent) in 1923 to 7,854,523 (46.8 per cent) in 1924. In addition to the growth in the electorate of about 447,927, there had been a very high turnout of 77.0 per cent in the poll (80.0 per cent in Wales) compared to 71.1 per cent recorded in 1923. In Aberavon, MacDonald held his seat with a reduced majority of

2000 – compared to 3500 in 1923 – in a straight fight with the Liberal candidate.[8]

Quite clearly MacDonald's handling of the Campbell Case had been poor and the Zinoviev Letter was a distraction from the main issues of the election. Owing to its minority position in the Commons, MacDonald's administration was always likely to fall once the Liberals had determined to oppose the Anglo-Soviet Treaties. Beatrice Webb told C. P. Scott that MacDonald had sought a dissolution as he knew the Liberals meant to defeat them on the Russian Treaty a month later and thought it was 'better for them to anticipate their fate.'[9]

However, the demise of the Labour ministry raised the immediate issues of MacDonald's leadership, relationships within the party, and future prospects for Labour – all of which proved more favourable than at first appeared on the evening of defeat. In fact, there was a sense of achievement and success in the Labour ranks at what government had accomplished in office. Despite the setback of the 1924 October election defeat, Labour's momentum was given a new impetus by the decline of the Liberal Party. 'For some time I felt things were shaping themselves towards the disappearance of the Liberal Party, but I did not think it would come so quickly,' Stanley Baldwin told Thomas Jones. The Tory leader believed that Labour should then eliminate the Communists: 'Then we shall have two Parties, the Party of the Right and the Party of the Left.'[10]

Of course, this was never to be entirely, or immediately, the case. The Liberal Party did re-emerge as a parliamentary force sufficient to support a second minority Labour government in 1929–31, after which it divided into three groups: a radical rump led by Lloyd George; the centrist free traders under Sir Herbert Samuel, who joined but later left the National government; and Sir John Simon, whose National Liberals eventually merged with the Conservative Party. In the 1920s the Liberal decline was, however, more immediately obvious at the local level where Liberalism survived in numbers and influence in the Celtic fringes of Britain, the West Country and in various English towns such as Huddersfield.[11]

The decline of local Liberal Parties was nowhere more evident than in one of its old heartlands – the textile district of the West Riding of Yorkshire. The industrial seats of this region had become a battleground where Liberal and Labour rivalry was fought out in the 1890s and the early twentieth century. What became obvious from this conflict was that the Liberal decline was not simply due to the internecine conflict that developed during the First World War. It was largely due to the fact that the Liberal Party had long neglected its working-class vote, which was now shifting to Labour. Faced with such a deteriorating situation, the constituency Liberal Parties were forced into municipal, and even parliamentary, alliances with the local Conservative Parties. Such pacts might have been temporarily advantageous but ultimately contributed to the further erosion of political support for the party. After 1924 the Liberals could no longer successfully challenge Labour in many urban constituencies where Liberal support had remained firm since 1918.[12]

By the 1920s, when many Liberals were feeling uncertain about the future of their party, there was confusion about which political direction to follow. Whilst many favoured a move to the Right rather than the Left, shortly after the 1924 general election disaster, Thomas A. Jones, the defeated Liberal candidate for Keighley, advised the local Divisional Liberal Council that 'the further we turn away from the right and from the patchwork of compromise . . . the more quickly we shall recover the confidence of the same and moderate workmen without whose support we shall never regain our ascendancy of our best days.'[13]

In some areas, the Conservatives also began to abandon their municipal alliances with the Liberals that had so dominated the politics of the West Yorkshire textile district since 1907. These pacts – known as Citizens or anti-Socialist alliances – were normally formalised affairs, supported by joint meetings and agreements, and continued in a few towns, such as Halifax and Huddersfield even until the 1960s. However, in the main, they broke down once the Liberals could no longer secure the municipal successes necessary to justify such an arrangement. In Leeds, for instance, the alliance worked well only until 1925, after which the local Conservatives encouraged some of the Liberal leaders and other councillors to defect to them in 1926. The Cabinet Committee of Leeds Liberal Federation then decided 'to urge all ward Liberal Associations in the City . . . to adopt a Liberal Candidate in each ward forthwith.'[14]

By the same token, Labour began to fill the gaps left by the Liberal Party at both parliamentary and local level. Of the 23 seats in the textile district of Yorkshire, Labour won an increasing and dominating proportion. Having won one seat in the 1918 general election, it secured ten in 1922, ten in 1923 and 11 in 1924. The Liberals declined, correspondingly, from 11 in 1918 (ten Coalition Liberals and one Liberal) to six (five Liberal and one Coalition Liberal) in 1922, to nine Liberals in 1923 and four in 1924. The Labour Party had replaced the Liberals to become the largest parliamentary party in the Yorkshire woollen and worsted textile region of Yorkshire.[15]

This Labour success was also evident at local level in a number of West Yorkshire towns where the party won a steady rise in number of municipal seats – from 82 (November 1923), to 90 (November 1924) and 106 (November 1925), reaching a peak of 161 in November 1928.[16] In Bradford Labour was the largest municipal party in 1919 and again between 1926 and 1929, after being on an equal footing with the Liberals and Conservatives combined in 1923 and 1924. From 1926–29 Labour was easily the largest party on the Bradford council. By 1929 Labour had achieved this position in Wakefield with 22 seats and was then equal to the Conservatives and Liberals combined. In Leeds Labour fortunes improved by the late 1920s, making the party the largest group on the council.[17] During the 1930s Labour controlled many towns and cities in the West Yorkshire textile district, despite the demoralising impact on the labour movement of the collapse of the second Labour administration and the controversial formation of the National government headed by MacDonald.[18] Labour's electoral victories in the 1920s in the textile district of West Yorkshire are not necessarily untypical of the rest of the country. There is significant evidence of Labour success and Liberal decline in other areas.

In the Black Country in the West Midlands, Labour won four of the ten parliamentary seats in 1918, and the same number in the 1922, 1923 and the 1924 elections before gaining nine of ten seats in 1929. Although the *Birmingham Gazette*, after the 1924 general election felt that the Zinoviev Letter 'had not increased the confidence of the electorate in Mr. MacDonald and the Russian Treaty', it is clear Labour had not done badly, despite its Black Country parliamentary vote falling from 41 per cent to 37.8 per cent between the 1923 and 1924 general elections.[19] Surprisingly, and against the national trend, the total parliamentary vote of the Liberals in the ten Black Country seats rose from 15.89 per cent in 1923 to 19.5 per cent in 1924, although this can be accounted for by various local factors. However, the Liberal Party posed little long-term threat to Labour, although its temporary improvement might well have been at the expense of Labour. Even the Conservative challenge might not have made much difference. Of the 1924 general election, John Ward has concluded that 'From these figures it is apparent that the Labour vote in the Black Country was not significantly affected by the Conservatives' Red Scare Campaign.'[20] Both nationally and locally, as we have seen, the Labour Party had not done badly in the 1924 election since its vote had increased and it had moved decisively ahead of the Liberal Party, despite losing parliamentary seats. Labour was soon recapturing any lost support and its success in this respect can be seen in the 1929 general election when the number of its MPs, down from 191 in 1923 to 151 in 1924, rose to 287 in 1929.

In complete contrast, the 1924 election was particularly profitable for the Conservative with their vote increasing from 5.5 million to almost 8 million and 419 MPs returned to Westminster – the greatest number in the party's history. Baldwin formed his second administration, offering the Foreign Office to Austen Chamberlain while Birkenhead took the India Office. Interestingly, Winston Churchill became a Chancellor of the Exchequer who could attract dissident Liberals to the Conservative fold. As Minister of Health, Neville Chamberlain pursued his interest in solid reform as an alternative to socialism. As John Charmley has written: 'This was the "beef" behind the Baldwinian rhetoric: Stanley soothed the customers and Neville provided them with the goods.'[21]

In 1924 MacDonald's first ministry created problems for the Labour Party and the PLP in the new relationship established during the period in office. There was a growing feeling within the Labour rank and file that the administration had not achieved what was expected or required. The formation of a liaison committee to act between the government and the PLP had not always worked effectively and, as we have seen, internal tensions had built up, particularly over Iraq and the sniping of the *Daily Herald*, as well as the general awkwardness of Labour left-wing MPs. The MFGB, and the miners' MPs in the Commons, were openly critical of the likely impact that the Dawes Report on the British coal industry. Disappointment grew within the Women's Sections of the Labour Party over Labour's official attitude towards birth control. Yet, at the same time party loyalty to MacDonald remained strong. As David Howell has stated, trade unionists, Labour conferences, divisional parties, the PLP and other sections of the Labour Party, increasingly supported Ramsay MacDonald's leadership during the 1920s.[22]

Within the PLP party loyalism was most evident, even after the disappointment of defeat in the 1924 election. Some critical voices were raised at first, however, over MacDonald's leadership – especially his mishandling of the Zinoviev Letter – as became evident on 3 December 1924 when the PLP met to elect its new officers. MacDonald observed, 'The Left Wing were out for my blood, and had not the sense to restrain itself' – implying that some of these were Labourites still disappointed at not obtaining office in 1924.[23] 'I should not be surprised if before Baldwin appeals to the electorate again, MacDonald will be out of the leadership of His Majesty's Opposition,' Beatrice Webb declared once the smoke of battle began to clear after the 1924 election. She added: '[I]f he is saved it will by the loyalty of Henderson, Clynes, and Sidney (Webb) and other members of the right wing.' In normal circumstances it would have been expected that MacDonald, the leader of the PLP and former

Prime Minister, should have been returned unopposed. However, the ILP MPs Jimmy Maxton and R. C. Wallhead, bitter that MacDonald had not brought forward a socialist programme during 1924, put forward George Lansbury's name for the leadership. Though the Poplar socialist refused to accept the nomination, there was also an attempt to postpone the election by Ben Smith and Jack Hayes of the Transport and General Workers' Union (TGWU), who felt that the decision should be held over until an inquiry into the Zinoviev Letter and the Soviet Treaty had been conducted. This initiative was probably driven by Ernest Bevin, the General Secretary of the TGWU, but was withdrawn when both MacDonald and Henderson accepted the need for an inquiry.[24]

In the event, MacDonald was re-elected as party leader with only 'five dissidents'.[25] David Howell suggests that there were 30 abstentions and that the five dissidents were Jimmy Maxton, George Buchanan, and Campbell Stephens, (all Clydesiders), George Barker, a South Wales miner who opposed the Ruhr settlement, and the Reverend Herbert Dunnico, the MP for Consett.[26] Even then, it was not all plain sailing for MacDonald. The new PLP Executive elected on 9 December 1924, included George Lansbury at the top of the poll with 67 votes. Bob Smillie, Snowden and Thomas, who might be relied upon to support the Labour leader, were second and third, but Jimmy Maxton and John Wheatley, the ILP representatives, were fourth and fifth equal on 52 and 51 votes, thus obtaining 20 or so votes more than their ILP strength would suggest. The loyal Arthur Henderson was returned a poor tenth, with 38 votes – possibly a reflection on his performance as Home Secretary.[27] While the majority of those returned to the PLP executive could be reckoned as MacDonald's supporters, there remained a small core – numbering at least three or four – persistently critical of MacDonald's record in office.

There was some volatility within Labour and PLP ranks throughout 1925, but the predominant trend was that MacDonald gradually regained total control of the Labour Party. In 1925 he and Henderson, the Party Secretary, dominated the annual party conference at Liverpool. The election of the PLP Executive in December 1925 demonstrated that the restoration of MacDonald's authority as party leader was complete. Snowden was now returned at the top of the poll with 104 votes, followed by William Graham (98) and Jimmy Thomas (86). Jimmy Maxton refused to stand again; John Wheatley was defeated with only 38 votes. Of MacDonald's main critics only George Lansbury, with 51 votes, was returned, but in tenth place.[28] During the next few years this position fluctuated, but the balance of power remained firmly with

MacDonald. The PLP Executive that began to emerge was effectively the one that formed the core of the second Labour government of 1929–31. The wholesale loss of PLP members into the government meant that an entirely different PLP emerged. A Consultative Committee was being formed in place of the Executive staffed by backbenchers.[29]

The PLP clearly came into line with MacDonald and so did the national Labour Party shortly after the fall of the first Labour government. There was some frustration from local constituency Labour Parties and trade union organisations that the Labour government had achieved so little in office. This was displayed, though dismissed, at the Labour Party Conference in the autumn of 1925. C. T. Cramp, the general secretary of the National Union of Railwaymen and President of Conference, in an adeptly stage-managed affair reiterated the successes of the Labour government. At the 1924 conference, Cramp had argued that the government had proved itself the 'equal of any of its predecessors in its fitness to undertake the responsibilities of government'.[30] With even greater praise he added that 'You have done good work, you have left your mark on history by what you have done, and we are going to do our part in the districts so that you are not only returned to office but to power.'[31] At the 1925 conference he continued with the same theme, but warned of 'unscrupulous and skilfully organised resistance' from the vested interests of capitalism, although he was quick to reject the revolutionary tactics of communists.[32] His great concern was that Labour must develop its policies, organisation and methods. However, his chief purpose was to pre-empt the criticism of the Labour government that was to emerge at the conference.

One of the main debates was not just about general policies, but 'if a Labour government came into office, how would it approach the problem of the Mines, the problem of Foreign Affairs, the problem of the Franchise, and so forth.'[33] The aim of the Labour Party Executive was that this would emerge and be discussed through the Party Conference and its established procedures. The main criticism came from George Simpson of the Wallasey Trades and Labour Party, who put forward an amendment to the National Executive Committee resolution criticising 'the inadequate declaration of the policy of the Party which exists to achieve the foundations of the Socialist State' and instructing the NEC to formulate detailed policies on the 'nationalisation of land, banks, mines, insurance and other fundamental questions'.[34] Claiming to represent the rank and file movement throughout the country, Simpson asked MacDonald to accept his amendment in the spirit of good advice and reflected that many grassroots Labour supporters 'had been compelled to sit in silence too long, while the Party leaders had been endeavouring to carry out a policy of gradualism and obscurantism whilst starvation has been staring the rank and file in the face'.[35] However, the amendment was opposed by C. P. Trevelyan and MacDonald and was lost.

Another amendment, presented by Arthur Ferguson of Glasgow Trades Council and Labour Party and representing the views of 15 local Divisional Labour Parties and 30 ILP branches in the Glasgow region, demanded the overthrow of capitalist society by revolt if necessary. Ferguson condemned the policies and actions of the first government, in the words of another delegate, as, 'A model example of crawling, slithering gradualism.'[36] Ferguson's amendment was, likewise, rejected.

This all pointed to disquiet amongst some constituency sections of the Labour Party about the performance of the first Labour government. However, Arthur Henderson controlled the Conference in such a way as to minimise the threat of revolt and to leave the conference able to pass resolutions to formulate policy in the time-honoured way. There was to be no revolt from the Labour Party rank and file, just as there was only limited and brief opposition from the PLP. Nevertheless, there was an element of division within the Labour leadership as a result of the first Labour government, most markedly between MacDonald and Snowden over foreign policy.

By the beginning of the 1920s, Snowden must have realised that there was only one person who could fill the niche within the Labour Party occupied by the ethical and non-trade unionist Ramsay MacDonald. Philip Snowden was never a serious candidate for the position of Chairman and leader of the Labour Party in 1922 but, in the leadership election, had voted for J. R. Clynes. Snowden did not feel that MacDonald would give the party 'a vigorous lead' and that his pre-war activities highlighted his 'passion for intrigue and compromise'.[37] These were comments probably written with the events of 1931 in mind but it is fair to recall that Snowden had come into conflict with MacDonald on this very matter at the ILP Conference in 1914. MacDonald and Snowden had clashed, over the implementation of the Dawes Report and the Geneva Protocol, although MacDonald seems to have considered Snowden Labour's only possible Chancellor of the Exchequer and was prepared to stick with him.

MacDonald and Snowden were also driven apart following the fall of the 1924 government. As we have seen, Snowden believed that the Campbell Case and the Zinoviev Letter affair were badly handled and that MacDonald was personally responsible for Labour's defeat.[38] During 1925, Snowden's name was mentioned, along with those of Arthur

Henderson and J. R. Clynes, as possible leaders of the Labour Party. Ernest Bevin and many other trade union leaders were beginning to wonder about the wisdom of continuing with MacDonald as leader and were toying with alternative names. But nothing came of this suggested palace revolution, although the soundings were indicative of the frustration that had developed towards MacDonald. Such feelings, as indicated by the changing mood of the PLP, were soon banished from thought.

Despite a sense of frustrated ambition, personal animosity and a drifting of Labour's course in the mid-term of Baldwin's Conservative government, Snowden attempted to heal the rift between MacDonald and himself. In 1927 he wrote a letter to MacDonald in which he argued that 'Now that the protocol has been buried at Geneva I do not see any reason why we cannot agree upon an agreed policy for securing its fundamental aims and disarmament.' But there were problems, and he continued:

> you must excuse me for writing quite plainly. I am expressing the feeling of all my colleagues who have talked with me on the subject. We are feeling somehow – it is difficult to explain – we cannot get inside you. You seem to be protected by some impenetrable barrier. I called it aloofness in my last letter. It was not so in the old days of the N.A.C.[39]

There is no record in MacDonald's correspondence of a response in Snowden's papers which were largely destroyed upon his death. Nevertheless, the matter became irrelevant as Labour geared itself up to the 1929 general election.

MacDonald emerged from the 1924 government with his reputation more or less intact and in a supreme and unchallenged position to lead the party to the next general election. The 1924 general election had strengthened the Labour Party at the expense of the Liberals and, despite some misgivings, MacDonald remained in a strong position as leader.

Within the Labour Party there were significant repercussions arising from the formation of the first Labour government despite moves, within the PLP and at Party Conference, to return quickly to normality. In particular, Labour leaders and the party were forced to think out their policies more clearly and to plan for the future when in office, despite their rejection of some of the criticisms at Party Conference. At the very least the Labour Party was now one of the two parties of government in Britain that could expect to win office and power. It was not surprising, therefore, that C. T. Cramp opened his presidential speech at the 1925 Party Conference as follows: 'the Labour movement as a whole is confronted with serious problems of policy, organisation, and methods of organisation that cannot be ignored and must be minimised by either the industrial or the political wing of our movement.'[40] Above all, he urged that a future Labour government to be clear on policies, mindful of the capitalist press which focused upon trivialities rather than principles, and aware of the inertia of public opinion and the opposition of vested interests. Drawing from his railway background, he argued that the Labour government's work had been preparatory like, 'the breakdown gang sent down the line to clear away the obstructions and to repair the track before the fast express sets out on its long nonstop run'.[41] In effect, the task of the Labour government had been to prepare the way, remove prejudice and misunderstanding, and to inspire the nation with confidence. However, this implied that a second Labour government would offer more detailed and considered policies that they would publicise well in advance of office, together with strategies to effect those policies despite the strong resistance of the vested interests of capitalism. Nevertheless, Labour was committed to working within the system and there would be no revolution by force.

Given the problems that the Campbell Case and the Zinoviev Letter posed for the Labour government, it is not surprising that the Labour Party had determined to detach itself from any unnecessary association with communism. As we have seen, the Labour Party took steps to limit the influence and power of communism at Labour Party conferences in the mid and late 1920s before seeking to eradicate Communist influence further in the 1930s. The CPGB was committed to affiliating to the Labour Party from its formation in 1920 until 1928, and again from 1933 onwards. However, the Labour Party had rejected any association with the CPGB and had made its first major thrust against the CPGB at its Edinburgh Conference in 1922, where, amongst other decisions, it was agreed that every person nominated to serve as a delegate would accept the constitution and principles of the Labour Party. This led to conflicts with some trade unions over the delegates they wanted and the need for some compromise.

This was not surprising given that the CPGB had criticised the Labour government over its failure to change British colonial attitudes towards the nationalist demands for independence in India and British imperial policy towards Iraq. Indeed, despite the Labour government's *de jure* recognition of Bolshevik Russia, the CPGB published 'The Future of the Labour Government – A Call to All Workers' in April 1924. It was a bitter condemnation of the administration's failure to use the power of the state to promote the interest of the working class in Britain and abroad. 'The Labour Government has shown itself the servant of the bourgeoisie...the Labour Cabinet had become the missionaries of a new imperialism' was typical of the critical language used in the pamphlet.[42] Despite this criticism the Sixth Congress of the CPGB in May 1924 had not abandoned its attempts to secure affiliation to the Labour Party but directed its criticisms squarely at Ramsay MacDonald rather than the Labour Party itself.[43] Nonetheless, the Labour Party had continued to distance itself from the CPGB and its supporters – much as it had done before the formation of the first Labour government.

On 2 September 1924, the NEC had endorsed two resolutions – that CPGB affiliation should be rejected and that no Communist should be allowed to stand as a parliamentary or local Labour Party candidate – which were put forward at the twenty-fourth annual Party Conference, held in London on 8 and 9 October 1924. A third NEC resolution was also put to conference stating 'That no member of the Communist Party shall be eligible for membership of the Labour Party.'

All three resolutions were bitterly fought. Frank Hodges, MP, presented the NEC case that the principles and objectives of the two parties were different: 'We cannot have as a Party, the obligation put upon us to give credentials to candidates for Parliament or candidates for Local Authorities who do not accept the fundamental view of our task and our progress.'[44] G. A. Spencer, MP, concurred, fearing the loss of electoral support if Labour did not disassociate itself from the revolutionary aims of the CPGB.[45] William Paul (Rusholme Labour Party) maintained that the CPGB wished to use all means to get rid of capitalism, but did not necessarily accept that Parliament 'was a constructive organisation for the working classes'.[46] Harry Pollitt, who later became the Secretary of the CPGB, stated that the three resolutions would simply split the Labour movement.[47]

The first two resolutions had been endorsed by the Conference, but Communist affiliation was overwhelmingly rejected by 4,115,000 to 224,000 in a climate influenced by the Campbell Case and the Zinoviev Letter.[48] At this point the Labour Party Conference added another rule to its Standing Orders which prevented resolutions, and thus affiliation, being voted on for another three years.[49] The third resolution was then referred back to the NEC which re-presented a new form of the resolution at the 1925 Labour Party Conference together with another asking that electing or appointing bodies should not select known Communists to represent them.[50]

The supporters of the CPGB attempted to get the new third resolution referred back to the NEC for further consideration, but there were only 321,000 votes in favour with 2,870,000 against.[51] In October 1924 MacDonald concluded the argument for the NEC, pointing out that there were 30 out of 600 Local Labour Parties 'using exactly the same language' in 'machine-made resolutions' of support for the CPGB.[52] It was clear that the Labour Party would never allow the CPGB to affiliate, especially in the climate of the CPGB's hostility to the first Labour Government. Further moves to exclude Communists were endorsed at the 1927 Labour Party Conference.

The CPGB's criticism of the TUC for calling off the General Strike of 1926, the formation of the National Left-Wing Movement within the Labour Party by the CPGB, and the previous reaction against the CPGB as a result of the Zinoviev Letter all strengthened the reaction against communism. These led to a wave of expulsions of Communist-dominated constituency Labour Parties in South Wales and London in 1927. Eventually, the CPGB wound up the National Left-Wing Movement. The emergence of the 'Class Against Class' policy for the CPGB and communism worldwide led to Communists rejecting the association with the Labour Party, damning it as the 'third capitalist' party in Britain.[53] While the Labour Party was always opposed to communism, its sense of hostility strengthened during and after the period of the first Labour government. Similarly, the trade unions reaction against Communist influence was strong. Walter Citrine, the Assistant General Secretary of the TUC at the time of the General Strike and subsequently General Secretary, wrote a pamphlet entitled *Democracy or Disruption: An Examination of Communist Influence on the Trade Unions*. In this he condemned the Minority Movement as a disruptive Communist organisation that 'owed its origin' to 'the Red International', which fought for 'the revolutionary overthrow by violence of the social system'. The trade union movement had, therefore, to abandon its negative attitude towards the Minority Movement and be prepared to confront it.[54] In fact, this is precisely what the TUC, Citrine and Ernest Bevin did throughout the rest of the inter-war years culminating in the Black Circulars of 1934 which banned Communists taking up official posts in unions and trades councils.[55]

Indeed, just as the first Labour government had been a major turning point in Labour attitudes towards the CPGB, so the General Strike of 1926 had acted as the catalyst for the residual trade union support for the CPGB. The nine days in May, when the TUC brought out up to two million workers in support of about 800,000 or so miners faced with wage reductions, had failed to secure the defence of wages and conditions of miners. In its wake, the CPGB had attacked the TUC leaders for perpetuating 'the greatest crime that has ever been permitted, not only against the miners but against the working class of Great Britain and the whole world.[56] Relations between the TUC leadership and the CPGB broke down over trade union activities, but even more so as it became obvious that after the failure of the General Strike, the trade union movement bagan to place its faith in the politics of Labour as much as the economics of the strike weapon.

In the wake of the demise of the first Labour government, there had been some minor moves to the Left and criticism of MacDonald. However, what emerged most strongly was how the Labour Party rallied around MacDonald and strengthened his leadership. The PLP and the Labour Party moved to the Right, developed policies which MacDonald and Henderson advocated and strongly rejected communism. The failure of trade unionism in the General Strike of 1926 merely strengthened MacDonald's hand and there were attempts to heal the rifts between MacDonald and other prominent Labour leaders. Underpinning all this was the fact that Labour was growing as a local political force, which became evident in the general election of May 1929 when Labour almost doubled its parliamentary representation in the House of Commons. Between defeat in October 1924 and the general election of May 1929, Labour strengthened greatly in organisation, unity and focus even though the first past the post structure of British parliamentary politics left it, once again, as a minority government. The compensation was that, by then, Labour was the largest party in British politics and its gains, in some senses, were partly derived from the confidence, image and strategy reaped from the experiences of 1924.

9
Conclusion

A quick résumé of the history of Britain's first Labour government would maintain that it was a minority administration, lucky to be in office, of short duration and achieved little in policy beyond the important Wheatley Housing Act that subsidised the building of local authority rented accommodation for the working class and securing fleeting successes in foreign policy in Europe. Indeed, Britain's first Labour government has generally been portrayed as a mere *cul de sac* in the overall history of the Labour Party.

This book challenges such notions and maintains that its true role is more central than this. Britain's first Labour government was a sensitive indicator of how much Labour had progressed from its formation in 1900 as the Labour Representation Committee. In particular, MacDonald's minority administration was a useful mile-post at which the party could assess its progress, scrutinise its policies and develop its organisational strategies and skills. Above all, 1924 legitimised Labour as the new representative of progressive forces in British politics, helped to dispatch the Liberal Party to political oblivion and shaped Labour, as Stanley Baldwin observed, as the leading British political party of the Left.[1] The first Labour government was thus vital in legitimising the new post-war democracy and in reshaping British parliamentary and local politics during the inter-war years – the realignment of political parties following the fall of the Lloyd George Coalition government in 1922. It is thus in terms of its long-term impact and influence, rather than just its immediate successes or failures, that we must judge its achievement.

However, governments and political parties have invariably been judged by their apparent immediate successes and failures. In the case of Britain's first Labour government, its achievements have normally been overlooked. However, although this administration was limited in

199

what it could achieve during its brief existence of 287 days, it was more successful than it is often portrayed as being. Although not avowedly socialist, in the way the post-war Attlee governments were, the first Labour government placed markers, modest as they were, of Labour's ultimate intent of implementing social reform. What then did it achieve?

Britain's first Labour government was immediately faced with one significant decision – what to do about its commitment to public ownership, the famed nationalisation of industry to which it had become pledged in 1918. Support for public ownership and the introduction of the Capital Levy were dropped at the outset, as the Labour leadership recognised that its minority position would not allow such policies to be achieved. In fact, it was part of the purpose of MacDonald's triumphalist January 1924 meeting held at the Albert Hall, on the eve of assuming power, to convey this message of moderation, gradualism and delayed expectation to its fervent and expectant supporters. It was also clear that the first Labour administration's *raison d'être* was to establish Labour's fitness to govern. Having made this decision, MacDonald committed his colleagues to pursuing existing government policy. There were Labour initiatives in education and housing, but they did not come to fruition until Labour was out of office. More significant was the realm of foreign policy where MacDonald, Snowden and the Labour leaders committed themselves to their long-held belief that a new climate of international cooperation had not to be engendered in order to avoid another Great War and that the German reparation issue, if not solved, could become a major source of future conflict.

All governments inherit some of the policies of their predecessors, which they can change or continue at their will either with the support of, or opposition from, the civil service and other political interests. Given its minority position the first Labour government was not mindful to much change in direction. It maintained, through default, the existing 'Zionist' policies in Palestine, although it extolled a more Liberal view than its predecessors. It retained the old imperialist attitudes towards India, even though many Labour leaders favoured the development of a federal constitution rather than the diarchy offered by the 1919 Act. It was determined to justify the RAF's bombing of tribesmen a hundred miles or so from Basra in Iraq. It finalised the detailed arrangements for the settlement in Ireland. Indeed, in foreign affairs it attached itself more to the Union Jack and Union Flag than the Red Flag.

Also, Arthur Henderson, the Home Secretary, proved as intransigent in dealing with the treatment of alien immigration and in industrial relations as any of his predecessors. Indeed, in dealing with the latter he was particularly insensitive. He was unwilling to reinstate the policemen dismissed for striking in 1919, despite his favourable attitude towards their position before assuming office and despite the pressure from Jack Hayes, the General Secretary of the Police and Prison Officers. Faced with a dock dispute, and a transport strike, he responded by introducing emergency measures, reactivating the Supply and Transport Committee – and by indicating that the government was prepared to use troops. Moreover, he threatened to use the Emergency Powers Act of 1920. His dealings with the Miners' Federation of Great Britain were no more tactful during their dispute. In fact, it would be fair to suggest that Henderson's continuance of the industrial policies of the previous government did little to endear him, or the first Labour government, to the trade union movement. Henderson's time as Home Secretary was not his finest moment, but he was not entirely to blame for its failure to promote improved industrial relations. The first Labour government passed an Agricultural Wages Bill through Parliament at the end of July 1924, but a Liberal amendment deprived it of its main purpose which was to set up a Central Board which could force local committees to impose county wage rates.[2]

This continuity with the past was equally evident, if not more so, in the economic policies adopted by the new government. Philip Snowden, the Chancellor of the Exchequer, was a 'Gladstonian' Liberal who believed in free trade and balanced budgets, and that socialist measures would come out of a surplus in budget income. He was therefore reluctant to spend substantial amounts of money on schemes to deal with unemployment, which he felt would be a waste if the world economy and free trade revived. As a result Labour's unemployment policy did little more than tidy over unemployment through the winter months by offering short-term public works schemes, much as previous governments had done. Labour's main concession to the unemployed was to introduce the 1924 National Insurance Act, which liberalised unemployment benefits by extending benefits from 26 to 41 weeks and standardising benefit arrangements, although the 'genuinely seeking work' clause was also introduced. The 'Housewife's Budget' was also overblown in its benefits for the working classes, though Snowden claimed that it was 'the greatest step ever taken towards the Radical idea of the breakfast table'.[3] In fact it did little beyond reducing indirect taxation by £29 millions, direct taxation by £14 millions and removing the McKenna Duties on motor cars. There were only modest measures for the working-class supporters of Labour.

Despite the importance of the women's movement within the Labour Party, the first Labour government did little to meet its needs. John Wheatley, the Minster of Health and Housing, would not commit the government to promoting birth control measures when he met a deputation of women in May 1924. Also, women's unemployment was to remain a neglected area of interest. Margaret Bondfield and Marion Phillips were both members of the philanthropic and voluntary Central Committee on Women's Training and Employment, an organisation financed by government which was committed to training unemployed working-class women for domestic employment. Involved in government or on the fringes of power, these two women ensured that the first Labour government continued with this subcontracting activity and increased Labour's financial involvement in its activities.[4] There was nothing new, then, in the first Labour government giving limited support to voluntary subcontracting bodies training a small number of unemployed women for unpopular, badly paid and uninsured domestic work.

There were, of course, some new initiatives and departures. The most lauded of these were to be found in housing and education. John Wheatley's Housing Act financed for ten years a boom in local authority rented accommodation, which went some way to meet the appalling shortage of rented accommodation and was far more relevant to working-class needs than the Chamberlain Act of 1923, which focused upon the subsidising of houses for sale. There were also improved tenancy rights. C. P. Treveleyan's educational schemes provided a little more money for education and increased the number of scholarship places available in secondary schools for local authority children. Snowden also began the process that led to the formation of the National Grid for electricity distribution, which ensured the more efficient use of electricity. These were all significant achievements in their own right and were certainly more lasting than developments in foreign policy, which many contemporaries felt were the crowning achievements of Labour's period in office.

MacDonald's accomplished handing of the Dawes Report on reparations, and his diplomacy with the Geneva Protocol, have drawn much approval. It is clear that the Inter-Allied talks in London in July and August 1924 paved the way for MacDonald's success in preparing the ground for progress on collective security through the League of Nations. Despite the battles involved, international security seemed more likely at the end of 1924 than at the beginning. Moreover, Robert Cecil, a former Conservative Under-Secretary at the Foreign Office and stalwart of the League of Nations, rightly reflected that MacDonald was supporting the French, making compromises and encouraging the climate of international co-operation security in which the League of Nations had a role to play.[5]

There were, of course, consequences to this comparative success. There was criticism from those like E. D. Morel, who was a leading figure in the Parliamentary Labour Party and had been a founder of the Union of Democratic Control during the Great War, that Parliament, rather than a Foreign Secretary and Foreign Office, should run the nation's foreign policy. In addition it was noted by the *Daily Herald* that whilst Britain had a good and successful Foreign Secretary in MacDonald it had the 'disadvantage of having no effective Prime Minister'.[6] In the end, of course, the first Labour government pushed one of its international policies too far for many Liberal MPs. Although staunchly anti-Communist, it pressed ahead too rapidly with the Soviet Treaties. As discussions continued they caused unease within Labour's own ranks but, more significantly, amongst the Liberal MPs who could, at a moment's notice, withdraw their support from the Labour government. In addition, the decision to prosecute J. R. Campbell under the Incitement to Mutiny Act for calling upon troops not to fire on strikers was the final straw. The hasty and mishandled decision to withdraw the prosecution was considered by many Liberal MPs to have been the result of the government's decision to bow to left-wing pressure. The Liberal motion in the Commons in October 1924 effectively became one of no-confidence in the government. Defeated on this vote, the first Labour government resigned and a general election was called. An exhausted MacDonald, who was under pressure from several quarters by this time, was probably happy at the turn of events and almost certainly aware that his party had little chance of securing a general election victory. However, the last few days of the election campaign were marked by the *Daily Mail* publishing the so-called 'Zinoviev Letter', a document purporting to come from the Executive Committee of the Communist International (the Comintern) urging the Communist Party of Great Britain to prepare for revolution by, amongst other things, infiltrating the Labour Party. Although almost certainly a forgery, this livened up an election which Labour would have lost in any case.

Yet there were far more significant and long-term consequences of the formation of a Labour government than the policies it initiated and pursued in office. In reality, the first Labour government was of immense importance to the whole Labour movement since it legitimised the Labour Party as a party of government. In less than 24 years from its formation, the Labour Party had assumed government office and destroyed the established two-party parliamentary political arrangement. Within six years of the 1918 Franchise Act, which had established the basis of modern British parliamentary democracy, it had formed a minority government, albeit in odd circumstances, after the Conservatives failed to secure an overall majority in the 1923 election. The Liberal Party, which had fallen behind Labour to become the third party in the Commons, generally gave its support to the new administration, although MacDonald was clear from the outset that he would not contemplate a Lib–Lab pact or understanding. In fact, he challenged his opponents to defeat his government on a substantial issue, if they wished to rid themselves of his administration, safe in the knowledge that it was unlikely the opposition parties wanted an early general election. Eventually, the Liberals' decision to defeat Labour proved unwise and costly at the 1924 election. At this point the inevitable had happened, the Liberal Party declined, never to recover to its former glory, and the Labour Party emerged even stronger to become the largest party in the House of Commons in 1929 and the progressive party of British politics.

The formation of the first Labour government also changed relationships within the Labour Party, making the party aware of the need to improve its communications with any future Labour government. The attempts to do this did not work in 1924, the Labour government failing to recognise the concerns of both the Labour Party and the Parliamentary Labour Party at the lack of coordination between it, the Government and its ministers. Of course, such a re-examination of relationships raised issues of primacy. Did Party and Conference have supremacy in deciding the policies and actions of a Labour government or was a Labour government responsible to the voters rather than the party? These questions became recurrent in British Labour history and the usual pattern was for the Labour Party Conference to impose limits on the actions of their leaders, which were largely ignored once a Labour Government was formed. This was most blatantly obvious when Clem Attlee formed a Labour government in 1945 without seeking the permission of the Labour Party, which had required such action after the departure of Ramsay MacDonald in 1931. This tension about primacy was apparent in the 1925 Labour Party Conference when moves to create a programme of Labour policies based upon conference resolutions and processed by a committee were rejected. Nevertheless, moves in the direction of considering and developing policy further continued apace, particularly under the leadership of Hugh Dalton in the 1930s and in the wake of MacDonald's ditching of the second Labour government in August 1931.

The first Labour government also made it clear that trade unions would not command any direct influence over government policies. Lewis Minkin in his book *Contentious Alliance* has argued that from the 1920s, and the time of the first Labour government, it was recognised that the Labour Party and trade unions existed in their separate spheres. Nevertheless, they were interconnected by a set of evolving rules which saw the Labour Party support the rights of trade unions to collective bargaining, and the need of the Labour Party and the Labour governments to maintain a degree of independence.[7] There were some obvious disagreements between the trade union leaders and the Labour Party, but often no obvious victor. The one stressed the democratic right to decide about wages and conditions of employment whilst the other claimed and operated a system of parliamentary privilege.[8] In the end, Labour governments and the trade-union base of the Labour Party have often travelled separately in their objectives – the one emphasising the needs of the British people whilst the other has generally protecting the sectional interests of their members. This separation, was already indicated in the industrial relations of the first Labour government and in the actions of Arthur Henderson.

The experiences of the first Labour government also finally shaped the attitude of Labour towards the Communist Party of Great Britain and, also, other political rivals on the Left of British politics. The Labour Party's rejection of the CPGB had begun before the 1924 Labour government came to office, but was considerably speeded up after the criticisms and actions of the communists whilst Labour was in power. It led, as we have seen, to Labour imposing restrictions upon trade unions, and other organisations, from sending Communist delegates to the Party Conference. Certainly, Harry Pollitt, Dr Saklatvala and other CPGB members were prevented from attending Labour Party conferences after 1925 as a result of the new resolutions. From then onwards Labour was wary of left-wing infiltration, whether by the CPGB, Militant Tendency or any other organisation, throughout is history. Morgan Phillips's 'Lost Sheep Files' of the 1940s are testament to that tradition of keeping a watching brief against infiltration, or entryism, by other left-wing organisations.[9] Stanley Baldwin, the Conservative Prime Minister, probably had it broadly correct in his assessment of politics in November 1924, when he informed Thomas Jones that 'For some time I felt things were shaping themselves towards the disappearance of the Liberal Party, but I did not think it would come so quickly. The next step must be the elimination of the Communists by Labour.'[10]

In many respects, then, the formation of the 1924 Labour government was a pivotal moment in the history of the Labour movement. It signalled the arrival of Labour as a major political force in British politics. It forced Labour to reconsider the need for improved communications within the party in times of office. It made Labour reconsider both its policies and their formulation. In addition, it required Labour to reconsider its precise relationship with trade unions and to eject political organisations who wished to use it as a platform for their own aims, most obviously the Communist Party of Great Britain. It gained many advantages as it conditioned itself to become an established party of government. In many respects it was assisted in these directions and initiatives by the fact that it was in office but not in power. The guilt of failure was not something that was going to stick to a government which was well short of a majority in Parliament.

This fact was soon recognised by C. T. Cramp, President of the Labour Party Conference in 1925, when having surveyed the triumph and pride of forming a government in 1924, and reflecting upon the problems of policy and organisation that confronted a Labour Party out of office, he maintained that 'in my deliberate judgement the events of the last twelve months as they affect the prospects of the Labour Party warrant neither pessimism, recrimination, nor doubts about the future'.[11] After reflecting upon the great successes and achievements of the Labour government, not least its willingness to stand for the community as a whole and its advocacy of international peace, Cramp concluded:

> We set our faces steadfastly against the attempt to divide our movement from within, and we will not suffer the enemy without to break the unity of the political and industrial that has been established. Two generations of effort and sacrifice in the building up of the working-class political organisation have brought us to the proud position we occupy to-day – the official Opposition in Parliament and the alternative Government to the one that holds power. The future is ours, if we are loyal to the spirit and ideals which brought the movement into existence. Nothing but our own dissensions can rob us of the victory that lies within our grasp.[12]

Cramp's reflections reveal the imminental feelings reverberating around the Labour Party. There was an immense sense of achievement and hope from a movement which had sensed what might be possible once there was a majority Labour government. The 1924 Labour government, despite limited success, was thus a vital mile-post, rather than a *cul de sac*, in the development of the viable and politically effective Labour movement that emerged in the rest of the twentieth century. As already indicated, in October 1924 MacDonald informed King George V that despite their lack of experience, the Labour ministers 'have acquitted themselves with credit'. This statement is a suitable epitaph for a government which served well in office even though it was not effectively in power.

Notes

Chapter 1   From foundation conference to government

1. Thomas Jones, *Whitehall Diary Volume 1: 1916–1925*, ed. Keith Middlemas (London: Oxford University Press, 1960), p. 266 (diary entry; 22 January 1924).
2. Donald Sassoon, *One Hundred Years of Socialism: The West European Left in the Twentieth Century* (New York: The New Press, 1996), ch. 2.
3. Interview with John Fisher (grandson of Andrew Fisher 1862–1928, Prime Minister of Australia in 1908, 1910–13, 1914–15 and a minister in the world's first Labour government in 1899), University of Sydney, 21 November 2003. For a photograph of Andrew and Margaret Fisher with Ramsay and Margaret MacDonald with their daughter Joan in 1911, see David Marquand, *Ramsay MacDonald* (London: Jonathan Cape, 1977), between pp. 352 and 353. For Chris Watson's 1904 government, see Ross McMullin, *So Monstrous A Travesty: Chris Watson and the world's first national labour* government (Melbourne: Scribe Publications); Mark Hearn 'Cultivating an Australian Sentiment: John Christian Watson's Narrative of White Nationalism', *National Identities, Vol. 9, No. 4*, December 2007, pp. 351–68.
4. Labour leader Arthur Henderson had been President of the Board of Education in Asquith's Coalition Cabinet and in Lloyd George's War Cabinet until succeeded by George Barnes in 1917. Other Labourites in wartime governments were: J. R. Clynes, John Hodge, George Roberts, William Brace, George Wardle and Stephen Walsh.
5. Robert Rhodes James (ed.), *Winston S. Churchill: His Complete Speeches, 1897–1963, Vol. III: 1914–1922* (New York and London: Chelsea House in association with R. R. Bowker, 1974), p. 2921.
6. Harold Nicolson, *King George V: His Life and Reign* (London: Constable, 1984), p. 384.
7. David Jarvis, 'Stanley Baldwin and the Ideology of the Conservative Response to Socialism 1918–1931' (University of Lancaster, PhD thesis, 1991), p. 139 quoted in Martin Pugh, ' "Class Traitors": Conservative Recruits to Labour, 1900–30', in *English Historical Review*, vol. cxiii, No. 450 (1998), p. 38.
8. Lloyd George to Megan Lloyd George, 4 February 1924, in Kenneth O. Morgan (ed.), *Lloyd George Family Letters, 1885–1936* (Cardiff: University of Wales Press, 1973), p. 202.
9. *New Leader*, 11 January 1924.
10. For the Gill Bennett Report, see Foreign and Commonwealth Office, '*A Most Extraordinary and Mysterious Business': The Zinoviev Letter of 1924* (London: Historians, LRD, No. 14, 1999).
11. For Margaret Bondfield, see Mary Agnes Hamilton, *Margaret Bondfield* (London: Leonard Parsons, 1924).
12. For Clement Attlee, see Robert Pearce, *Attlee* (London: Longman, 1997).

13. *Beatrice Webb's Diaries, 1912–24*, pp.17–18, quoted in R. T. McKenzie, *British Political Parties: The Distribution of Power within The Conservative and Labour Parties* (London: Mercury Books, 1963), p. 305.

14. D. Marquand, *Ramsay MacDonald*, particularly ch. 27; K. Laybourn, *The Rise of Labour: The British Labour Party, 1890–1979* (London: Edward Arnold, 1988), ch. 5.

15. Jonathan Lawrence, 'Labour – the myths it has lived by', in Duncan Tanner, Pat Thane and Nick Tiratsoo (eds), *Labour's First Century* (Cambridge: Cambridge University Press, 2000), pp. 351–4.

16. See David Marquand's entry on Ramsay MacDonald in the *Oxford Dictionary of National Biography* (Oxford: Oxford University Press, 2004); Marquand, *Ramsay MacDonald*, pp. 1–2, 647–55; Laybourn, *The Rise of Labour*, ch. 5.

17. Richard Lyman, *The First Labour Government* (London: Chapman & Hall, 1957).

18. *Labour Magazine*, November 1924.

19. David Howell, *MacDonald's Party: Labour Identities and Crisis, 1922–1931* (Oxford: Oxford University Press, 2002), p. 21.

20. Ralph Miliband, *Parliamentary Socialism: A Study in the Politics of Labour* (London: Merlin Press, 1972); Michael Newman, 'Ralph Miliband and the Labour Party: from Parliamentary Socialism to "Bennism"', in John Callaghan, Steven Fielding and Steve Ludlam, *Interpreting the Labour Party: Approaches to Labour Politics and History* (Manchester: Manchester University Press, 2003), ch. 4.

21. Paul Foot, *The Vote: How It Was Won and How It Was Undermined* (London: Viking, 2005), pp. 267–70, 427.

22. Marquand, *Ramsay MacDonald*, chs 14–16.

23. Ibid., p. 391.

24. Pat Thane, 'Labour and Welfare', in Duncan Tanner, Pat Thane and Nick Tiratsoo (eds), *Labour's First Century* (Cambridge: Cambridge University Press, 2000), pp. 90–4. For centenary histories, see also Brian Brivati and Richard Heffernan (eds), *The Labour Party: A Centenary History* (Basingstoke: Palgrave Macmillan, 2000); Keith Laybourn, *A Century of Labour: A History of the Labour Party, 1900–2000* (Stroud: Sutton Publishing, 2000).

25. Andrew Thorpe, *A History of the British Labour Party* (Basingstoke: Palgrave, 2001 edn), p. 51.

26. Howell, *MacDonald's Party, passim*.

27. Thorpe, *A History of the British Labour Party*, pp. 8–9.

28. Keith Laybourn, 'The Failure of Socialist Unity in Britain, c.1893–1914', *Transactions of the Royal Historical Society*, 6th series, vol. IV (London: Royal Historical Society, 1994), pp. 153–75.

29. *Labour Leader*, October 1924.

30. Ross McKibbin, *The Evolution of the Labour Party, 1910–1924* (Oxford: Oxford University Press, 1974), pp. 136–7. McKibbin gives slightly different figures but indicates that the union percentage was 60 per cent in the 1922 general election, 52 per cent in 1923 and 57 per cent in 1924.

31. For examples of socialist failure in the 1895 election, see David Howell, *British Workers and the Independent Labour Party, 1888–1906* (Manchester: Manchester University Press, 1983), pp. 129–282 *passim*.

32. John Shepherd, *George Lansbury: At the Heart of Old Labour* (Oxford: Oxford University Press, 2002), p. 77.
33. Kenneth O. Morgan (ed.), *Labour In Power, 1945–1951* (Oxford: Oxford University Press, 1985), p. 9; David Howell, 'When was "The Forward March of Labour?" ', *Llafur*, vol. 3, (1990), p. 59.
34. Jack Reynolds and Keith Laybourn, *Labour Heartland* (Bradford: University of Bradford, 1986), pp.75–82; Laybourn, *A Century of Labour*, pp. 52–3.
35. Robert Taylor, 'PLP's first 100 years', *Tribune*, 10 February 2006, pp. 8–9. See also, Geoff Hoon, ' "Organised socialism has risen in the night" ', ibid., pp. 10–11; David E. Martin, ' "The Instruments of the People? The Parliamentary Labour Party in 1906" ', in David E. Martin and David Rubinstein (eds), *Ideology and the Labour Movement: Essays Presented to John Saville* (London: Croom Helm, 1979), ch. 7.
36. John Shepherd, 'Labour and Parliament: The Lib.–Labs. as the First Working-Class MPs, 1885–1906', in Eugenio Biagini and Alastair Reid (eds), *Currents of Radicalism: Popular Radicalism, Organised Labour and Party Politics in Britain, 1850–1914* (Cambridge: Cambridge University Press, 1991), pp. 208–10.
37. Kenneth O. Morgan, 'The High and Low Politics of Labour: Keir Hardie to Michael Foot', in Michael Bentley and John Stevenson (eds), *High and Low Politics In Modern Britain* (Oxford: Clarendon Press, 1983), pp. 286–7.
38. Pamela M. Graves, *Labour Women: Women in British Working-Class Politics, 1918–1939* (Cambridge: Cambridge University Press, 1994), *passim*.
39. Bob Holton, *British Syndicalism, 1900–1914: Myths and Realities* (London: Pluto Press, 1978), *passim*.
40. Ross McKibbin, *The Evolution of the Labour Party 1910–1924* (Oxford: Clarendon Press, 1983), pp. 82–6.
41. Duncan Tanner, *Political Change and the Labour Party, 1900–1918* (Cambridge: Cambridge University Press, 1990), pp. 420–1.
42. Trevor Wilson, *The Downfall of the Liberal Party, 1914–1935* (London: Collins, 1966), pp. 84–92.
43. Margaret Cole, *Growing Up Into Revolution* (London: Longmans, 1949), p. 86.
44. Chris Wrigley, *Arthur Henderson* (Cardiff: University of Wales Press, 1990), 114–21; F. M. Leventhal, *Arthur Henderson* (Manchester: Manchester University Press, 1989), pp. 64–72.
45. McKibbin, *Evolution of the Labour Party*, ch. 5, pp. 88–111; *The Times*, 7 August 1914.
46. Kenneth D. Wald, 'Advance by Retreat? The Formation of British Labour's Electoral Strategy', *Journal of British Studies*, 27:3 (July 1988), pp. 284–5.
47. Arthur Henderson, 'The Outlook for Labour', *Contemporary Review*, CXIII, (February 1918), p. 122 (emphasis added).
48. G. D. H. Cole, *A History of the Labour Party From 1914* (London: Routledge & Kegan Paul, 1948), pp. 140–1.
49. For a recent study, see Matthew Worley (ed.), *Labour's Grass Roots: Essays on the Activities of Local Labour Parties and Members, 1918–45* (Aldershot: Ashgate, 2005).
50. *Daily Herald*, 13 December 1919.
51. *Labour Leader*, 13 October 1922.
52. For the Poplar Rates Revolt, see John Shepherd, *George Lansbury: At the Heart Of Old Labour* (Oxford: Oxford University Press, 2004), ch. 11.
53. Morgan, 'The High and Low Politics of Labour', pp. 285–312.

54. Herbert Morrison, 'London's Labour Majority', *Labour Magazine*, 8 (1929/30), p. 68, cited in Stefan Berger, 'Labour in Comparative Perspective', in Duncan Tanner, Pat Thane and Nick Tiratsoo (eds), *Labour's First Century* (Cambridge: Cambridge University Press, 2000), p. 315.
55. Dominic Wring, 'Selling Socialism: Marketing the Early Labour Party', *History Today* (May 2005), pp. 41–3.
56. The best history of *The Daily Herald* is Huw Richards, *The Bloody Circus: The Daily Herald and the Left* (London, Pluto Press, 1997).
57. Reynolds and Laybourn, *Labour Heartland*, pp, 43–6.
58. Duncan Tanner, 'The Labour Party and Electoral Politics in the Coalfields', in Alan Campbell, Nina Fishman and David Howell (eds), *Miners, Unions and Politics, 1910–47* (Aldershot: Scolar Press, 1996), pp. 59–92.
59. Kenneth O Morgan, *Consensus and Disunity: The Lloyd George Coalition Government, 1918–1922* (Oxford: Clarendon Press, 1986), pp. 213–15.
60. David Powell, *British Politics, 1910–1935: The Crisis of the Party System* (London: Routledge, 2004), pp. 118–23.
61. Harold Laski to O. W. Holmes, 13 December 1923, in Mark DeWolfe (ed.), *Holmes-Laski Letters: The Correspondence of Mr. Justice Holmes and Harold J. Laski, 1916–1935* (London: Oxford University Press, 1953), pp. 569–70.
62. Michael Newman, *Harold Laski: A Political Biography* (Basingstoke: Macmillan – now Palgrave Macmillan, 1993), pp. 69–71; Isaac Kramnick and Barry Sheerman, *Harold Laski: A Life on the Left* (London: 1993), *passim*.
63. There is an extensive literature. The main works include: Ross McKibbin, *Evolution*; Keith Laybourn and Jack Reynolds, *Liberalism and the Rise of Labour, 1890–1918* (Beckenham: Croom Helm, 1984); Keith Laybourn, 'The Rise of Labour and the Decline of Liberalism: The State of the Debate', *History*, 80 (June 1995), pp. 207–26; P. F. Clarke, *Lancashire and the New Liberalism* (Cambridge: Cambridge University Press, 1971); Wilson, *Downfall*; Kenneth O. Morgan ' The New Liberalism and the Challenge of Labour: The Welsh Experience, 1885–1929', in Kenneth D. Brown (ed.), *Essays in Anti-Labour History: Responses to the Rise of Labour* (London: Macmillan, 1974), pp. 159–82; Michael Bentley, *The Climax of Liberal Politics: British Liberalism in Theory and Practice* (London: Edward Arnold 1987); Duncan Tanner, *Political Change and the Labour Party, 1900–1918* (Cambridge: Cambridge University Press, 1990).
64. Lyman, *The First Labour Government*; Marquand, *Ramsay MacDonald*; Howell, *MacDonald's Party*; Maurice Cowling, *The Impact of Labour* (Cambridge and London, Cambridge University Press, 1971).
65. Duncan Tanner, 'Socialist Parties and Policies', in Martin Pugh (ed.), *A Companion to Modern European History, 1871–1945* (Oxford: Blackwell, 1997), pp.144–50.
66. James Joll, *Intellectuals in Politics: Three Biographical Essays* (London: Weidenfeld & Nicolson, 1960), pp. 26–8. We are grateful to Professor Kenneth O. Morgan for this reference. See also, Sassoon, *One Hundred Years of Socialism*, pp. 52–3.
67. Sidney Webb to William Robson, 16 December 1923, Norman Mackenzie (ed.), *The Letters of Sidney and Beatrice Webb, Volume 111: Pilgrimage, 1912–1947* (Cambridge: Cambridge University Press, 1978), p. 186.
68. Egon Wertheimer, *Portrait of The Labour Party* (London: G. P. Putnam's Sons, 1930), pp. 275, 284.

69. J. R. MacDonald, *Socialism and Society* (Independent Labour Party: 1905), p. xix.
70. Richard Lyman, *The First Labour Government* (1957), pp. 14–15.
71. *New Leader*, 14 December 1923.
72. Lord Stamfordham to George V, 28 December 1923, RA PS/GV/K 1918/84.
73. C. R. Attlee, *As It Happened* (London: Heinemann, 1954), pp. 58, 62.
74. J. H. Thomas, *When Labour Rules* (London: Collins, 1920), pp. 7, 9.
75. Jonathan Davis, 'Left Out in the Cold: British Labour Witnesses the Russian Revolution', *Revolutionary Russia*, 18:1 (June 2005), pp. 71–81.
76. J. R. MacDonald to George V, 10 October 1924, RA PS/GV/K1958/26.

Chapter 2 'Over the threshold'

1. Labour Party, *Report of the Annual Conference*, 1923, p. 175.
2. 'Over the Threshold' is taken from the title of the 'Report to the Executive Committee, 1923–4', published in the Labour Party, *Annual Report*, 1924, p. 3.
3. Labour Party, *Report of the Annual Conference* (1923).
4. Paul Ward, *Red Flag and Union Jack: Englishness, Patriotism and the British Left, 1991–1924* (Woodbridge: The Royal Historical Society, 1998), pp. 167–9.
5. Matthew Worley, *Labour Inside the Gate: A History of the British Labour Party between the Wars* (London: I. B. Taurus, 2005), pp. 23–4.
6. Ben Pimlott (ed.), *The Political Diary of Hugh Dalton, 1918–40, 1945–60* (London: Jonathan Cape. In Association with the London School of Economics and Political Science, 1986), pp. 10–11. See also Greg Rosen, 'Willie Adamson', in Greg Rosen *Dictionary of Labour Biography* (London: Politicos, 2001), pp. 6–7.
7. Kenneth O. Morgan, *Consensus and Disunity: The Lloyd George Coalition Government, 1918–1922* (Oxford: Oxford University Press, 1986), p. 213.
8. Keith Laybourn, *A Century of Labour: A History of the Labour Party* (Stroud: Sutton Publishing, 2000), pp. 38–40.
9. Worley, *Labour Inside the Gate*, pp. 60–4.
10. *Labour Party General Election Manifesto*, 1923.
11. Keith Laybourn, *Philip Snowden: A Biography* (Aldershot: Temple Smith/Gower/Wildwood, 1988), p. 99.
12. Parliamentary Debates, 5th series, vol. 168, 15 December 1923, col. 479.
13. David Marquand, *Ramsay MacDonald* (London: Jonathan Cape, 1977), pp. 299–302.
14. Ross McKibbin, *The Evolution of the Labour Party, 1910–1924* (Oxford: Clarendon Press, 1983), pp. 159–60.
15. *Liberal Magazine*, XXXI (December 1923), p. 705
16. Richard Lyman, *The First Labour Government* (London: Chapman & Hall, 1957), p. 70. F. W. S. Craig gives slightly different figures for the 1922 and 1923 elections, including the Conservatives contesting 54 (rather than 64) more seats in 1923 compared to 1922. F. W. S. Craig, *British Electoral Facts, 1885–1975* (London and Basingstoke: Macmillan, 1976), pp. 12–14.
17. G. D. H. Cole, *A History of the Labour Party From 1914* (London: Routledge & Kegan Paul, 1969), p. 153.
18. Michael Kinnear, *The British Voter: An Atlas and Survey since 1885* (London: Batsford, 1981), pp. 43–4.

19. Chris Cook, *The Age of Alignment: Electoral Politics in Britain, 1922–1929* (London: Macmillan, 1977), p. 168.
20. H. W. Massingham article in *Nation*, 6 February 1924; Labour Party, National Executive Committee, Minutes, Box VI. According to George Lansbury, in the *Daily Herald*, 9 January 1924, Massingham ran the *Star*, along with T. P. O'Connor.
21. Robert. E. Dowse, *Left In the Centre: The Independent Labour Party, 1893–1940* (London: Longmans, 1966), p. 102.
22. *The Times*, 1 October 1914; Marquand, *Ramsay MacDonald*, ch. 10, entitled 'Public Enemy'.
23. P. Snowden's pamphlets included *A Plea for Peace* (Blackburn: Blackburn Labour Party, 1916), *Labour in Chains* (London: National Labour Press, 1917), *How to Pay for the War – Tax the Unearned Income of the Rich* (London: 1916), and *War and Peace* (London: National Labour Publications, 1918).
24. Laybourn, *Philip* Snowden, ch. 5.
25. A. J. P. Taylor, *English History* (London: Penguin, 1975), pp. 198–9.
26. Gordon Brown, *Maxton* (Glasgow: Collins/ Fontana, 1988), pp. 122–3.
27. Dowse, *Left in the Centre*, pp. 93–4
28. Independent Labour Party, *Conference Report, 1923*, p. 91.
29. *New Leader*, 6 July 1923; F. M. Leventhal, *The Last Dissenter: H. N. Brailsford and His World* (Oxford: Clarendon Press, 1985), pp 180–1.
30. Arthur Ponsonby Diary, 11 December 1923.
31. *New Leader*, 21 December 1924.
32. Ibid., 11 January 1924.
33. *Forward*, 26 April 1924.
34. 'Report to the Executive Committee, 1923–1924', Labour Party, *Annual Report, 1924* (London: Labour Party, 1924), p. 3.
35. Ibid., p. 4, quoting from the Executive of the Labour Party statement for January 1924.
36. NEC of the Labour Party, Minutes, 2 September 1924, outlines the issues from 1922 to 1924.
37. James Klugmann, *History of the Communist Party of Great Britain: Formation and Early Years*, vol. 1: *1919–1924* (London: Lawrence & Wishart, 1968), pp. 166–81, traces the moves made by the CPGB to gain affiliation to the Labour Party, and Labour's response, in immense detail.
38. Pollitt Papers, CP/IND/POLL/3/1, 'The New Phase in Britain and the Communist Party' (draft by R. P. Dutt), p. 29.
39. Labour Party, *Annual Report, 1924*, p. 127.
40. Andrew Thorpe, ' "The Only Effective Bulwark Against Reaction and Revolution": Labour and the Frustration of the Extreme Left', in Andrew Thorpe (ed.), *The Failure of Political Extremism In Inter-War Britain* (Exeter: University of Exeter, 1989), pp. 11–27.

Chapter 3   Labour takes office

1. Frederick Maurice, *Haldane 1915–1928* (London: Faber & Faber, 1929), *passim*.
2. The Earl of Oxford and Asquith, *Memories and Reflections 1852–1927*, vol. 2 (London: Cassell, 1928), pp. 207–8.
3. *Memorandum By Lord Stamfordham*, 10 December 1923, RA PS/GV/K 1918/34

4. Kenneth Young, *Baldwin* (London: Weidenfeld & Nicolson, 1976), pp. 54–5.
5. Harold Nicolson, *King George V: His Life and Reign* (London: Constable, 1984), p. 382.
6. Ibid., p. 383.
7. MacDonald Diary, 8–9 December 1923.
8. *Forward*, 15 December 1923.
9. John Shepherd, *George Lansbury: At the Heart of Old Labour* (Oxford: Oxford University Press, 2002), p. 208.
10. Beatrice Webb, *The Diary of Beatrice Webb: Volume Three, 1905–1924* (London: Virago & BLPES, 1984) pp. 430–1. (Diary entry, 12 December 1923.)
11. Jim Middleton to Frank Hughes, 15 February 1924, MacDonald Papers PRO 30/69/1169.
12. Sidney Webb, 'The First Labour Government', *Political Quarterly*, 32 (1961), pp. 7–9.
13. *Manchester Guardian*, 19 December 1923.
14. Philip Williamson, 'The Labour Party and the House of Lords, 1918–1931' *Parliamentary History*, vol. 10, pt 2 (1991), 317–41.
15. MacDonald to Massingham, 24 December 1924, Massingham Papers. For Massingham, see Alfred Havighurst, *Radical Journalist*: H. W. Massingham (Cambridge: Cambridge University Press, 1974), ch. 11.
16. MacDonald Diary, 10 December 1923; MacDonald to Massingham, 19 December 1923; Massingham to MacDonald, 21 December 1923, Massingham Papers.
17. Massingham to MacDonald, 21 December 1923; MacDonald to Massingham, 24, 29 December 1923, ibid.
18. For the *Report of the Machinery of Government Committee* (1918), see Peter Hennessey, *Whitehall* (London: Fontana, 1990), pp. 292–9 (emphasis added); Peter Hennessey, *The Prime Minister: The Office and Its Holders since 1945* (London: Allen Lane, 2000), p. 338; Hans Daalder, *Cabinet Reform in Britain* (Stanford, CA: Stanford University Press, 1964) pp. 273–7.
19. Harold Wilson, *A Prime Minister on Prime Ministers* (London: Michael Joseph, 1977), p. 198.
20. Beatrice Webb, *Diary*, 15 January 1924.
21. Ibid., 3, 15 January 1924.
22. Philip Viscount Snowden, *An Autobiography: Volume Two, 1919–1934* (London: Nicolson & Watson, 1934), pp. 594–8.
23. J. H. Thomas, *My Story* (London: Hutchinson, 1937), pp. 74–5.
24. Richard Lyman, *The First Labour Government* (London: Chapman & Hall, 1957), pp. 99, 101–2.
25. For a scathing attack on MacDonald, see L. Macneill Weir, *The Tragedy of Ramsay MacDonald* (London: Secker & Warburg, 1938), pp. 167–8.
26. J. R. MacDonald, *A Policy for the Labour Party* (1920).
27. MacDonald Diary, 10 December 1923.
28. Ibid., 10 January 1924.
29. *Socialist Review*, XXIII:124 (January 1924).
30. David Marquand, *J. Ramsay MacDonald* (London: Jonathan Cape, 1977), pp. 50–3,131–5 J. R. MacDonald, *Margaret Ethel MacDonald: A Memoir* (London: Hodder & Stoughton, 1913), *passim*.
31. M. A. Hamilton, *Ramsay MacDonald* (London: 1929); *The Times*, 22, 23 December 1923.

32. *The Times*, 23 December 1923.
33. MacDonald Papers PRO 30/69/1258.
34. Haldane to Mary Haldane, 13 December 1923, Haldane Papers MS 6006.
35. MacDonald to Haldane, 23 December 1923, Haldane Papers, MS 5916.
36. Haldane to MacDonald, 24 December 1923, printed in Richard Burdon Haldane, *An Autobiography* (London: Hodder & Stoughton, 1929), pp. 321–3.
37. Robert Keith Middlemas, *The Clydesiders: A Left-Wing Struggle for Parliamentary Power* (London: Hutchinson, 1967), p. 137. Hennessey, *Whitehall*, pp. 292–3.
38. Haldane, *Autobiography*, pp. 321–3.
39. Brigadier General Thomson was a leading pioneer of airships in the 1920s. In 1924 his friend, Ramsay MacDonald – also a flying enthusiast – appointed a Cabinet Committee which recommended dual state and private company construction of the R100 and R101 airships by the Air Ministry and Vickers Ltd. The novelist and aeronautical engineer Nevil Shute in 1924 worked at Cardington on the early design of the R101. In 1930 Lord Thomson, Secretary of State for Air in the Second Labour Cabinet, died tragically in the R101 disaster. Neville Shute, *Slide Rule: The Autobiography of an Engineer* (London: Heinemann, 1954). We are grateful to Peter Hore for this reference. For Lord Thomson and the R101, see John Shepherd, *George Lansbury: At the Heart of Old Labour* (Oxford: Oxford University Press, 2004), pp. 263–4.
40. Williamson, 'The Labour Party and the House of Lords', 317–25.
41. Haldane, *Autobiography*, pp. 324–5.
42. Haldane to Mary Haldane, 12/13 January 1924, Haldane Papers MS 6007; Haldane to Elisabeth Haldane, 11 January 1924, Haldane Papers MS 6013.
43. Thomas Jones, *Whitehall Diary: Volume 1, 1916–1925*, ed. Keith Middlemas (London: Oxford University Press, 1969), pp. 264–7.
44. Neil MacLean to Ramsay MacDonald, 8 February 1924, MacDonald Papers PRO 30/69 1169.
45. Neil Maclean to Ben Spoor, 26 January 1924, ibid.
46. *The Political Dairies of C. P. Scott, 1911–1928*, ed. Trevor Wilson (London: Collins, 1976), Diary entry 6 January 1924.
47. Ibid.
48. Lord Parmoor, *A Retrospect: Looking Back on the Life of More than Eighty Years* (London: Heinemann, 1936), p. 194.
49. Haldane to Elisabeth Haldane, 11 January 1924, Haldane Papers MS 6013.
50. Middlemass, *The Clydesiders*, pp. 139–40.
51. William Gallacher, *The Rolling of Thunder* (London: Lawrence & Wishart, 1947), pp. 65–6.
52. MacDonald Diary, 21 January 1924.
53. For the Union of Democratic Control, see Martin Schwarz, *The Union of Democratic Control* (Oxford: Oxford University Press, 1971).
54. Raymond A. Jones, *Arthur Ponsonby: The Politics of Life* (London: Christopher Helm, 1989), pp. 140–1.
55. Ponsonby to MacDonald, 11 December 1923, MacDonald (JRM) Papers, PRO (69)/196 30/69/196.
56. Jones, *Whitehall Diary: Volume 1, 1916–1925*, p. 264.
57. Colin Cross, *Philip Snowden* (London: Barrie & Rockliff,1966), pp. 190, 195–6.
58. Keith Laybourn, *Philip Snowden* (Aldershot: Temple Smith, 1988), p. 107.
59. J. R. Clynes, *Memoirs, 1924–1937* (London: Hutchinson, 1937), ch. 1.

60. G. D. H. Cole, *A History of the Labour Party* (London: Kegan & Paul, 1948), p. 159.
61. Henderson to MacDonald, 18 December 1923, MacDonald (JRM) Papers, PRO 30/69/196.
62. MacDonald to Henderson, 22 December 1923, ibid.1169.
63. Fenner Brockway, *Socialism over Sixty Years: The Life of Jowett of Bradford (1864–1944)* (London: Allen & Unwin, 1946), pp. 206–8.
64. David Howell, *MacDonald's Party: Labour Identities and Crisis, 1922–1931* (Oxford: Oxford University Press, 2002), pp. 102–3.
65. Quoted in Peter Slowe, *Manny Shinwell* (London: Pluto Press, 1993), p. 123.
66. Emanuel Shinwell, *Conflict Without Malice* (London: Odhams, 1955), pp. 90–1.
67. Welsh to MacDonald, 26 January 1924, MacDonald Papers PRO 30/69 1709.
68. Wilson to MacDonald, 25 January 1924, MacDonald Papers PRO30/69/1169.
69. MacDonald to Wilson, 26 January 1924, ibid.
70. Henry Slesser, *Judgement Reserved* (London: Hutchinson, 1941), pp. 92-4.
71. Patrick Hastings, *The Autobiography of Sir Patrick Hastings* (London: Heinemann, 1948), p. 235.
72. W. Martin, P. Dollan, D. Kirkwood and W. Stewart to Ramsay MacDonald, 31 January, 14 February 1924; MacDonald to H. P. Macmillan, 13 February 1924; Rosslyn Mitchell to MacDonald, 25 January 1924; MacDonald to Mitchell, 11 February 1924, MacDonald Papers, PRO 30/69/689.
73. Robert Smillie to Ramsay MacDonald, 20 December 1923, MacDonald (JRM) Papers, PRO 30/69/1169. See also Robert Smillie, *My Life for Life* (London: Mills & Boon, 1924), pp. 303–4.
74. George Lansbury to Arthur Henderson, 15 January 1924, Lansbury Papers, vol. 28, fo. 162.
75. George Lansbury to Ramsay MacDonald, 18 Jan. 1924, ibid., fo. 163.
76. It is not clear if this meeting at MacDonald's home took place, since neither party later mentioned it publicly. MacDonald Notebooks and Diaries, MacDonald Papers, RMD/2/22 (John Rylands Library).
77. *The Times*, 9 January 1924.
78. *Daily Mail*, 22 January 1924.
79. *Manchester Guardian*, 7 January 1924; Memorandum by Lord Stamfordham, RA, GV 1918/164. See also Nicolson, *King George V*, p. 384.
80. For the episode of Labour ministers and court dress, see Nicolson, *King George V*, pp. 391–2. See also Anne Perkins, *A Very British Strike* (Basingstoke: Macmillan, 2006), pp. 38–41.
81. J. R. Clynes, *Memoirs, 1869–1924* (London: 1937), p. 347
82. G. D. H. Cole, *A History of the Labour Party from 1914* (London: Routledge & Kegan Paul, 1948), p. 159
83. Andrew Thorpe, *A History of the British Labour Party* (Houndmills: Macmillan – now Palgrave, 1997), p. 57
84. Robert E. Dowse, *Left In The Centre: The Independent Labour Party, 1893–1940* (London: Longmans, 1966), p. 102.
85. M. Margaret Patricia McGarran, *Fabianism In The Political Life of Britain, 1919–1931* (Chicago: Heritage Foundantion, 1954).
86. *The Times*, 24 January 1924.
87. *Daily Graphic*, 24 January 1924.
88. *Manchester Guardian*, 23 January 1924.

89. *Morning Post*, 23 January 1924.
90. House to Haldane, 6 February 1924, Haldane Papers, MS 5916.
91. Lytton to Haldane, 6 February 1924, ibid.
92. *Sydney Morning Herald*, 23 and 24 January 1924.
93. *Sun*, 24 January 1924.
94. *Lyttleton Times*, 24 January 1924.
95. *Australian Worker*, 30 January 1924. For Beatrice Webb's controversial contri-
    butions to 'the social side of the first Labour Government' by the creation
    of the Half-Circle Club to educate ministers and their wives in the ways of
    Westminster and the Parliamentary Labour Club, see Margaret Cole (ed.),
    Beatrice Webb's Diaries, 1924–1932 (London: Longmans, 1956), p. viii and
    diary entries 7, 8 February, 17 March 1924.
96. Jean Bonner, 'The Four Labour Cabinets', *Sociological Review* 6 (1958),
    38–9.

Chapter 4   Domestic policies

1. *Daily Mail*, 21 January 1924.
2. J. H. Thomas and C. T. Cramp to NUR Members, 18 January 1924, TUC
   Archives, MSS 292/251.12.
3. The best account of the Emergency Powers Act (1920) and anti-strike
   machinery in the inter-war years is Jane Morgan, *Conflict and Order: The Police
   and Labour Disputes in England and Wales, 1900–1939* (Oxford: Clarendon
   Press, 1987).
4. For the Supply and Transport Organisation, see Ralph H. Desmarais,
   'Strikebreaking and the Labour Government of 1924', *Journal of Contemporary
   History*, 8: 4 (October 1973), pp. 165–75. For the wider issues, see Morgan,
   Conflict and Order, pp. 111 ff.
5. Robert Rhodes James, *Memoirs of a Conservative: J. C. C. Davidson's Memoirs
   and Papers, 1910–1937* (London: Weidenfeld & Nicolson, 1969), pp. 178–80.
6. Josiah C. Wedgwood, *Memoirs of a Fighting Life* (London: Hutchinson, 1941),
   p. 186.
7. Cabinet 23/47(13)(24), 13 February 1924; Alan Bullock, *The Life and Times
   of Ernest Bevin*, vol. 2 (London: Heinemann, 1967), pp. 237–62.
8. A. Hutt, *The Post-War History of the British Working Class* (London: Left Book
   Club/Gollancz, 1937), p. 84.
9. *The Times*, 25 March 1924.
10. Cabinet 23/47(22)(24), 26 March 1924; Alan Bullock, *The Life and Times of
    Ernest Bevin*, vol. 1 (London: Heinemann, 1967), pp. 237–42.
11. PLP, Minutes of Special Meeting, 28 March 1924.
12. Cabinet 23/47(23)(24), 27 March 1924.
13. Report of the Emergency Committee, 24 March and 27 March 1924, see
    Cabinet 23/47(23)(24), 27 March 1924. See also Desmarais, 'Strikebreaking',
    pp. 165–75; K. Jefferys and P. Hennessy, *States of Emergency: British Govern-
    ments and Strikebreaking since 1919* (London: Routledge & Kegan Paul, 1982);
    pp. 78–86; and Richard Lyman, *The First Labour Government* (London:
    Chapman & Hall, 1957), pp. 218–23.

14. *Hansard, Parliamentary Debates*, 5th series, vol. 171, 28 March 1924, cols 1680–4.
15. Cabinet 23/47(12)(24), 12 February 1924; Bullock, *Bevin*, vol. 1, p. 237.
16. Quoted in Chris Wrigley, *Arthur Henderson* (Cardiff: University of Wales Press, 1990), p. 148.
17. Cabinet 23/47(24)(24), 2 April 1924, CAB 23-47-365/6.
18. For the British Empire Exhibition, see Denis Judd, *Empire: The British Imperial Experience from 1765 to the Present* (London: Harper Collins, 1996), ch. 21.
19. M. Cole (ed.), *Beatrice Webb's Diaries, 1924–1932* (London: Longmans, Green, 1956), entry 3 April 1924, p. 18.
20. Cabinet 23/47(24)(24), 2 April 1924.
21. *Hansard, Parliamentary Debates*, 5th series, vol. 169, 12 February 1924, col. 751.
22. J. Ramsay MacDonald, *Socialism: Critical and Constructive* (London: Cassell, 1924), p. vii.
23. John Shepherd, *George Lansbury: At the Heart of Labour* (Oxford: Oxford University, 2002), pp. 215–16.
24. Marion Phillips (ed.), *Women and the Labour Party* (London: Headley Bros, 1918).
25. Pat Thane, 'The Women of the British Labour Party and Feminism, 1906–1945', in Harold L. Smith (ed.), *British Feminism in the Twentieth Century* (Aldershot: Edward Elgar, 1990), pp. 124–5.
26. *Woman's Leader and the Common Cause*, 1 February 1924.
27. Ibid., 25 January 1924.
28. Ibid., 1 February 1924.
29. David Howell, *MacDonald's Party: Labour Identities and Crisis, 1922–1931* (Oxford: Oxford University Press, 2002), pp. 336–7.
30. *Parliamentary Debates*, 5th series, vol. 169, 21 January 1924, cols 601–6.
31. Pamela Graves, *Labour Women: Women in British Working-Class Politics, 1918–1939* (Cambridge: Cambridge University Press, 1994), pp. 32, 39.
32. Harold L. Smith, *The British Women's Suffrage Campaign, 1886–1928* (London: Longman, 1998), pp. 70–3.
33. Ibid., pp. 81–98.
34. Lesley A. Hall, 'Sexuality', in Ina Zweiniger-Bargielowska (ed.), *Women in Twentieth-Century Britain* (Harlow: Longman, 2001), pp. 55–7.
35. *The Labour Woman*, June 1923. This monthly paper was edited by Dr Marion Phillips.
36. Dora Russell, *The Tamarask Tree*, quoted in Howell, *MacDonald's Party*, p. 349.
37. National Executive Committee, Minutes of Labour Party, Box 6, 27 February 1924.
38. Marion Phillips, 'Birth Control: A Careful Consideration', *The Labour Woman*, March 1924. Also note that in the same issue, a pro-birth-control information declaration signed by Rose Witcop-Aldred, Majory Allen, Ruth Dalton, Frida Laski, Leah L'Estrange Malone, Joan Malleson and Dora Russell.
39. Russell, *Tamarisk Tree*, pp. 171–2, quoted in Howell, *MacDonald's Party*, p. 350.
40. Ibid., pp. 172–3.
41. *Labour Woman*, June 1924.
42. Ibid., July 1925.
43. *Labour Party Conference Report*, 1925, pp. 191–2. The vote was 1,824,000 for the platform and 1,053,000 against.

44. British Library of Political and Economic Science, Violet Markham Papers 3: 1–7, Central Committee on Women's Training and Employment (CCTWE), Minutes, 1914–1940; Report of the Standing Committee of Industrial Women's Organisations, 27 February 1924.
45. Keith Laybourn, *Unemployment and Employment with Particular Reference to Women in Britain, c.1900–1951* (Lampeter: Edwin Mellen, 2002); Keith Laybourn, ' "Waking up to the Fact that there are any Unemployed": Women, Unemployment and the Domestic Solution in Britain, 1918–1939', *History*, 88: 4 (2003), pp. 608–23.
46. British Library of Political and Economic Science, Violet Markham Papers 3: 1–7, Central Committee on Women's Training and Employment (CCWTE), Minutes, 1914–1940.
47. CCWTE, Minutes, 29 February 1940.
48. Ibid., 28 January 1921.
49. Ibid., 11 February 1926; Laybourn, *Unemployment and Employment*, pp. 80–85.
50. Ibid., 28 February 1924. Approval was given by the Ministry of Labour for many of these schemes on 8 May 1924 and evidence of this appears in the minutes of later meetings.
51. LP/DOM/23 1ii.; Ibid., 23/2–3 letter, 11 April 1923; Ibid., 23/7 letter, 8 June 1923.
52. Ibid., 23/12, Marion Phillips to Mrs. McCleverty, 13 March 1924.
53. LP/DOM/23/1–66, Domestic Service General 1923–1930.
54. *The Labour Woman*, June 1923.
55. Howell, *MacDonald's Party*, pp. 356–61.
56. Harriet Jones, 'The State and Social Policy', in Zweiniger-Bargielowska, *Women in Twentieth-Century Britain*, pp. 324–5.
57. National Executive Committee of the Labour Party, Box 6, published material on the National Conference of Labour Women, 13 and 14 May 1924.
58. Ibid., leaflet advertising Women's Day.
59. For Haldane's appointments, see 'Justices' Advisory Committees' (November 1924), Haldane Papers. MS 5916, pp.177–84. For the role of the advisory committees, see 'Selection of Justices under the Advisory Committee System and Ashton-under-Lyne' (1918), Duchy of Lancaster papers (DLP); Richard Burdon Haldane, *An Autobiography* (London: Hodder & Stoughton, 1929), p. 324.
60. Crawford to Shuttleworth, 19 July 1920, DLP,
61. For a typical example, see N. R. Warwick to Arthur Bennett, 15 September 1924, DLP Warrington Box.
62. For local opposition to government direction, see correspondence between Duchy of Lancaster Office and Bury Advisory Committee, 26 March, 30 April, 4, 18, 30 July 1924, DLP, Bury Box B.
63. Tom Snowden to Oswald Mosley, 12, 14 March 1930, DLP, Accrington Box.
64. *Labour Party Conference Report*, 1924, p. 195.
65. Ibid., p. 107.
66. Norman and Jean Mackenzie (eds), *The Diary of Beatrice Webb: Volume Three, 1905–1924* (London: Virago in Association with the London School of Economics and Political Science, 1984), Diary entry 12 December 1923.
67. Quoted in Colin Cross, *Philip Snowden* (London: Barrie & Rockcliffe, 1966), p. 185.

68. *Hansard, Parliamentary Debates*, 5th series, vol. 161, 20 March 1923, cols, 2472–8.
69. R. Skidelsky, *Politicians and the Slump: The Labour Government of 1929–1931* (London: Macmillan, 1967), p. 69.
70. Keith Laybourn, *Philip Snowden: A Biography* (Aldershot: Temple Smith/Gower/Wildwood. 1988), first two chapters.
71. Ibid.
72. Ibid., p. 38.
73. A. Booth and M. Pack, *Employment, Capital and Economic Policy* (Oxford: Basil Blackwell, 1985), p. 136.
74. Philip Snowden, *Labour and National Finance* (London: Leonard Parsons, 1920).
75. Philip Snowden, *An Autobiography*, 2 vols (London: Ivor Nicholson & Watson, 1934), p. 595.
76. Philip Snowden, *The Socialist Budget* (London: George Allen & Unwin, pamphlet, 1907).
77. Archives of the Labour Party (on microflm), *The Big Business Budget* by Philip Snowden, 1924/94, p. 5.
78. Ibid.
79. *Manchester Guardian*, 29 April 1924.
80. *The Times*, 30 April 1924.
81. Archives of the Labour Party, *The Housewife's Budget* [the 1924 Labour Budget] by Philip Snowden.
82. Ibid., p. 5.
83. *Morning Post*, 30 April, 1 May 1924.
84. *Daily Herald*, 30 April 1924.
85. *Hansard, Parliamentary Debates* (1924), vol. 174, cols 2091–114.
86. Cabinet 23/47(11)(24), 10 February 1924.
87. Jones, *Whitehall Diary*, entry 1 February, Friday, p. 269.
88. *Hansard, Parliamentary Debates*, 5th series, vol. 174, cols 645–60; Cabinet 23/47(27)(24), 15 April 1924; Cabinet 23/47(35)(24), 30 May 1924.
89. Cabinet 23/47(40)(24) 9 July 1924 and *Hansard Parliamentary Debates*, 5th series, 30 July 1924, vol. 176, cols 2091–114.
90. Cabinet 23/47(47)(24), 5 August 1924.
91. *Labour Party Conference Report*, 1924, p. 102.
92. Parliamentary Labour Party (PLP), minutes, 29 May 1924, report on unemployment.
93. Ibid., 10 July 1924.
94. NEC Minutes of the Labour Party, Box 6, Report of Arthur Henderson to the House of Commons, 25 March 1924.
95. F. M. Leventhal, *Arthur Henderson* (Manchester: Manchester University Press, 1989), p. 126.
96. Cabinet 25 (24), 7 April 1924, CAB 23-47-387.
97. PLP Minutes, 29 May 1924. For the background to the police unrest, see Chris Wrigley, *Lloyd George and the Challenge of Labour: The Post War Coalition, 1918–1922* (Hemel Hempstead: Harvester Wheatsheaf, 1990), ch. 4.
98. Cabinet 31 (24), 14 May 1924, CAB 24-48-89.
99. *Hansard Parliamentary Debates* (1924), vol. 174, cols 1667–98, 15 May 1924.
100. PLP Minutes, 29 May 1924, report on 'Police and Prison Officers'.

101. Norman and Jean Mackenzie (eds), *The Diary of Beatrice Webb: Volume Four, 1924–1943* (London: Virago in association with the London School of Economic and Political Sciences, 1985), entry 23 June 1924, p. 30.
102. Quoted in Wrigley, *Henderson*, p. 147, who draws this comment from Bert William's pamphlet, *The Record of the Labour Government* (1924), pp. 12–13.
103. Howell, *MacDonald's Party*, p. 142.
104. PLP Minutes, 25 March 1924.
105. MFGB Annual Conference, 1924, pp. 17–22; *MFGB Records*, 1924.
106. LP/MIN/19/14, LP/MIN/19/15.
107. LP/MIN/19/16/I, ii.
108. *Mineworker*, 20 September 1924.
109. D. Cesarini, 'An Alien Concept? The Continuity of Anti-Alienism in British Society before 1940', *Immigrants and Minorities*, III: 3 (November 1992), 39.
110. *Hansard Parliamentary Debates*, 1919, vol. 114, 15 April 1919, cols 2777, 2782–3, 2795; J. Jenkinson, 'The 1919 Riots', in P. Panayi (ed.), *Racial Violence in Britain in the 19th and 20th Centuries* (Leicester: Leicester University Press, 1993).
111. For a critical view of this legislation, see C. Holmes, *John Bull's Island. Immigration and British Society, 1871–1971* (London: Macmillan, 1988), especially p. 114; Cesarini, 'An Alien Concept?'; P. Panayi, *Immigration, Ethnicity and Racism in Britain, 1815–1945* (Manchester: Manchester University Press, 1994), p. 43.
112. This passage draws on material in the Middleton Papers, JSM/HOM/1–26.
113. JSM/HOM/8, 'Alien Orders'.
114. Most of the material can be found in the Labour Party archive and is located in the L. P. Middleton Papers, JSM/HOM/1–26.
115. JSM/HOM/12, a six-page letter from Arthur Henderson to J. S. Middleton dated 7 August 1924.
116. *Hansard, Parliamentary Debates*, vol. 172, 24 April 1924.
117. Labour Party General Election Manifesto 1923, in Iain Dale (ed.), *Labour Party General Election Manifestos, 1900–1997* (London: Politicos, 1998), pp. 24–5.
118. David Howell, *A Lost Left: Three Studies in Socialism and Nationalism* (Manchester: Manchester University Press, 1986.), pp. 237–8.
119. *Hansard, Parliamentary Debates*, 24 April 1924, 269–70.
120. For Wheatley's Housing Act, see Richard W. Lyman, *The First Labour Government* (London: Chapman and Hall, 1957), ch. VIII; Ian Wood, *John Wheatley* (Manchester: Manchester University Press, 1990), pp.131–9; Robert Keith Middlemas, *The Clydesiders: A Left Wing Struggle for Parliamentary Power* (New York: Augustus M. Kelley, 1965), pp. 146–51; Iain Mclean, *The Legend of Red Clydeside* (Edinburgh: John Donald Publishers), pp. 216–18.
121. *Hansard Parliamentary Debates*, 5th series, vol. 171, 26 March 1924, cols 1466–7.
122. B. B. Gilbert, *British Social Policy, 1914–1939* (London, Batsford, 1973), pp. 197–203.
123. Cole, *Beatrice Webb's Diaries, 1924–1932*, p. 11 (29 February 1924).
124. Ibid., p. 31 (23 June 1924).
125. Wood, *John Wheatley*, pp. 141–4.
126. For Wheatley's Evictions Bill, see Ian MacLean, *The Legend of Red Clydeside* (Edinburgh: John Donald Publishers, 1983), pp. 214–16; Wood, *John Wheatley*.

127. Gordon Brown, *Maxton* (Glasgow: Collins/Fontana, 1988), pp. 159–62.
128. Maclean, *The Legend of Red Clydeside*, pp. 207–9; Wood, *John Wheatley*, pp. 149–50.
129. Maurice Bruce, *The Rise of the Welfare State: English Social Policy, 1601–1971* (London, Weidenfeld & Nicolson, 1973), p. 233.
130. Keith Laybourn, 'The Issue of School Feeding in Bradford, 1904–1907', *Journal of Educational Administration and History*, 14:1 (1982), p. 37
131. Keith Laybourn, *The Evolution of British Social Policy and the Welfare State* (Keele: Ryburn Publishing and Keele University Press, 1995), pp. 119–20.
132. Labour Party, *Secondary Education for All: A Policy for Labour* (reproduced by The Hambledon Press, 1988).
133. Cole, *Beatrice Webb's Diaries, 1914–1932*, pp. 1, 3 (8 January 1924, but should be 19 January 1924).
134. *Labour Magazine*, March 1924.
135. Charles Trevelyan to Molly Trevelyan, 4 March 1924, C. P. Trevelyan Papers, Ex 118, ff. 3–4.
136. Snowden to Trevelyan, 22 August 1924, CPT 108, f. 92.
137. *Labour Party Conference Report, 1924*, p. 125.

Chapter 5   Minority government

1. For Liberal–Labour relations, see Trevor Wilson, *The Downfall of the Liberal Party, 1914–1935* (London: Collins, 1966), ch.14; David Dutton, *A History of the Liberal Party in the Twentieth Century* (Basingstoke: Palgrave Macmillan, 2004). ch. 2; Chris Cook, *The Age of Alignment: Electoral Politics in Britain, 1922–1929* (London: Macmillan, 1975); Robert Self, *The Evolution of the British Party System, 1885–1940* (Harlow: Longman, 2000), pp. 156–9; C. J. Wrigley, 'Lloyd George and the Labour Party after 1922', in Judith Loades, *The Life and Times of Lloyd George* (Bangor: Headstart, 1991), ch. 4.
2. E. D.Simon Papers, M11/11, diary entry 21 January 1924.
3. Trevor Wilson (ed.), *The Diaries of C. P. Scott, 191–1928* (London: Collins, 1970).
4. Harold Spender to Ramsay MacDonald, n.d. (December 1923), cited in Harold Spender, *The Fire of Life* (London: Hodder & Stoughton, 1926), p. 277.
5. MacDonald Diary, 9 May 1924.
6. Ibid.
7. Kenneth O. Morgan, *Lloyd George* (London: Weidenfeld & Nicolson, 1974), pp. 170–8.
8. C. J. Wrigley, 'Lloyd George and the Labour Party after 1922', pp.50–3.
9. Michael Bentley, *The Liberal Mind, 1914–1929* (Cambridge: Cambridge University Press, 1977), pp. 90–1.
10. Austen Chamberlain to Hilda Chamberlain, 29 December 1923, quoted in Robert C. Self (ed.), *The Austen Chamberlain Letters: The Correspondence of Sir Austen Chamberlain with his Sisters Hilda and Ida, 1916–1937* (Cambridge and London: Cambridge University Press; The Royal Historical Society, 1995).

11. *Manchester Guardian*, 7 February 1924.
12. C. P. Scott's Diary, Add Mss 50, 907 (27 November 1924).
13. John Campbell, *Lloyd George: The Goat in the Wilderness, 1922–1931* (Aldershot: Gregg Revivals, 1993), ch. 3.
14. Morgan, *Lloyd George*, pp. 170–2.
15. *Liberal Magazine*, April 1924.
16. Thomas Jones, *Whitehall Diary*, ed. Keith Middlemas (London: Oxford University Press, 1969), pp. 277–8 (diary entry 27 April 1924).
17. *Manchester Guardian*, 23 April 1924.
18. Grigg to Bailey, 20 March 1924, Grigg Papers.
19. Hobhouse to Scott, 7 November 1924, C. P. Scott Papers.
20. J. M Kenworthy, *Sailors, Statesmen – And Others* (London: Rich & Cowan, 1933), pp. 213–15.
21. Stansgate Dairy, 11 March 1924, Stansgate MSS ST/66. For a personal view of his father, see Tony Benn, *Dare To Be A Daniel: Then and Now* (London: Arrow Books, 2004), chs 1–2.
22. This section draws heavily on Chris Cook, 'By-Elections of the First Labour Government', in Chris Cook and John Ramsden (eds), *By-Elections in British Politics* (London: Macmillan, 1973), pp. 44–71.
23. Chris Wrigley, *Arthur Henderson* (Cardiff: GPC Books University of Wales, 1990), pp. 151–2.
24. Ross McKibbin, *The Evolution of the Labour Party, 1910–1924* (Oxford: Oxford University Press, 1983), pp. 193–6; Cook, 'By-Elections of the First Labour Government', pp. 64–6.
25. Ben Pimlott, *Hugh Dalton* (London: Jonathan Cape, 1985), pp. 147–8.
26. Cook 'By-Elections of the First Labour Government', pp. 69–71.
27. *The Times*, 18 July 1924.
28. Kenneth Young, *Stanley Baldwin* (London: Weidenfeld & Nicolson, 1976), p. 55.
29. Jones, *Whitehall Diary*, pp. 257 (diary entry 28 November 1923).
30. Robert Rhodes James, *Bob Boothby: A Portrait* (London: Headline, 1992), pp. 55–7.
31. John Ramsden, *An Appetite for Power: A History of the Conservative Party since 1830* (London: HarperCollins, 1998), p. 260.
32. Ibid., p. 213.
33. John Ramsden, *The Age of Balfour and Baldwin* (London: Longman, 1978), p. 211.
34. R. Blake, *The Conservative Party from Peel to Thatcher* (London: Fontana, 1985 edn); Keith Middlemas and John Barnes, *Baldwin* (London: Weidenfeld & Nicolson, 1969); H. Montgomery Hyde, *Baldwin: The Unexpected Prime Minister* (London: Hart-Davis, MacGibbon, 1973).
35. Margaret Cole (ed), *Beatrice Webb's Diaries, 1924–1932* (London: Longmans. Green, 1956), p. 13 (diary entry 15 March 1924).
36. Ibid., pp. 9–10 (diary entries 15, 29 February 1924).
37. *The Times*, 30 May 1924.
38. Stansgate Papers ST/66, diary 8 October 1924.
39. PLP Minutes, 28 July 1924.
40. *Daily Herald* cutting, no date, in LP/DH/1-489, 1st box, vol. 3.
41. *Manchester Guardian*, 8 February 1924.

42. Vivian Phillipps to C. P. Scott, 19 July 1924, quoted in Wilson, *The Political Diaries of C. P. Scott, 1911–1928*, p. 462.
43. Ibid., pp. 470–1 (diary entry 29 November 1924).
44. PLP Minutes, 22 January 1924.
45. Ibid.
46. Ibid.
47. Ibid., 26 February 1924 The 12 members of the new Executive were R. Smillie, G. Lansbury, R. C. Wallhead, E. D. Morel, Miss Jewson, J. R. Hayes, G. Edwards, J. Maxton, Miss Lawrence, H. Snell, J. Scurr and T. Johnston. See also David Howell, *MacDonald's Party: Labour Identities and Crisis, 1922–1931* (Oxford: Oxford University Press, 2002), p. 30.
48. MacDonald Diary, 3 February 1924.
49. Ibid.
50. PLP Minutes, 11 February 1924.
51. Ibid., 8 April 1924.
52. PLP Minutes, 26 February 1924.
53. MacDonald Diary, 21 March 1924.
54. *Hansard Parliamentary Debates*, 5th series. vol. 171, 17 March 1924, cols 83–194.
55. PLP Minutes, 28 March 1924.
56. Ibid., 7 May 1924.
57. Howell, *MacDonald's Party*, p. 32.
58. PLP Minutes, 29 May 1924. This quotation is taken from Arthur Henderson's Home Office letter, dated 12 April 1924.
59. PLP Minutes, 29 May 1924.
60. Ibid., 29 May and 10 July 1924.
61. Ibid., 29 May and 4 June 1924.
62. MacDonald Diary, 30 September 1924.
63. LP/DH/24/3.
64. LP/DH/24/4.
65. LP/DH/24/5.
66. LP/DH/24/6.
67. *Daily Herald*, 13 August 1924.
68. Ibid., 14 August 1924. The article also contains a reference to the mistake of the Attorney-General in prosecuting Mr Campbell 'under some murky old act'.
69. Ibid., 16 August 1924 and LP/DH/24/12.
70. Ibid., 11 July 1924.
71. *Daily Herald*, 21–22 November 1922.
72. John Shepherd, *George Lansbury: At the Heart of Old Labour* (Oxford: Oxford University Press, 2002), pp. 209–11.
73. Ibid., p. 212.
74. *Daily Herald*, 19 May 1924.
75. Ibid., 20 May 1924.
76. LP/DH/302-388, Letter dated 23 June 1924 from George Lansbury to J. S. Middleton.
77. Letter from J. Ramsay MacDonald to Fenner Brockway, 1 August 1924, in the possession of Jeni Freeman, of Fordyke House, Little Hale, Sleaford, Lincolnshire. NG34 9BA.

78. Quoted in Richard Lyman, *The First Labour Government* (London: Chapman & Hall, 1957), p. 164.
79. *Hansard Parliamentary Debates*, 5th series vol. 173, 22 May 1924, cols 2059–11 (emphasis added).

Chapter 6   Foreign and imperial policy

1. Harold Nicolson, *King George V: His Life and Reign* (London: Constable, 1984) p. 385. Salisbury was Prime Minister and Foreign Secretary in 1885, 1886; 1895–1900.
2. *Hansard Parliamentary Debates*, 12 February 1924, vol. 169, col. 767.
3. For an outstanding account, see Kenneth O. Morgan, *Consensus and Disunity: The Lloyd George Coalition Government, 1918–1922* (Oxford: Clarendon Press, 1986), chs 5, 13.
4. Kenneth O. Morgan, *Labour People: Leaders and Lieutenants: from Hardie to Kinnock* (Oxford: Oxford University Press, 1987), pp. 43–4.
5. For the Union of Democratic Control, see Sally Harris, *Out of Control: British Foreign Policy and the Union of Democratic Control, 1914–1918* (Hull: Hull University Press, 1996).
6. Casper Sylvest, ' "A Commanding Group?" Labour's Advisory Committee on International Questions, 1918–1931', in Paul Carthorn and Ian Davis (eds), *The British Labour Party and the Wider World* (London: I. B. Taurus, 2006); Henry R. Winkler, 'The Emergence of a Labour Foreign Policy in Great Britain, 1918–1929', *The Journal of Modern History*, 28:3 (1956); Henry R. Winkler, *Paths Not Taken: British Labour and International Policy in the 1920s* (Chapel Hill, NC: University of North Carolina Press, 1994; and Henry K. Winkler, *British Labour Seeks a Foreign Policy, 1910–1940* (London: Transaction Publishers, 2005).
7. Ramsay MacDonald to Gilbert Murray, 12 July 1923, Murray Papers, f.23; Rose Rosenberg to Gilbert Murray, 23 June 1924, ibid., f.34; Donald S. Birn, *The League of Nations Union, 1918–1945*(Oxford: Clarendon Press, 1981), ch. III.
8. For an important survey of the Labour Party and foreign affairs in the 1920s, see Winkler, *Paths Not Taken*. Also see Winkler, *British Labour Seeks a Foreign Policy*.
9. Rhiannon Vickers, *The Labour Party and the World: Volume 1, The Evolution of Labour's Foreign Policy, 1900–1951* (Manchester: Manchester University Press, 2004), p. 3.
10. A. Hutt, *The Post-War History of the British Working Class* (London: Left Book Club, Gollancz, 1937), p. 91.
11. Arthur Ponsonby to Dorothy Ponsonby, 21 January 1924. Shulbrede Mss, Box 9.
12. For a recent study of the Ruhr Crisis, see Elspeth Y. O'Riordan, *Britain and the Ruhr Crisis* (Basingstoke: Palgrave in association with King's College London, 2001).
13. MacDonald Diary, 3 February 1924.
14. Hutt, *The Post-War History of the British Working Class*, p.88.
15. Hankey to Smuts, 1 April 1924, Hankey Papers 4/16.

16. R. Lyman, *The First Labour Government 1924* (London: Chapman & Hall, 1957), p. 160.
17. Cabinet 23/47(8)(24), 28 January 1924.
18. *The Times*, 3 March 1924.
19. D'Abernon to MacDonald, 11 February, 4 March 1924, D'Abernon Papers Add Ms 48926 ff. 9–11; 13–14.
20. MacDonald Diary, 10 April 1924.
21. D. Marquand, *Ramsay MacDonald* (London: Jonathan Cape, 1977), pp. 334–9.
22. Cabinet 23/47(26)(24), 10 April 1924.
23. T. Jones, *Whitehall Diaries*, vol. 1, 1916–1925, ed. Keith Middlemass (London: Oxford University Press, 1968) 20 March 1924 entry, p. 273.
24. Ibid., 9 April 1924, pp. 276–7.
25. Hankey to Smuts, 1 April 1924, Hankey Papers 4/16.
26. Robert Cecil to Lady Cavendish, 18 February 1924, Cecil Papers Add Ms. 51164. f. 4.
27. Robert Cecil to Gertrude Bell, 22 February 1924, Ibid. f. 9.
28. Marquand, *Ramsay MacDonald*, p. 341.
29. *Daily Herald*, 11 July 1924.
30. Hutt, *The Post-War History of the British Working Class*, p. 89.
31. R. E. Dowse, *Left in the Centre* (London: Longmans, 1966), p. 102.
32. H. L. Lindsay to MacDonald, 4 July 1924, quoted in Marquand, *Ramsay MacDonald*, p. 342.
33. PLP Minutes, 4 June 1924.
34. Hankey Diary, 11 October 1924. Hankey attributed his late diary entry 'partly because I had an attack of writer's cramp... partly because I cannot write of what happens at Cabinet owing to my Oath as Clerk of the (Privy) Council...'. See also, John F. Naylor, *A Man and an Institution: Sir Maurice Hankey, the Cabinet Secretariat and the Custody of Cabinet secrecy* (Cambridge: Cambridge University Press, 1984), pp. 133–5.
35. Lyman, *First Labour Government*, pp. 211–13.
36. *Daily Herald*, 15 July 1924.
37. Ibid.
38. Catherine Ann Cline, 'E. D. Morel and the Crusade Against the Foreign Office' *Journal of Modern History*, 39:2 (June 1967), 126–37.
39. A. Ponsonby, *Brief Glimpses: E. D. Morel*. (n.d.) Shulbrede Mss. See also, Morel to Parmoor, 2 February 1924, Morel Papers F.2. 1/12; Ponsonby to Morel, 23 May 1924, ibid. F8/123, *Foreign Affairs*, May 1924.
40. *Proceedings of the London Reparations Conference*, cmnd 2270, vol. 1, pp. 1–2
41. Ibid., vol. 2, pp. 160–3, 167.
42. Ibid., pp. 175–9.
43. MacDonald, Dairy, 8 August 1924.
44. Marquand, *MacDonald*, p. 349.
45. Ibid.
46. Jones, *Whitehall Diary*, vol. 1, entry 8 August 1924, p. 290.
47. *Proceedings of the London Reparations Conference*, vol. 2, pp. 185–92.
48. MacDonald to Snowden, 2 a.m., 14 August 1924, MDP1/127, quoted in Marquand, *Ramsay MacDonald*, pp. 349–50.
49. MacDonald's Diary, 14 August 1924.
50. Ibid., 15 August 1924.

51. *Proceedings of the London Reparations Conference*, vol. 2, pp. 7–8.
52. Labour Party Archives, LP/DH/24/6.
53. *Daily Herald*, 14 August 1924.
54. Prime Minister's Private Office Papers, 1, 37, quoted in D. Howell, *MacDonald's Party: Labour Identities and Crisis* (Oxford: Oxford University Press, 2002), p. 144. Howell's book contains more evidence on this point on pages 144–5.
55. Gregory Blaxland, *J. H. Thomas: A Life for Unity* (London: Frederick Muller, 1969), p. 169.
56. Howell, *MacDonald's Party*, p. 9.
57. Sidney Webb, 'The First Labour Government', *Political Quarterly*, 32 (1961), pp. 18–20.
58. For Olivier, see Francis Lee, *Fabianism and Colonialism: The Life and Political Thought of Lord Sydney Olivier* (London: Defiant Books, 1988), especially ch. 5.
59. Webb, 'The First Labour Government', p. 21.
60. For the Amritsar Massacre, see Denis Judd, *Empire: The British Imperial Experience, from 1765 to the Present* (London: HarperCollins, 1996), ch. 20.
61. James Ramsay MacDonald, *The Awakening of India* (1910), p. 187, quoted in Marquand, *Ramsay MacDonald*, p. 118.
62. Denis Judd, *The Lion and the Tiger: The Rise and Fall of the British Raj* (Oxford: Oxford University Press, 2004), ch. 8.
63. Lee, *Fabianism and Colonialism*, pp. 145–9.
64. Jones, *Whitehall Diary*, vol. 1, 20 March 1924, p. 274.
65. Sir Gilbert Clayton to Walford Selby, 3 March 1924, cited in the Curzon Papers (PRO FO 800/156/177 ff., quoted in Bermard Wasserstein, *The British in Palestine: The Mandatory Government and the Arab-Jewish Conflict, 1927–1929* (London: The Royal Historical Society, 1978), p. 148. Returning to British politics Samuel played an important role in the events of the 1926 General Strike.
66. Joseph Gorny, *The British Labour Movement and Zionism, 1917–1948* (London: Frank Cass, 1983), ch. 3; Bernard Wasserstein, 'Samuel, Herbert Louis, first Viscount Samuel (1870–1963)', *Oxford Dictionary of National Biography*, ed. Colin Mathew and Brian Harrison (Oxford: Oxford University Press, 2004), pp. 819–20.
67. Ibid., p. 264.
68. Leeds City Labour Party, Minutes, 18 June 1930.
69. Jacques Berque, *Egypt: Imperialism and Revolution* (London, Faber & Faber, 1972), pp. 372–3.
70. Ibid., p. 388.
71. Marquand, *Ramsay MacDonald*, p. 339, quoting from the Foreign Office record of Chequers talks.
72. League of Nations, *Official Journal, Records of the Fifth Assembly, Text of Debates* (Geneva, 1924), pp. 41–5.
73. Marquand, *Ramsay MacDonald*, p. 353.
74. MacDonald, *Diary*, 21 September 1924.
75. *The Times*, 27 September 1924.
76. Lord Parmoor, *A Retrospect* (1936), pp. 196–7.
77. Marquand, *Ramsay MacDonald*, p. 354.
78. Ibid., p. 342.

79. *The Times*, 13 October 1924.
80. Chris Wrigley, *Arthur Henderson* (Cardiff: GPC Books/University of Wales Press, 1990), p. 154.
81. Snowden to MacDonald, 14 October 1927, MacDonald Papers, PRO 30/69/1753.
82. MacDonald to Massingham, 19 December 1923; Massingham to MacDonald, 21 December 1923, Massingham Papers.
83. Rakovsky to MacDonald, 22 January 1924, MacDonald Papers PRO 30/69/1264.
84. *Hansard Parliamentary Debates* (1924), vol. 169, cols 768–9
85. Hutt, *The Post-War History of the British Working Class*, pp. 90–1.
86. For Ponsonby's declining relations with MacDonald, see Ponsonby Diary, 3 March, 7 June, 13, 25 August, 24 September, 31 October, 8 November 1924, Shulbrede MSS.
87. Cabinet 44 (24), 30 July 1924.
88. Ponsonby Diary, 13 August 1924.
89. *Manchester Guardian*, 3 September 1924.
90. Ponsonby to MacDonald, 14 September 1924, MacDonald Papers PRO30/69/1264.
91. MacDonald Diary, 26 September 1924.
92. *The Times*, 29 September 1924.
93. Lyman, *The First Labour Government*, 1924, p. 164.
94. *The Austen Chamberlain Dairy Letters: The Correspondence of Sir Austen Chamberlain with his sisters Hilda and Ida, 1916–1937*, ed. Robert C. Self, Camden 5th series, vol. 5 (Cambridge, Cambridge University Press, 1995), AC5/1/334, letter to Ida, 5 October 1924.

Chapter 7   Downfall

1. Margaret Cole, *Beatrice Webb Diaries, 1924–1932* (Longmans: 1956), p. vii.
2. Lucy Masterman, *C. F. G. Masterman* (London: Nicolson & Watson, 1939), p. 351.
3. Sidney Webb to Beatrice Webb, 2 October 1924, in Norman Mackenzie (ed.), *The Letters of Sidney and Beatrice Webb, Volume IV: Pilgrimage, 1912–1947* (Cambridge: Cambridge University Press and the London School of Economics, 1978), pp. 216–7.
4. G. D. H. Cole, *A History of the Labour Party* (London: Routledge & Kegan Paul, 1948).
5. For the legal issues in the Campbell Case, see F. H. Newark, 'The Campbell Case and the First Labour Government', *Northern Ireland Legal Quarterely*, 1:1 (1969), 19–42.
6. *Workers' Weekly*, 25 July 1924.
7. *Hansard Parliamentary Debates*, 5th series, vol. 176, 29 July 1924, col. 1897.
8. N. and J. Mackenzie (eds), *The Diary of Beatrice Webb, Volume 4: 1924–1943: The Wheel of Life* (London: Virago and the London School of Economics, 1985), pp. 19–20.
9. *Hansard Parliamentary Debates*, 5th series, vol. 176, 6 August 1924, cols 2928–30; 7 August 1924, col. 3080.

10. Trevor Barnes, 'Special Branch and the First Labour Government', *Historical Journal*, 22:4 (1979).
11. *Parliamentary Debates*, 5th series, vol. 176, 8 August 1924.
12. Ibid.
13. Ibid., 25 July 1924.
14. Barnes, 'Special Branch and the First Labour Government'.
15. As Chancellor of the Duchy of Lancaster, Josiah Wedgwood knew of these plans, but said and did nothing about them.
16. Alexander to Kell, 7th August 1924, PRO KV 2/1186.
17. PRO KV 2/1186 Admiralty Reference Sheet, 11 August 1924.
18. Cabinet 48 (24) 6 August 1924, CAB 23/48.
19. For the pre-First World War 'Don't Shoot!' campaign, and the Labour protests over the prosecution of Fred Crowsley, Tom Mann, Guy Bowman, Benjamin and Charles Buck, see John Shepherd, *George Lansbury: At the Heart of Old Labour* (Oxford: Oxford University Press, 2002), pp. 108–9.
20. *Workers' Weekly*, 15 August 1924.
21. C. L. Mowat, *Britain between the Wars, 1918–1940* (London: Methuen, 1955), p. 183.
22. H. Montgomery Hyde, *Baldwin* (London: Hart-Davis, MacGibbon, 1973), pp. 219–20.
23. *Hansard Parliamentary Debates*, 5th series, vol. 177, 30 September 1924, cols. 8–15.
24. Ibid., col. 16.
25. T. Jones, *Whitehall Diary*, Vol. 1: 1916–1925, ed. Keith Middlemas (London: Oxford University Press, 1969), p. 296, entry for 15 October 1924.
26. For the Cabinet meeting of 6 August 1924, see ibid., pp. 287–90: see also D. Marquand, *Ramsay MacDonald* (London: Jonathan Cape, 1977), pp. 364–70. For MacDonald's explanation to the King, see H. Nicolson, *King George V: His Life and Reign* (London, Constable, 1952), pp. 398–9.
27. MacDonald to Stamfordham, 22 August 1924, RA PS/GV/K 1958/4.
28. Jones, *Whitehall Diary*, pp. 295–97.
29. Kenneth O. Morgan, *Consensus and Disunity: The Lloyd George Coalition Government, 1918–1922* (Oxford: Oxford University Press, 1986), pp. 133–7, 308–14.
30. Gill Bennett, *'A most extraordinary and mysterious business': The Zinoviev Letter of 1924* (London: Foreign and Commonwealth Office, Historians LRD) no. 14, January 1994.
31. Arthur Ponsonby, 'Brief Glimpses: J Ramsay MacDonald' (typescript, n.d.) Shulbrede Ms.
32. Ponsonby Diary, 7 June, 1924, Shulbrede MSS.
33. *The Times*, 4 July 1924.
34. Arthur Ponsonby to Dorothy Ponsonby, 31 July 1924, Shulbrede Ms. Box 10.
35. Arthur Ponsonby to Dorothy Ponsonby, 21 July 1924, ibid.
36. *Foreign Affairs*, September 1924.
37. R. A. Jones, *Arthur Ponsonby: The Politics of Life* (London: Christopher Helm, 1989), pp. 149–51. For Ponsonby's detailed recollections, see Ponsonby Diary, 18 August 1924, Shulbrede MSS. See also E. D. Morel, 'How the Anglo-Russian Conference Was Saved by the Labour Back Benchers: Secret History of the Events of August 5, 6, 7, 1924', Morel MSS F2 3/1; Richard Lyman, *The First Labour Government* (London: Chapman & Hall, 1957),

pp. 193–5, which is based mainly on Morel's account in *Foreign Affairs*, September 1924.

38. Chris Cook, *The Age of Alignment: Electoral Politics in Britain, 1922–1929* (Basingstoke: Macmillan, 1975), pp. 269–72.

39. Lucy Masterman, *C. F. G. Masterman: A Biography* (London: Nicolson & Watson, 1939), p. 349.

40. David Dutton, *Simon: A Political Biography of Sir John Simon* (London: Atrum Press, 1992), pp. 64–7.

41. Cited in Stephen Koss, *Asquith* (London: Allen Lane, 1976), p. 266.

42. From Chequers MacDonald wrote to Baldwin asking for 'a good photograph of you here in the study... Your predecessor is here and puts the Devil into me and makes me feel anything but proud of my job.' MacDonald to Baldwin, 29 March, Baldwin papers, vol. 159, f. 230.

43. *Westminster Gazette*, 8 July 1924; *Daily Chronicle*, 8 August 1924.

44. John Campbell, *Lloyd George: The Goat in the Wilderness, 1922–1931* (Aldershot: Gregg Revivals, 1977,1999 edn), pp. 85–9.

45. Lloyd George to Megan Lloyd George, 2 October 1924, Kenneth O. Morgan (ed.), *Lloyd George Family Letters, 1885–1936* (Cardiff and London: University and Wales Press and Oxford University Press, 1973), p. 204.

46. Margaret I. Cole (ed.), *Beatrice Webb Diaries, 1924–1932*, ed. Margaret I. Cole (London: Longman, 1956), p. 44.

47. Ibid.

48. MacDonald to Stamfordham, 2 October 1924, RA PS/GV/K 1958/4.

49. Trevor Wilson (ed.), *The Political Diaries of C. P. Scott, 1911–1928* (London: Collins, 1970), pp. 475–7, diary entry 4 March 1925.

50. Henry Slesser, *Judgement Reserved: The Reminiscences of the Right Honourable Sir Henry Slesser* (London: Hutchinson, 1941), pp. 104–5.

51. Ibid.

52. J. R. Clynes, *Memoirs, 1924–1937* (London: Hutchinson, 1937), pp. 64–5.

53. Philip Snowden, *An Autobiography: Volume Two, 1919–1934* (London: Nicolson & Watson, 1934).

54. Ibid.

55. Thomas Johnstone, *Memories* (London: Collins, 1952), pp. 57–8.

56. Emanuel Shinwell, *Conflict without Malice* (London: Odhams, 1955), p. 96.

57. Richard Burdon Haldane, *An Autobiography* (London: Hodder & Stoughton, 1929), pp. 328–9.

58. G. D. H. Cole, *A History of the Labour Party from 1914* (London: Routledge & Kegan Paul, 1948), pp. 164–5.

59. A. Thorpe, *A History of the British Labour Party* (Basingstoke: Palgrave, 1997 and 2000), pp. 59–60.

60. Baron Beaverbrook, 'Who Killed Cock Robin?', draft article, *Sunday Express*, 23 November 1924, Beaverbrook Papers, BBK/G/12/6.

61. Cabinet 23/48(53)(24), 8 October 1924.

62. Cabinet 23/48(54)(24), 8 October 1924.

63. Nicolson, *King George V* (1952 and 1984 edns), pp. 398–400.

64. David Dutton, *A History of The Liberal Party in the Twentieth Century* (Basingstoke: Palgrave, 2004), pp. 100–1.

65. A. H. Booth, *British Hustings, 1924–1950* (London: Muller, 1956).

66. *Daily Mail*, 25 October 1924.

67. Gabriel Garodetsky, *The Precarious Truce: Anglo-Soviet Relations* (Cambridge: Cambridge University Press, 1977), pp. 35–6.
68. Ibid., p. 38.
69. Foreign and Commonwealth Office, '*A Most extraordinary and mysterious business*', which contains a detailed bibliography. See especially Lewis Chester, Stephen Fay and Hugo Young, *The Zinoviev Letter: A Political Intrigue* (London: Heinemann, 1967); Nigel West and Oleg Tsarev, *The Crown Jewels: The British Secrets at the Heart of the KGB Archives* (London: HarperCollins, 1998).
70. Jonathan Pile, 'Red Letter of Deception', *Tribune*, 5 November 2004.
71. Joseph Ball Papers, Ms. Eng c 6652–3.
72. For 'The Plot Against Harold Wilson', see John Booth, 'Elected by the People, Undone by the Plotters', *Tribune*, 17 March 2006.

Chapter 8   Political aftermath

1. Philip Snowden to Fred Jowett, 31 October, 18 November 1924, cited in Fenner Brockway, *Socialism over Sixty Years: The Life of Jowett of Bradford (1864–1944)* (London: George Allen & Unwin, 1946), pp. 222–3, 410.
2. Colin Cross, *Philip Snowden* (London: Barrie and Rockliff, 1966), p. 213.
3. Thomas Jones, *Whitehall Diary*, ed. Keith Middlemas (London: Oxford University Press, 1969), pp. 298–9.
4. Ibid., pp. 299–300; David Marquand, *Ramsay MacDonald*, (London: Jonathan Cape, 1977).
5. 'The Fall of the Labour Government', *Beatrice Webb's Diaries, 1924–1932* (London: Longman, 1956), p. 50.
6. F. W. S. Craig, *British Electoral Facts, 1885–1975* (London: Macmillan, 1976), pp. 13–14; for slightly different figures, see *Labour Party Conference Report, 1925* (London: Labour Party, 1925), p. 305, which provides a complete breakdown of the general election result, mainly from the Labour perspective.
7. David Dutton, *A History of the Liberal Party in the Twentieth Century* (Houndmills: Palgrave Macmillan, 2004), p. 102.
8. Marquand, *Ramsay MacDonald*, p. 387.
9. C. P. Scott Diary, 27 November 1924.
10. Jones, *Whitehall Diaries*, Vol. 1, entry 4 November 1924, p. 301
11. Jack Reynolds and Keith Laybourn, *Labour Heartland: A History of the Labour Party in West Yorkshire During the Inter-War Years, 1918–1939* (Bradford: University of Bradford Press, 1987), pp. 33–64.
12. Michael Kinnear, *The British Voter: An Atlas and Survey since 1885*, 2nd edn (London: Batsford, 1981), p. 112.
13. Keighley County Divisional Liberal Party, Minutes, 13 December 1924.
14. Leeds Liberal Federation, Cabinet Committee, 19 July 1926.
15. Reynolds and Laybourn, *Labour Heartland*, ch. 2, and particularly pp. 36 and 54.
16. Ibid., p. 57.
17. Ibid., pp. 58–62.
18. Ibid., pp. 158–61.
19. *Birmingham Gazette*, 28 October 1924.

20. John Ward, 'The Development of the Labour Party in the Black Country, 1918–1929', unpublished PhD of the University of Wolverhampton, 2004, p. 188.
21. John Charmley, *A History of Conservative Politics, 1900–1995* (Basingstoke: Macmillan – now Palgrave Macmillan, 1998), pp. 74–5.
22. David Howell, *MacDonald's Party: Labour Identities and Crisis, 1922–1931* (Oxford: Oxford University Press, 2002), p. 89.
23. MacDonald Diary, 30 September 1924.
24. PLP, Minutes, 3 December 1924.
25. *Ibid.*, 3 December 1924.
26. D. Howell, *MacDonald's Party: Labour Identities and Crisis* (Oxford: Oxford University Press, 2002), p. 34, also referring to a letter from T. E. Naylor to MacDonald, 5 December 1924, enclosing a copy of the *Westminster Gazette* report, MacDonald Papers,PRO 30/69/1170.
27. PLP Minutes, 9 December 1924.
28. Ibid., December 1925.
29. Ibid., 27 June 1929.
30. *The Labour Party Conference Report, 1924* (London: Labour Party, 1924), p. 113.
31. Ibid., p.115.
32. *The Labour Party Conference Report, 1925* (London: Labour Party, 1925), p. 172.
33. Ibid., p. 219.
34. Ibid.
35. Ibid.
36. Ibid., p. 221.
37. Philip Snowden, *An Autobiography* (London: Ivor Nicholson & Watson, 1934), vol. 2, p. 573.
38. Cross, *Philip Snowden*, p. 212.
39. MacDonald Diary, PRO 30/69/1753.
40. *Labour Party Conference, 1925*, p. 172.
41. Ibid., p. 173.
42. *Workers Weekly*, 25 April 1924.
43. Report of the Congress of the CPGB, Swalford, Manchester, 16–18 May 1924.
44. *Labour Party Conference Report*, 1924, p. 123.
45. Ibid., p. 128.
46. Ibid., p. 123.
47. Ibid., p. 127.
48. J. Klugmann, *History of the Communist Party of Great Britain: Formation and Early Years*, vol. 1, 1919–1924 (London: Lawrence & Wishart, 1968), pp. 166–181 traces in great detail the moves by the CPGB to achieve affiliation.
49. Harry Pollitt Papers, CP/IND/POLL/3/1, 'The New Phase in Britain and the Communist Party' (draft by R. P. Dutt), p. 29.
50. MacDonald Papers, John Rylands Library, RMD 1/5/2, a statement signed by Arthur Henderson.
51. *Labour Party Conference Report*, 1925, p. 187.
52. Ibid.
53. Keith Laybourn and Dylan Murphy, *Under the Red Flag* (Stroud: Sutton, 1999), pp. 50–74.
54. MacDonald Papers, John Rylands Library, RMD 1/5/13.
55. Laybourn and Murphy, *Under the Red Flag*, pp. 88, 99–100.

56. *Workers' Bulletin*, 13 May 1926. Also see Keith Laybourn, *The General Strike of 1926* (Manchester: Manchester University Press, 1993); and Keith Laybourn, *The General Strike: Day by Day* (Stroud: Sutton, 1996).

Chapter 9   Conclusion

1. Thomas Jones, *Whitehall Diary: Volume 1, 1916–1925* (London: Oxford University Press, 1969), p. 301.
2. PLP Minutes, 28 July 1924.
3. Philip Snowden,*The Housewife's Budget* (London: Labour Party, 1924).
4. Keith Laybourn, *Unemployment and Employment with Particular Reference to Women in Britain c. 1900–1951* (Lampeter: Edwin Mellen, 2002), particularly chs 3 and 4; Keith Laybourn, 'Waking up to the Fact that there are any unemployed': Women, Unemployment and the Domestic Solution in Britain, 1918–1939', *History*, 88:4 (2003), 607–23.
5. Robert Cecil to Lady Cavendish, 18 February 1924, Cecil Papers, Add Ms 51164 f.4.
6. *Daily Herald*, 14 August 1924.
7. Lewis Minkin, *The Contentious Alliance: Trade Unions and the Labour Party* (Edinburgh: Edinburgh University Press, 1991).
8. Ibid., pp. 30–4.
9. The General Secretary's Papers (Morgan Phillips), 'Lost Sheep Files', Box 4, such as GS/LS/49 to GS/LS/72 which contain material on Nye Bevan.
10. Jones, *Whitehall Diary*, entry date 3 November 1924, p. 301.
11. *Labour Party Conference Report*, 1925, p. 172.
12. Ibid., p. 177.

Bibliography

A Unpublished primary sources

1 Private Papers

Stanley Baldwin Papers (Cambridge University Library)
Sir Joseph Ball Papers (Bodleian Library)
Lord Beaverbrook Papers (House of Lords Record Office)
John Burns Papers (British Library)
Sir Robert Cecil Papers (British Library)
Lord D'Abernon Papers (British Library)
David Lloyd George Papers (House of Lords Record Office)
Viscount Gladstone Papers
Grigg Papers (Bodleian Library)
Lord Haldane Papers (National Library of Scotland)
Sir Maurice Hankey Papers (Churchill Archives, Cambridge)
J. R. MacDonald Papers (John Rylands Library)
J. R. MacDonald Papers (The National Archives)
Violet Markham Papers (British Library of Political and Economic Science)
J. S. Middleton Papers (Nuffield College Library)
E. D. Morel Papers (British Library of Political and Economic Science)
Gilbert Murray Papers (Bodleian Library)
Harry Pollitt Papers (Labour History Archive and Study Centre, Manchester)
Lord Ponsonby Papers (Bodleian Library)
The Royal Archives (Windsor)
C. P. Scott Papers (British Library)
E. D. Simon Papers (Manchester Reference Library)
Lord Simon Papers (Bodleian Library)
Lord Stansgate Papers (House of Lord Record Office)
J. St Loe Strachey Papers (House of Lords Record Office)
J. H. Thomas Papers (Kent Record Office)
Charles P. Trevelyan Papers (Robinson Library, Newcastle University)
Sidney and Beatrice Webb/Lord Passfield Papers (British Library of Political and
     Economic Science)
Josiah Wedgwood Papers (Keele University Library)

2 Other Papers (in private possession)

Lord Ponsonby Papers (Shulbrede Priory: courtesy of Ponsonby family)
James Ramsay MacDonald correspondence (courtesy of Jeni Freeman, Fordyke
     House, Little Hale, Sleaford, Lincolnshire)

3 Official sources

The National Archives
CABINET CONCLUSIONS FOR 1924
CAB 21, 23
FO 371
PREM 1
Hansard (Parliamentary Debates)

4 Labour Party sources (Labour History Archive and Study Centre, Manchester)

Advisory Committee on International Questions
Advisory Committee on Local Government
Annual Conference Reports
Departmental Correspondence
General Correspondence
General Secretaries' Papers
National Executive Committee Minutes
Parliamentary Labour Party Minutes

5 Trade union and political party sources

Keighley County Divisional Liberal Party Minutes, 1924
Leeds Liberal Federation Minutes of the Executive Committee.
Miners' Federation of Great Britain records, 1924
Trades Union Congress archives, 1924.
Yorkshire Liberal Federation Minutes and Annual Report.

6 Other collections

Central Committee on Women's Training and Employment (CCWTE) Minutes (Violet Markham Collection, British Library of Political and Economic Science)
Communist Party of Great Britain archive (Labour History Archive and Study Centre, Manchester)
Magistrates Papers, Duchy of Lancaster Office

B Published primary sources

1 Contemporaneous material including memoirs, books, pamphlets and reports

Angell, N., *After All: The Autobiography of Norman Angell* (London: Hamish Hamilton, 1951).
Attlee, C. R., *As It Happened* (London: Heinemann, 1954).
Clynes, J. R., *Memoirs, 1924–1937* (London: Hutchinson, 1937).
Cole, M., *Growing up into Revolution* (London: Longman, 1949).
Gallacher, W., *The Rolling of Thunder* (London: Lawrence & Wishart, 1947).
Holmes-Laski Letters: The Correspondence of Mr. Justice and Harold J. Laski, 1916–1935, ed. M. De Wolfe (London: Oxford University Press, 1953).

Haldane, R. B., *An Autobiography* (London: Hodder & Stoughton, 1929).

Independent Labour Party, *Conference Report, 1923* (London: Independent Labour Party, 1923).

ILP Summer School, Bryn Corach, Conway, N. Wales, June 30th to July 13th 1919 (London: ILP, 1919).

Johnstone, T., *Memories* (London: Collins, 1952).

Jones, T., *Whitehall Diary*, vol. 1, 1916–1925, ed. Keith Middlemas (London: Oxford University Press, 1968).

Kenworthy, J. M., *Sailors, Statesmen – And Others* (London: Rich & Cowan, 1933).

Labour Party *General Election Manifesto, 1923* (London: Labour Party, 1923).

Labour Party, *Secondary Education for All: A Policy for Labour* (London: Labour Party, 1922, reproduced by Hambledon Press, 1988).

League of Nations, *Official Journal of the Records of the Fifth Assembly: Text of Debates* (Geneva, 1924).

MacDonald, J. R., *Socialism and Society* (London: Independent Labour Party, 1905).

MacDonald, J. R., *The Awakening of India* (London: Hodder & Stoughton, 1910).

Miners' Federation of Great Britain, *Annual Conference, 1924*.

Parmoor, Lord, *A Retrospect: Looking Back on the Life of More than Eighty Years* (London: Heinemann, 1936).

Proceedings of the London Reparation Conference (London: HMSO, 1924, cmnds 2270), vols 1 and 2.

Report of the Congress of the CPGB, 1925 (London: CPGB, 1925).

Scott, C. P., *The Political Diaries of C. P. Scott, 1911–1928*, ed. Trevor Wilson (London: Collins, 1970).

Shinwell, E., *Conflict Without Malice* (London: Odhams, 1955).

Simon, Sir J., *Three Speeches on the General Strike* (London: HMSO, 1926).

Slesser, H., *Judgement Reserved* (London: Hutchinson, 1941).

Snowden, P.,*The Socialist Budget* (London: George, Allen & Unwin, 1907).

Snowden, P., *A Plea for Peace* (Blackburn: Blackburn Labour Party, 1916).

Snowden, P., *How to Pay for the War – Tax the Unearned Income of the Rich* (London: 1916).

Snowden, P., *Labour in Chains* (London: National Labour Press, 1917).

Snowden, P., *War and Peace* (London: National Labour Publications, 1918).

Snowden, P., *Labour and the National Finance* (London: Leonard Parsons, 1920).

Snowden, P., *The Big Business Budget*, in the Labour Party Archives (London: Labour Party, 1924).

Snowden, P., *The Housewife's Budget* (London: Labour Party, 1924).

Snowden, P. *An Autobiography, Volume Two: 1919–1934* (London: Nicolson & Watson, 1934).

Spender, H., *The Fire of Life* (London: Hodder & Stoughton, 1926).

The Austen Chamberlain Diary Letters: The Correspondence of Sir Austen Chamberlain with his sisters Hilda and Ida, ed. Robert C. Self, Camden 5th series, vol. 5 (Cambridge: Cambridge University Press, 1995).

The Earl of Oxford and Asquith, *Memories and Reflection,s 1852–1923*, vol. 2 (London: Cassell, 1928).

The Political Diaries of C. P. Scott, 1911–1928, ed. Trevor Wilson (London: Collins, 1976; and London: Leonard Parsons, 1920).

Thomas, J. H., *When Labour Rules* (London: Collins, 1920).

Thomas, J. H., *My Story* (London: Hutchinson, 1937).

Webb, B., *The Diary of Beatrice Webb, Volume Three: 1905–1924*, ed. N. and J. Mackenzie (London: Virago & BLPES, 1984).
Webb, B., *The Diary of Beatrice Webb, Volume Four: 1924–1943*, ed. N. and J. Mackenzie (London: Virago & BLPES, 1985).
Webb, B., *Beatrice Webb's Diaries, 1924–1932*, ed. Margaret I. Cole (London: Longman, 1956).
Webb, S., and B., *The Letters of Sidney and Beatrice Webb, III: Pilgrimage, 1912–1947*, ed. N. Mackenzie (Cambridge: Cambridge University Press and the London School of Economics, 1978).
Wedgwood, J. C., *Memoirs of a Fighting Life* (London: Hutchinson, 1941).
Weir, L. MacNeill, *The Tragedy of Ramsay MacDonald* (London: Secker & Warburg, 1938).
Williams, B., *The Record of the Labour Government* (London: 1929).

2   Articles

Morrison, H., 'London's Labour Majority', *Labour Magazine* 8 (1929/1930).
Phillips, M., 'Birth Control: A Careful Consideration', *The Labour Woman*, March 1924.

C   Secondary sources

1   Books and contributions to books

Bennett, G., *'A Most extraordinary and mysterious business': The Zinoviev Letter of 1924* (London: Foreign and Commonwealth Office, Historians LRD, No. 14, January 1924).
Bentley, M., *The Liberal Mind, 1914–1929* (Cambridge: Cambridge University Press, 1977).
Bentley, M., *The Climax of Liberal Politics: British Liberalism in Theory and Practice* (London: Edward Arnold, 1987).
Birn, D. S., *The League of Nations Union, 1918–1945* (Oxford: Clarendon Press, 1981).
Booth, A., and Pack, M., *Employment, Capital and Economic Policy* (Oxford: Basil Blackwell, 1985).
Blaxland, G., *J. H. Thomas: A Life of Unity* (London: Frederick Muller, 1969).
Brivati, B., and Heffernan, R. (eds), *The Labour Party: A Centenary History* (Basingstoke: Palgrave Macmillan, 2000).
Brockway, F., *Socialism over Sixty Years: The Life of Jowett of Bradford (1984–1944)* (London: Allen & Unwin, 1946).
Brown, G., *Maxton* (Glasgow: Collins/Fontana, 1988).
Bruce, M., *The Rise of the Welfare State: English Social Policy, 1601–1971* (London: Weidenfeld & Nicolson, 1973).
Bullock, A., *The Life and Times of Ernest Bevin*, vol. 1 (London: Heinemann, 1967).
Campbell, J., *Lloyd George: The Goat in the Wilderness, 1922–1931* (Aldershot: Gregg Revivals, 1977, 1999 edns).
Carlton, D., *MacDonald Versus Henderson: The Foreign Policy of the Second Labour Government* (London: Macmillan, 1970).
Charmley, J. *A History of Conservative Politics, 1900–1995* (Basingstoke: Macmillan – now Palgrave Macmillan, 1998).

Clarke, P. F., *Lancashire and the New Liberalism* (Cambridge: Cambridge University Press, 1971).

Cole, G. D. H., *A History of the Labour Party from 1914* (London: Kegan & Paul, 1948).

Cook, C., *The Age of Alignment: Electoral Politics in Britain, 1922–1929* (Basingstoke: Macmillan, 1975).

Cowling, M., *The Impact of Labour, 1921–1926* (Cambridge and London: Cambridge University Press, 1971).

Cross, C., *Philip Snowden* (London: Barrie & Rockcliffe, 1966).

Daalder, H., *Cabinet Reform in Britain* (Stanford: Stanford University Press, 1964).

Englefield D., Seaton, J., and White, I., *Facts About British Prime Ministers: A Compilation of Biographical and Historical Information* (New York: H. W. Wilson, 1998).

Dowse, R. E., *Left in the Centre* (London: Longman, 1966).

Dutton, D., *A History of the Liberal Party in the Twentieth Century* (Basingstoke: Palgrave, Macmillan, 1975).

Dutton, D., *Simon: A Political Biography of Sir John Simon* (London: Atrum Press, 1992).

Garodetsky, G., *The Precarious Truce: Anglo-Soviet Relations* (Cambridge: Cambridge University Press, 1977).

Graves, P., *Labour Women in British Working-Class Politics, 1918–1939* (Cambridge: Cambridge University Press, 1994).

Hamilton, M. A., *Margaret Bondfield* (London: Leonard Parsons, 1924).

Hamilton, M. A., *Ramsay MacDonald* (London: 1929).

Harris, K., *Attlee* (London: Weidenfeld & Nicolson, 1982).

Harris, S., *Out of Control: British Foreign Policy and the Union of Democratic Control, 1914–1918* (Hull: The University of Hull Press, 1996).

Holmes, C., *John Bull's Island: Immigration and British Society, 1871–1971* (Basingstoke: Macmillan – now Palgrave Macmillan, 1998).

Holton, B., *British Syndicalism, 1906–1914: Myths and Realities* (London: Pluto Press, 1978).

Howell, D., *British Workers and the Independent Labour Party, 1888–1906* (Manchester: Manchester University Press, 1983).

Howell, D., *A Lost Left: Three Studies In Socialism and Nationalism* (Manchester: Manchester University Press, 1986).

Howell, D., *MacDonald's Party: Labour Identities and Crisis* (Oxford: Oxford University Press, 2002).

Hutt, A., *The Post-War History of the British Working Class* (London: Left Book Club/Gollancz, 1937).

Hyde, H. M., *Baldwin* (London: Hart-Davis, MacGibbon, 1973).

James, R. R., *Winston Churchill: His Complete Speeches* (Leicester: Windward, 1981).

Jefferys, K., *Leading Labour: From Keir Hardie to Tony Blair* (London: I. B. Tauris, 1999).

Jefferys, K., and Hennessy, P., *States of Emergency: British governments and Strikebreaking since 1919* (London: Routledge & Kegan Paul, 1982).

Jenkinson, J., 'The 1919 Riots', in P. Panayi (ed.), *Racial Violence in Britain in the 19th and 20th centuries* (Leicester: Leicester University Press, 1993).

Jones, R. A., *Arthur Ponsonby: The Politics of Life* (London: Christopher Helm, 1989).

Judd, D., *Empire: The British Imperial Experience, from 1765 to the Present* (London: Harper Collins, 1996).

Judd, D., *The Lion and the Tiger: The Rise and Fall of the British Raj* (Oxford: Oxford University Press, 2004).

Klugmann, J., *History of the Communist Party of Great Britain: Formation and Early Years, Volume 1: 1919–1924* (London: Lawrence & Wishart, 1968).

Koss, S., *Asquith* (London: Allen Lane, 1976).

Krammick, I., and Sheerman, B., *Harold Laski: A Life on the Left* (London: 1993).

Lancaster, B., *Radicalism, Co-operation and Socialism: Leicester Working-Class Politic, 1860–1906* (Leicester: Leicester University Press, 1987).

Lawrence, J., 'Labour – the myths it has lived by', in Duncan Tanner, Pat Thane and Nick Tiratsoo (eds), *Labour's First Century* (Cambridge: Cambridge University Press, 2000).

Laybourn, K., *Philip Snowden: A Biography* (Aldershot: Temple Smith/Gower. Wildwood, 1988).

Laybourn, K., *The Evolution of British Social Policy and the Welfare State* (Keele: Ryburn Publishing and Keele University Press, 1995).

Laybourn, K., *A Century of Labour* (Stroud: Sutton, 2000).

Laybourn, K., *Unemployment and Employment with Particular Reference to Women in Britain, c.1900–1951* (Lampeter: Edwin Mellen, 2002).

Laybourn, K., and Murphy, D., *Under the Red Flag* (Stroud: Sutton, 1999).

Lee, F., *Fabianism and Colonialism: The Life and Political Thought of Lord Sydney Olivier* (London: Defiant Books, 1988).

Leventhal, F. M., *Arthur Henderson* (Manchester: Manchester University Press, 1989).

Lyman, R., *The First Labour Government* (London: Chapman & Hall, 1957).

McFarlane, L. J., *The British Communist Party: Its Origins and Development until 1929* (London: MacGibbon & Kee, 1966).

Mackenzie, R. T., *British Political Parties: The Distribution of Power within the Conservative and Labour Parties* (London: Mercury Books, 1963).

Marquand, D., *Ramsay MacDonald* (London: Jonathan Cape, 1977).

Martin, D., ' "The Instruments of the People?" The Parliamentary Labour Party in 1906', in David E. Martin and David Rubinstein (eds), *Ideology and the Labour Movement: Essays Presented to John Saville* (London: Croom Helm, 1979).

Masterman, L. C. F. G., *Masterman* (London: Nicolson & Watson, 1939).

Maurice, F., *Haldane, 1915–1928* (London: Faber & Faber, 1929).

McKibbin, R., *The Evolution of the Labour Party* (London and Oxford: Oxford University Press, 1974).

Middlemas, R. K., *The Clydesiders: A Left-Wing Struggle for Parliamentary Power* (London: Hutchinson, 1967).

Miliband, R., *Parliamentary Socialism: A Study in the Politics of Labour* (London: Merlin Press, 2002).

Miller, K. E., *Socialism and Foreign Policy: Theory and Practice in Britain to 1931* (The Hague: Martinus Nijhoff, 1967).

Minkin, L., *The Contentious Alliance: Trade Unions and the Labour Party* (Edinburgh: Edinburgh University Press, 1991).

Morgan, K. O., *Lloyd George* (London: Weidenfeld & Nicolson, 1974a).

Morgan, K. O., 'The New Liberalism and the Challenge of Labour: The Welsh Experience, 1885–1929', in Kenneth D. Brown (ed.), *Essays in Labour History: Responses to the Rise of Labour* (London: Macmillan, 1974b).

Morgan, K. O., 'The High and Low Politics of Labour: Keir Hardie to Michael Foot' in Michael Bentley and John Stevenson (eds), *High and Low Politics in Modern Britain* (Oxford: Clarendon Press, 1983).

Morgan, K. O., *Labour in Power, 1945–51* (Oxford: Oxford University Press, 1985).

Morgan, K. O., *Consensus and Disunity: Lloyd George Coalition Government, 1918–1922* (Oxford: Clarendon Press, 1986).

Mowat, C. L., *Britain between the Wars, 1918–1940* (London: Methuen, 1955).

Naylor, J. F., *A Man and an Institution: Sir Maurice Hankey, the Cabinet Secretariat and the Custody of Cabinet Secrecy* (Cambridge: Cambridge University Press, 1984).

Newman, M., *Harold Laski: A Political Biography* (Basingstoke: Macmillan, 1993).

Newman, M., 'Ralph Miliband and the Labour Party: From Parliamentary Socialism to "Bennism"', in J. Callaghan, S. Fielding and Steve Ludlum (eds), *Interpreting the Labour Party: Approaches to Labour Politics and History* (Manchester: Manchester University Press, 2003).

Nicolson, H., *King George V: His Life and Reign* (London, Constable, 1952).

Oxford Dictionary of National Biography (Oxford: Oxford University Press, 2004).

O'Riordan, Elspeth V., *Britain and the Ruhr Crisis* (Basingstoke: Palgrave, 2001).

Panayi, P., *Immigration, Ethnicity and Racism in Britain, 1815–1945* (Manchester: Manchester University Press, 1994)

Pearce, R., *Attlee* (Harlow: Addison Wesley Longman, 1997).

Powell, D., *British Politics, 1910–1935 : The Crisis of the Party System* (London: Routledge, 2004).

Reynolds, J., and Laybourn, K., *Labour Heartland: A History of the Labour Party in West Yorkshire During the Inter-War Years, 1918–1939* (Bradford: Bradford University Press, 1987).

Sassoon, D., *One Hundred Years of Socialism: The West European Left in the Twentieth Century* (New York: The New Press, 1996).

Schwarz, M., *The Union of Democratic Control* (Oxford: Oxford University Press, 1971).

Self, R., *The Evolution of the British Party System, 1885–1929* (London: Macmillan, 1975).

Shepherd, J., 'A Life on the Left: George Lansbury (1859–1940): A Case Study in Recent Labour Biography' *Labour History* (University of Sydney), no. 87, November 2004.

Shepherd, J., *George Lansbury: At the Heart of Old Labour* (Oxford: Oxford University Press, 2002).

Shepherd, J., 'Labour in Parliament: The Lib-Labs as the first working-class MPs, 1895–1906', in Eugenio Biagini and Alistair Reid (eds), *Currents of Radicalism: Popular Radicalism, Organised Labour and Party Politics, 1850–1914* (Cambridge: Cambridge University Press, 1991).

Shepherd, J., 'Ramsay MacDonald and Britain's first Labour government: influences in the making of British foreign and imperial policy', in P. Corthorn and J. Davis (eds), *The Labour Party and the Wider World* (London: I. B. Taurus, 2008).

Simon, B., *Education and the Labour Movement, 1870–1920* (London: Lawrence & Wishart, 1965).

Simon, B. *The Politics of Educational Reform, 1920–1940* (London: Lawrence & Wishart, 1974).

Skidelsky, R., *Politicians and the Slump: The Labour Government of 1929–1931* (London: Macmillan, 1967).

Slowe, P., *Manny Shinwell* (London: Pluto Press, 1993).
Sylvest, C., ' "A Commanding Group?" Labour's Advisory Committee on International Questions, 1918–1931', in Paul Carthorn and Ian Davis (eds), *The British Labour Party and the Wider World* (London: I. B. Tauris, forthcoming).
Tanner, D., *Political Change and the Labour Party, 1900–1918* (Cambridge: Cambridge University Press, 1990).
Tanner, D., 'The Labour Party and electoral politics in the coalfields' in Alan Campbell, Nina Fishman and David Howell (eds), *Miners, Unions and Politics, 1910–47* (Aldershot: Scolar Press, 1996).
Tanner, D., 'Socialist Parties and Policies' in Martin Pugh (ed.), *A Companion to Modern European History, 1871–1945* (Oxford: Blackwell, 1997).
Thane, P., 'Labour and welfare' in Duncan Tanner, Pat Thane and N. Tiratsoo (eds), *Labour's First Century* (Cambridge: Cambridge University Press, 2000).
Thorpe, A., *A History of the British Labour Party* (Basingstoke: Palgrave Macmillan, 1997 and 2000).
Vickers, R., *The Labour Party and the World, Volume 1: The Evolution of Labour's Foreign Policy, 1900–1951* (Manchester: Manchester University Press, 2004).
Ward, Paul, *Red Flag and Union Jack: Englishness, Patriotism and the British Left, 1881–1924* (Woodbridge: The Royal Historical Society and the Boydell Press, 1998).
Wilson, H., *A Prime Minister on Prime Ministers* (London: Michael Joseph, 1977).
Wilson, P., *The International Theory of Leonard Woolf: A Study in Twentieth-Century Idealism* (Basingstoke: Palgrave, 2003).
Wilson, T., *The Downfall of the Liberal Party, 1914–1935* (London: Collins, 1966).
Windrich, E., *British Labour's Foreign Policy* (Stamford, CA: Stamford University Press, 1952).
Winkler, Henry K., *Paths Not Taken: British Labour and International Policy in the 1920s* (Chapel Hill, NC: University of North Carolina Press, 1994.
Winkler, Henry K., *British Labour Seeks a Foreign Policy, 1910–1940* (London: Transaction Publishers, 2005).
Winter, J. M., *Socialism and the Challenge of War: Ideas and Politics in Britain, 1912–1918* (London: Routledge & Kegan Paul, 1974).
Worley, Matthew, *Labour Inside the Gate: A History of the British Labour Party between the Wars* (London: I. B. Tauris, 2005a).
Worley, Matthew (ed.), *Grass Roots: Essays on the Activities of Local Labour Parties and Members, 1918–1945* (Aldershot: Ashgate, 2005b).
Wrigley, C., *Arthur Henderson* (Cardiff: University of Wales Press, 1990).
Wrigley, C. J., 'Lloyd George and the Labour Party after 1922', in Judith Loades (ed.), *The Life and Times of Lloyd George* (Bangor: Headstart, 1991).
Wrigley, C. 'James Ramsay MacDonald', in K. Jefferys (ed.), *Leading Labour: From Keir Hardie to Tony Blair* (London: I. B. Tauris, 1999).
Young, K., *Baldwin* (London: Weidenfeld & Nicolson, 1976).

2 Articles

Barnes, T., 'Special Branch and the First Labour Government', *Historical Journal*, 22:4 (1979).
Bonner, J., 'The Four Labour Cabinets', *Sociological Review*, 6 (1958).
Brooks, J. R., 'Labour and Educational Reconstruction, 1916–1926: A Case Study in the Evolution of Policy', *History of Education*, 20:3 (1991).

Cesarini, D., 'An Alien Concept? The Continuity of Anti-Alienism in British Society before 1940', *Immigrants and Minorities*, II:3 (November, 1992).

Cline, C. A., 'E. D. Morel and the Crusade Against the Foreign Office', *Journal of Modern History*, 39:2 (June 1967).

Davis, J., 'Left out in the Cold: British Labour Witnesses the Russian Revolution', *Revolutionary Russia*, 8:1 (June 2005).

Desmarais, R., 'Strike Breaking and the Labour Government of 1924', *Journal of Contemporary History*, 8 (1973).

Douglas, R., 'Labour in Decline, 1910–1914', *Essays in Anti-Labour History* (1974).

Dowse, R. E., 'The Left Wing Opposition During the First Two Labour Governments', *Parliamentary Affairs*, Autumn 1960.

Golant, W., 'C. R. Attlee in the First and Second Labour Governments', *Parliamentary Affairs*, 26 (1972–3).

Hart, P., ' "Operation Abroad": The IRA, 1919–1923', *English Historical Review*, 115 (2000).

Hoon, G., 'Organised socialism has risen in the night', *Tribune*, 10 February 2006.

Laybourn, K., 'The Issue of School Feeding in Bradford, 1904–1907', *Journal of Educational Administration and History*, 14:1 (1982).

Laybourn, K., 'The Failure of Socialist Unity in Britain, c.1883–1914', *Transactions of the Royal Historical Society*, 6th series, vol. IV (London: Royal Historical Society, 1994).

Laybourn, K., 'The Rise of Labour and the Decline of Liberalism: The State of the Debate', *History*, 80 (June 1995).

Laybourn, K., ' "Waking up to the Fact that there are any Unemployed": Women, Unemployment and the Domestic Solution in Britain, 1918–1939', *History*, 88:4 (2003).

Newark, F. H., 'The Campbell Case and the First Labour Government', *Northern Ireland Legal Quarterly*, I:1 (1969).

Pugh, M., ' "Class Traitors": Conservative Recruits to Labour, 1900–1931', *English Historical Review*, CXIII:450 (1998).

Shepherd, J., and Laybourn, K., 'Labour's Red Letter Day' *BBC History Magazine*, December 2004.

Taylor, R 'PLP's first 100 years', *Tribune*, 10 February 2006.

Wald, K. D., 'Advance by Retreat'? The Formation of British Labour's Electoral Strategy', *Journal of British Studies*, 27:3 (July 1988).

Webb, S., 'The First Labour Government', *Political Quarterly*, 32 (1961), pp. 18–22.

Winkler, H. R., 'The Emergence of a Labour Foreign Policy in Great Britain, 1918–1929', *The Journal of Modern History*, 28:3 (1956).

Wring, D., 'Selling Socialism: Marketing the Early Labour Party', *History Today* (May 2005).

D   Newspapers and journals

Australian Worker
Birmingham Gazette
Daily Chronicle
Daily Graphic
Daily Herald

Daily Mail
Foreign Affairs
Forward
Labour Leader
Labour Magazine
Labour Woman
Leeds Weekly Citizen
Liberal Magazine
Lyttleton Times
Manchester Guardian
Mineworker
Morning Post
Nation
New Leader
Socialist Review
Sun
Sunday Express
Sydney Morning Herald
The Times
The Times Educational Supplement
The Times Higher Education Supplement
Westminster Gazette
Workers' Weekly

E Theses

Jarvis, D., 'Stanley Baldwin and the Ideology of the Conservative Response to Socialism, 1918–1931', PhD thesis (Lancaster, 1991).

Rose, G., 'Locality, Politics and Culture: Poplar in the 1920s', PhD thesis (London, 1988).

Rowlett, J. S., 'The Labour Party in Local Government: Theory and Practice in the Inter-War Years', D. Phil thesis (Oxford, 1979).

Ward, J., 'The Development of the Labour Party in the Black Country, 1918–1929', PhD thesis (Wolverhampton, 2004).

Index